LIVING WELL
on Practically Nothing

To my dear wife, Sara.

Revised and Updated Edition

LIVING WELL

on Practically Nothing

Edward H. Romney

PALADIN PRESS
BOULDER, COLORADO

Living Well on Practically Nothing: Revised and Updated Edition
by Edward H. Romney

Copyright © 2001 by Edward H. Romney

ISBN 1-58160-282-0
Printed in the United States of America

Published by Paladin Press, a division of
Paladin Enterprises, Inc.
Gunbarrel Tech Center
7077 Winchester Circle
Boulder, Colorado 80301 USA
+1.303.443.7250

Direct inquiries and/or orders to the above address.

PALADIN, PALADIN PRESS, and the "horse head" design
are trademarks belonging to Paladin Enterprises and
registered in United States Patent and Trademark Office.

Visit our Web site at www.paladin-press.com

Table of

Contents

Acknowledgments

Many people helped me in this work. Anita Girard Allen made the drawings. Darius Robinson critiqued it and supplied valuable information about houseboats, his father's antiques business, and Depression lifestyles. He also took the boat pictures. Bill Kallio helped a lot with the housing chapter and on painting contracting. Charles Swimmer showed how to convert a bookmobile into a rugged motor home. Much of the outdoor information in the book is taken from Francis H. Buzzacott's *Sportsman's Encyclopedia* of 1905. My dear wife Sara's contribution to the food and clothing section was great. She was willing to pose for the pictures wearing flea-market clothing, which many women would not do. She is most tolerant of the sacrifices and the ups and downs that come with my being self-employed. Kathy Wirtes and the people at Paladin Press edited the manuscript and did the layout work and book design. It was a pleasure working with them.

Whatever defects the work has are mine and whatever merit it has is a gift from the God who created me.

Introduction

This book is for people who need to live on a lot less money. If you have lost your job or expect to, or had to take a much lower-paying job, or if you have ever wondered how you would survive if you were poor, this book is for you. It is based upon the experiences of real people known to the author who live on small incomes—and do very well at it. Teachers, preachers, retired members of the military, widows, people on small inheritances, country people, old people who survived the Great Depression, farmers, writers, artists—all have contributed their know-how in economical living.

Poverty is more a state of mind than an economic condition. If you have the will to survive you will live quite well, no matter what the economic conditions. This book gives you the skills you need. The author comes from a whole family of penny-pinching New Englanders whose unique and sometimes droll lifestyle is detailed in this book. He remembers the 1930s Depression as a small boy. In later years his father never let him forget it. As a freelance writer, salesman, antiques trader, former teacher in technical schools and colleges, and survivor of a messy divorce, he has learned to count the pennies with the best of them—and enjoy doing it. He has used the methods described in this book and been successful enough so that he is no longer poor.

This 2001 revised edition contains much new information on making money or learning new things using computers and the Internet; starting new businesses; investing and saving; converting motor homes and school buses—and much more. All the information in the original 1992 edition has been carefully checked and brought up to date.

This book will help you if you have been fired, demoted, retired, divorced, widowed, bankrupted, or swindled. If you want to live on the interest from money gained from the sale of your house, if you hate your present job or hate where you have to live in order to work, or if you just want to be ready if disaster strikes, this book is for you. Many families today would like to learn to live on less money so the wife could quit her job and be a full-time homemaker and perhaps home-school the kids. This book is for them, too.

Living Well on Practically Nothing: Revised and Updated, will show you how to save $12,000 a year or more—even how to *live* on $12,000 a year. And one chapter tells you how to vanish into the woods and live on no money at all! The book tells you about nice, low-crime places to live where rents are $300 a month and houses are $40,000 or less, where you can walk everywhere and seldom need a car. It tells how to get along with country people and make them your friends. It shows how to buy good cars for less than $1,500, dress a husband and wife for $600 a year, buy secondhand appliances, eliminate heat, light, and telephone bills, and even educate and entertain yourself at low cost in your leisure time. This book tells you how to use government benefits without letting the government use you and drag you into hopeless poverty. It tells about new careers and profitable small businesses you can enter with only a few thousand dollars invested. It is an inspiring book. Most people who cut their living costs way down and change their lifestyles will be happier than ever before. It is all in the book. Go to it and good luck!

Chapter 1

Keep Your Self-Respect While Poor

The hardest part of losing your wealth may be when you also lose the respect of friends and relatives. If you lose your money, some people will have nothing to do with you. When you give up your golf club membership you lose your golfing buddies. If you stop going to the gym you lose track of your physical-fitness friends. If you get rid of your sailboat or antique car, there go the yachting and old-car people. When you meet former coworkers in the coffee shop, they are ill at ease and have nothing to say because they are embarrassed by your misfortune.

GETTING USED TO THE CHANGES

If you sell your house and move to an apartment, your neighbors from the previous neighborhood seldom come to visit you. It can be quite a shock. You are no longer considered for positions in the community, offices in church and service clubs, and are no longer asked to lead charity fund-raising drives. In-laws can hurt you badly with their criticism. If you are forced to cut down your kids' lessons and activities to save money, it hurts you because they are hurting. Even people who retire with money find they are no longer taken seriously in their hometowns. This is one reason people move to Florida or New Mexico.

You must recognize this problem. It may help to know that it happens to most people in your situation. The hurt, like all hurts, lessens with time. You may quicken the process by deciding to no longer compete or interact with your old environment and circle of acquaintances. You find another group to relate to, either locally or by moving, who accept you as you are because they never knew you when you had money.

HARD TIMES CHANGE PEOPLE

Dad was influenced by the Depression long after it was over. He never spent freely again. Even after World War II ended, he expected the

A WORD TO THE READER. You can tell that this author likes to save money. And you know New England people like to save words. So this book is written to contain the maximum number of important facts in the smallest number of pages. I left out obvious things you know already— things like saving money by insulating your house or setting the thermostat lower. It is not puffed up and padded like many books. I have digested and condensed it to save paper and save your time reading it. Be sure you read this book much more closely than an ordinary book so you won't miss anything.

Depression to return. He lived very economically, avoiding all debt and driving a VW Beetle as long as he lived. His investments were conservative, but wise in the long run. He could have bought farmland and wood lots for $10 an acre and made a lot more money (as a cousin, the economist Roger Babson, advised him). But he did recover most of his losses by the 1950s. If you do not remember the 1930s, his experiences may help you. More investment information is in Chapter 15, which has been greatly expanded for this new edition. This book is not just for really poor people.

SHOULD YOU ACCEPT FEDERAL HELP?

There is no absolute answer to this question. The problem with welfare is that it can keep you dependent forever. It takes so much time to apply for food stamps, rent subsidies, fuel assistance, low-cost housing, mortgage assistance, vocational rehabilitation, disability, Medicare and Medicaid, unemployment payments, Social Security, child care, and many more government programs than we can list here, that you have time for little else. To obtain benefits you must travel from one office to another and take a number, sit or stand in line for an hour or two, tell your clerk your problems, argue, get sent to another clerk and another line—and so on forever. It breaks people's spirits to depend on the government and makes them welfare dependents for life.

The first U.S. social programs were developed by the old Bureau of Indian Affairs in the Interior Department. Its policies and methods were used as guidelines to set up all other government social programs. People from Indian Affairs were brought in to staff Health, Education, and Welfare (HEW) and the War on Poverty in the Kennedy and Johnson years. I know because I was a poverty warrior then myself. I have worked under former Indian Affairs people. The Indian reservations, their schools and everything about them are a total fiasco. Reservation Indians live like prisoners exploited by poverty, alcohol, organized crime, gambling, and drugs. They stay unemployed and their children do poorly in school and on achievement tests. The government has broken the reservation Indian's spirit with their social programs.

Indians are bright, honest, brave people. If the government can break their spirits with its social programs, it can surely break yours. The bureaucrats care nothing about rehabilitating people; that would reduce their caseloads. They try to keep them as high as possible so their jobs will be secure.

Another problem with the government programs is they make you do foolish things to get the benefits. It is possible to get government incentives for locating your home or business in a depressed, high-crime area where it is not safe to live or work. Two young men I know, unmarried, with poor job prospects and tiny salaries, were induced by an FHA-guaranteed loan to buy a well-worn $60,000 house with taxes of $1,500 a year with $2,000 down borrowed from their parents. It was in a declining high-crime area and would be nearly impossible to resell. Another example: you can be paid to rebuild in the exact spot where a river has overflowed its banks previously and flooded you out. Surely it will happen again.

In yet another example of government foolishness, a woman with children gets few benefits if her husband lives at home. Women are induced to put men out of the home to get the federal handouts. This is bad for the children and can lead to promiscuity. You lose benefits if you own a tiny house or have money in the bank. This policy keeps poor people renting forever and keeps them from saving any money. Some people have cashed in savings accounts and bought silver or gold coins in order to meet poverty guidelines. Others withdraw their savings and hide the cash. Some people give their money to relatives or friends to hold for them so they can qualify for benefits, and often they are cheated out of it. It is a pity to have to do tricks to meet government regulations.

The number of people who wait to look for a job until their unemployment benefits are gone runs into the millions. When they fill out a job application with these characteristic gaps of several months in the work record, any interviewer knows that here is a worker who is not particularly ambitious, a person who is just along for the easy ride. So the best advice, probably, is to *use the government if you must, but never let it use you.* Never become known as a welfare person. Don't feel guilty about unemployment insurance, food stamps, or surplus food. But if you want to build or buy a small house, get married, or start a new career never let a possible loss of federal benefits stop you.

****

Here are some things to do to help you keep your self-respect while poor:

1. LIVE WITHIN A TIGHT BUDGET. If you are bringing in $1,000 a month and spending $2,000, and your savings are only $6,000, there will come a day six months from now when all your money will be gone. Conditions like this have made people commit suicide. You must cut expenses using the methods in this book so your condition is a steady state and there will be no ominous doomsday in the near future when you wake up with nothing left. You *must* live within a budget.

2. DON'T LOWER YOUR MORAL STANDARDS. In his famous study of social class in Elmstown, U.S.A. (actually Muncie, Indiana) A. Hollingshead, found there were two types of poor people.[1] The upper-lower class was described as "poor but honest" by themselves and other townspeople. They tried to keep clean and neat. They were religious. They avoided heavy drinking and stayed out of the criminal court system. They tried to pay their bills as best they could and valued hard work and education.

   The lower-lower class was called by the rest of the people, "those people who live like animals." They filled the courts, the jails, and the social work agencies. They had children out of wedlock and were sexually promiscuous. They admired people who broke the law. They felt the world was rigged against them, that they had no hope of bettering their condition through honest work.

   If you have been unjustly fired from your job or cheated of your

WHAT HAPPENED TO PEOPLE IN THE GREAT DEPRESSION? Dad was hard hit in the stock market crash in 1929 and he lost his job, too. The older relatives were good to us and remained friendly, but those his own age—30—definitely looked down on us.

As a small boy I overheard Dad telling my mother of a visit to some cousins. They were stockbrokers who had somehow kept their fortune intact. He dropped in unannounced. They were having a party so they sent him around to the back door and talked with him briefly in the kitchen. They kept him away from the important guests and had the servants feed him at the kitchen table.

My dad was badly hurt by having friends and relatives snub him. Many years later, after he made most of his money back, he still avoided people who had been unpleasant to him. He loved to wear old clothes long after there was any need to save money. "When you wear old clothes you know what people really think of you," he would say after an encounter with a nasty clerk or waitress. "When you dress up, they treat you well because they think you have money." A good point to remember.

savings it is tempting to stop playing by the rules—to shoplift or cut loose sexually or with alcohol or drugs in a way that would be disastrous to a person holding a middle-class job. But such decisions will make your poverty permanent. The courts, lawyers, and bail bondsmen are the real winners when a person goes bad. Many poor people pay $1,500 a year, or more, on lawyer's fees, fines, and bail bonds. Many of them have to walk everywhere due to DUI convictions. Only higher levels of crime seem to pay. You can keep your head up no matter how poor you are if you keep your honor.

3. KEEP YOUR RELIGIOUS FAITH. Christians should remember and keep the Ten Commandments. Find a church where they still teach the Bible. Strengthen your religious faith and worship regularly. When you are born again it really *does* change your life, if you are sincere. You should hear my personal testimony. Do not worry about the expense of church. They do not expect a fortune. It is inspiring when the poorest people in church put money in the collection plate; often it is only a dollar. Like the widow's mite, it is the spirit that counts. Prayer does work—even in these days.

4. YOU ARE NEVER TOO POOR TO HELP OTHERS. Even when we were the poorest, my mother saved my clothes when I outgrew them and gave them to the children of other poor relatives and neighbors. All children outgrow clothing faster than they wear it out. We also had poor people, tramps, and men who lived in tiny shacks who we let into the kitchen to warm themselves. We fed them when we could. In about 1935 Bill Miller, a retired lumber worker who lived in a shack nearby until it burned one cold night, got so close to our wood stove that he set his pants on fire. When Uncle John let tramps sleep in his barn, he always searched them and took away matches and cigarettes so they would not set the barn afire. He gave them back their things in the morning.

5. DO NOT GAMBLE. Do not play lotto, the numbers game, or the racehorses. There is no Divine Principle of Luck in the universe that favors those who are most needy. Gambling is simply a system for increasing risk, just as insurance is a system for decreasing risk. If you have lost once, you will probably lose again. The more you play, the more likely you will show a loss equal to the house take. This is a law of statistics I learned in college. Why it is not taught to everyone I simply cannot understand. The drowning man who grasped at a straw died anyway. There are no long shots. If you lose once more you will feel even more a failure than you do now. This also applies to taking chances with bald tires, bad wiring, cheap portable kerosene heaters that fume and explode, and wandering at night alone in crime-filled streets.

6. LEARN THE DIFFERENCE BETWEEN WANTS AND NEEDS. Know which things are wanted for vanity and which are essential. A kid must have shoes, but a pair of $100 Nikes is a want, not a need. You may have to own a car to get around in the country. A used 10-year-old Honda Civic meets a need—a new Buick Riviera is a want; oatmeal boiled from cheap rolled oats is a need—Kellogg's Froot Loops cereal is a want; potatoes that you peel and bake are a need—

potato chips or French fries are wants. The definition of being poor is being hungry all the time and underweight, lacking proper clothing to keep warm and dry, and having no place to live. By this definition almost no one in America is poor. Reassure yourself and your family that you are not in poverty if this definition does not apply to you. You can give your kids a great gift if you can teach them to be immune to peer pressure to spend more than they can afford.

7. KEEP NEAT AND CLEAN. Keep your home or apartment neat and clean inside. Detergent, bleach, and scouring powder cost very little, and labor is free when you do it yourself. If you cannot afford to buy flowers for the table, raise them yourself or use silk flowers. You keep your self-respect by staying attractive. The difference between a slum and a fancy historic district is mainly in the maintenance given the homes. We must hedge slightly on our advice to beautify the outside of a house since it sometimes causes the tax assessment to rise, and it can also attract burglars. Some New Englanders, particularly in Massachusetts, leave the outside of fairly good homes unpainted because they fear the tax collector. The insides of an ordinary looking little New England ranch house can have a finished cellar with a Jacuzzi and a projection TV in a fine, paneled recreation room. You'd be surprised what these Yankees will do.

8. YOU AND YOUR FAMILY MUST STICK TOGETHER. There is a tendency to displace frustration with aggression within the family. It is like the rats in the experimental cage that fight each time the cage is electrified to give them all a shock. Many families break up under economic stress. They blame each other for not being more successful. It is particularly important not to use Freudian psychological terms as weapons in an argument. I am not cheap because I am an "anal retentive" who was severely toilet trained. Your wife is not critical of you because she is a "castrating woman." All that stuff is cult nonsense. Your family must be sincere and work together.

9. All these eight points above are important, but the three most important rules for avoiding poverty and living a stable happy life are:
   AVOID ALL DEBT
   AVOID ALL DEBT
   AVOID ALL DEBT. Debt was called usury in the Bible and was considered a sin. Henry Ford, who became one of the richest men in the world in less than 20 years, credited his success to the fact he avoided borrowing money. My friend Charles Bristol, vice president of a large bank in Wyoming, told me that when people borrow money to start a business they never get it back. The money just stays in the business; they have simply bought themselves a job. After his retirement, he also explained that bankers could only survive if they lent you money you did not need. If you really needed it the loan was too risky. You might not pay it back.

HOW TO STAY OUT OF DEBT

When you borrow money, you have spent money *that isn't there*. It is like writing a bad check. You have to find money to replace it before it is

Long ago in New Hampshire, the people used to say there were three kinds of lower-class people. The best of these drank beer and carried the empty bottles out to the trash. The next best kind threw their beer bottles out the window where the snow covered them until spring (quite a mess of bottles would be discovered when the snow finally melted in spring). The worst of all threw their beer bottles out the window but didn't bother to open the window. They would replace the broken pane with a piece of cardboard.

too late. What an anxious insecure way to live! When you use leverage you are adding to risk! It is just that simple. When you borrow, you are actually stealing from your future to dissipate yourself in the present.

The Professors Have About Ruined Us

Modern liberal economic theory taught in colleges today states that businesses are controlled so well by computers that they can run much higher debt ratios than previously thought safe. These theories enabled junk bonds to be sold and caused the junk bond and savings and loan crises. The government has tax policies to reward debt, too, which can entrap you.

Debt can be useful if an individual or a company is growing rapidly. For instance, if you make $30,000 a year and are certain you will be making $60,000 a year in five years, it makes sense to buy the kind of upscale house that a $60,000 salary will allow. But the $30,000 person is just as likely to be fired or bankrupt in five years as to be making $60,000. And if you don't *know* the future is going to be better, now is *not* the time to borrow anything. That is the way times are today.

I am not completely against debt. I've had VA and FHA loans years ago myself at 6 percent interest. But in these times—*never*! What wonderful peace of mind it is to know that no one can ever take your house, or your car, or your good name away.

Credit Cards Are Addictive

Ordinary people have huge expenses due to interest on credit cards. These cards, developed by clever, greedy bankers, use the principle of "automatic interest." Credit card interest is added automatically each month, and most people never realize how much the interest costs them. Paying 18 percent interest on a credit-card debt of $3,000, which is common, means that $540 is simply thrown away for nothing every year.

Debt is an addiction, like cigarettes or overeating. Maybe you'd better stop using all your credit cards. Bankers like to keep you in debt by telling you ridiculous things such as urging you to borrow just to keep your credit rating good, or for frivolous things like vacations on cruise ships. Even worse are the ways bankers persuade farmers to buy more land than they can pay for and then repossess their farms. Many a family farm has been lost this way and gobbled up by the big agricultural interests. Also, the banks can be faulted for the way they promote home equity loans for questionable purposes like sending a lazy kid to college. To stay out of big trouble remember this last sentence: *Just say no to the bankers and stay out of debt!*

Get a Nest Egg

To stay out of debt, you need a reserve fund of at least $2,000 (preferably more) for big purchases. You never know when the washing machine is going to burn out or you will be told you either have to buy a new car or do a $1,500 repair on your old car. Often you find nice things like a 10-year-old car with 30,000 miles on it for sale by the roadside for $1,200. If you lack the ready cash to buy, you cannot take advantage of these sudden opportunities. Keep the money in a savings account with a passbook to reduce the temptation to spend it. (If you must keep it in cash, keep it well hidden.) Train yourself to build the account back up after you have drawn from it. If you dip into your savings for small purchases, you are simply cheating yourself out of any hope for your future. The usual way a small business is started is for both the husband and wife to work. One salary is spent, the other is saved. In a few years they have enough money to start a store, a restaurant, or a used-car lot. Then they are free. Get the willpower to do this.

MAKE THINGS LAST

I've written manuals on repair, trained repair people, and made a study of how long things last and why they wear. (I'm referring to cameras, radios, cars, furniture, and things like that). I found there are astonishing differences from one family to another regarding how much they spend on these items and how long they keep them.

Most things do not wear out; rather, they are destroyed willfully so a newer model may be purchased. When things are brand new we treat them gently and always wipe the dust off the finish and keep them polished. As they get older, dirt dulls the newness and they are taken for granted. Now we bang and scrape and dent them. We cannot see the damage because of the dust. Now they look really old in appearance but still are fine in operation. But we now call them the "old" car, the "old" TV, or whatever, and we really abuse them and break them up. We force their controls, slam them angrily when performance is less than ideal, refuse to spend for maintenance, and start saying the item is about done for and begin shopping for a new one. On a car, some people come to this last stage in about three years or 50,000 miles. More successful people keep cars running well for six or seven years and 100,000 miles or more. Similar ratios hold with furniture, TVs, stereos, kitchen appliances, and most of all with toys. Some clever families spend half as much money because they keep their things twice as long. You should be like this.

A BETTER LIFE

People who read this book are often lacking more than money. I received many heart-rending accounts of grief from readers of the first edition of this book. They were people who had lost faith and hope. Several people, after reading the book, decided to move or change their lifestyles greatly.

I have been part of the mobile society of academic, corporate, and governmental middle-level people myself. I've lived in the typical ranch-house neighborhood where I knew only one or two neighbors and the people stayed indoors and drove everywhere in cars. I've been to those parties where the guests, once they get full of drink, immediately become your best friends. You think you have met some real buddies, people who understand you, whom you can share confidences with. The next day when they are sober they hardly recognize you. Often we have

When my mother was a young girl, around 1925, she had never seen skywriting before. So when a message appeared high in the skies written in white smoke, at first she thought it was a miracle from heaven. But when the old biplane formed the letters and she saw that the first word was "Lucky," for Lucky Strike cigarettes, she knew it was no miracle, because there is no Divine Principle of Luck in the universe. She recorded the event in her diary. I have always remembered this point.

made good friends with a couple and in a few months they are transferred somewhere else.

I am particularly upset by those organizational power structures where people are kind to you only if they want something from you—or fear you. I am tired of people who call you by your first name and obviously don't want to know your family name. Much of middle-class suburban America is a very lonely place. I was outraged at a corporate family who, when they were transferred cross-country, had the kids' cocker spaniel, "Taffy," put to sleep by the vet and purchased an identical new spaniel at their new location to save the bother of transporting the dog by air. The wife chattered about it enthusiastically. She said the kids never knew the difference. I think she was a murderer. I want no more of sick people like that, even if I have to sacrifice to live away from them.

Wouldn't you like to move to a place where the families are like the Waltons on TV? Would you like to find a small town like Thornton Wilder's *Our Town*? Wouldn't you like to meet people like the Swiss Family Robinson or know a banker like James Stewart in *It's a Wonderful Life*? Well, you can, and I and many other people have done so. These people actually exist. I know real people like that and I have found them in such diverse places as Cheyenne, Wyoming; Nashua, New Hampshire; Galesburg, Michigan; Drayton, South Carolina; Arcadia, Virginia; Clinton, Iowa; Pittsford, Vermont; Vineland, New Jersey; Globe, Arizona; Joshua Tree, California; Truth or Consequences, New Mexico, and all over the United States in many smaller cities and towns. You can find towns with nice people too, if you just open your eyes and look.

There are still fine towns where people leave their doors unlocked, where there are schools with strong academic tradition and good moral training. You'll locate fine churches attended by kind-hearted, gentle people who still sing those wonderful old hymns, where you will be moved to tears, as I am at our homecoming when they all sing *Blessed Be the Tie that Binds*. You'll love the fellowship of service clubs like Kiwanis. You can help fight fires with the volunteer fire department, aid the rescue squad, march in the parade with the American Legion, help the Boy Scouts earn merit badges, and serve a pancake supper with the Grange. It is all still there in Middle America much as Norman Rockwell painted it—and you can be part of it.

Becoming a Country Person

It may not be all that easy for you to become a country person, however. Many small-town people who've traveled to certain cities have had bad experiences, such as being ridiculed for asking directions or when trying to buy something. Country people like the way they are and they don't like being humiliated by those people with a lot of education but little decency and kindness. They are suspicious of newcomers—with good reason. To be accepted by them, you have to adopt their lifestyle, go to their churches and club meetings and join after a reasonable time.

In a town where everyone knows everyone else, people do not dress to impress. The biggest landowner may wear bib overalls in town. You may also be surprised to find the people more intelligent and educated than you first believed. There will be artists and writers living quietly in the hills, retired doctors and army colonels, and greatly overqualified teachers in the schools with advanced degrees from famous universities who simply enjoy the life there and can do without the money. You cannot tell what kind of people they are from their clothing; they look just the same as the rest of the local people.

To succeed in a new lifestyle, what you need most is a willingness to learn from country people, to adopt their ways completely without holding back, to actually be a country person just like them. In satisfaction, happiness, freedom from stress, good health, by all criteria except monetary, you will be better off.

SAVING IS MUCH HARDER THAN YOU MIGHT THINK

As my friend Arch Newton points out, one must learn to march to a different drummer to resist economic pressure and advertising. Here is some real help: When you are tempted to buy some novelty item—such as a towel roll with a music box in it—visualize it in a pile of junk at a yard sale with a 50-cent price tag on it. I can do this with most everything in mail-order catalogs. Poor people and wage-earning spendthrifts think of money as if it were something perishable, like ice, that they have to get rid of fast by spending it all. Investors, even small investors, think of money as power, as capital, as a reserve.

There Is No Real Status In Spending

When the Eliots saw their New Hampshire neighbor had bought a Mercedes, they said with considerable scorn, "He must be dipping into his principal." The car may have cost $60,000, but it was not real status because that was $60,000 no longer earning interest. We who buy antiques and settle estates are amazed when the heir buys a Rolex, a Corvette, a Weatherby rifle, and a Prevost motor home and takes a year-long vacation and all the money is gone. It takes real willpower to have the money available to buy something really nice and not to spend it. That kind of willpower made America great. It made families wealthy for generations. It is something you need to work on.

Salespeople intimidate customers into buying a more expensive product than they planned to buy. They are *afraid* to admit they cannot afford something. It is astonishing what people can be persuaded to buy these days. Here is one common example: In the prosperous parts of the South, there are great numbers of expensive sports-utility vehicles. You start with a Ford Explorer, then you are persuaded to trade for an Expedition, and then when your neighbor gets the biggest $50,000 Ford Excursion, you cannot be happy until you own one, too. And next you want the Lincoln Navigator! There is almost no snow in Atlanta, no real need for four-wheel drive. Yet you see more of these vehicles there than you do in snowy, mountainous New Hampshire. These SUVs are costly, top-heavy, and hard for women in skirts to climb into. You never see one with any mud on it from traveling in the boondocks. It is incredible how people have been brainwashed into buying expensive things like this just for status. You must resist sales pressure. You will probably never see that particular sales person again. He or she does not know your boss, your landlord, or your snooty in-laws, and will not tell them you are cheap. So just say *no* and refuse to buy. Be a winner and keep your money for better things. Always say no when you are being pressured. Wait and the price may come down.

Fighting Consumer Mentality

The urge to spend all you make is called *consumer mentality*. Keep this term in your vocabulary. You must ask yourself, am I using consumer mentality when I want this or that? Evaluate your friends and relatives in terms of consumer mentality. Try to get *investment mentality* instead. Learn to regard your capital—your net worth—as the most important criterion. Resist the urge to spend money on what economists call "non-income producing depreciating assets"—such luxuries as fiberglass motorboats or ATVs.

You can learn to see through advertising and status. Don't pay for the sizzle, just the steak. For example, I have two suits. One cost $5 in the thrift shop but looks new and is a fine Hart Schaffner & Marx. The other really cost a lot. Both look and fit equally well. But even though I resist the feeling, I feel more expensively dressed in the new suit. However, I do wear both suits and I take as good care of the flea-market suit as the store-bought one, so I have made some progress.

The Anti-Spendthrift Checklist

It may help to have a mental checklist to run down when you want to buy something. You should ask yourself these questions:

1. Can I buy it cheaper later? Do I have to have it now?
2. Can I buy it used?
3. Can I rent or borrow it?
4. Will I feel stupid after I buy it?
5. Will it be a lot of bother and trouble and need constant care and repair?
6. Where will I store it?
7. Can I do without?
8. Do I really need it?

Renting Things Instead of Buying

We never buy seldom-used items like post-hole diggers, circular saws, wheel pullers, hoists, cement mixers, slide and movie projectors, punch bowl sets, and extra folding chairs. We rent these seldom-used items from an equipment rental store. We like the Taylor Rental Stores. There may be different stores in your area.

Who Needs All That Clutter?

I hate to see the useless clutter of junk that people buy and keep simply because they cannot resist advertising. Many people devote a whole room in a house or apartment to keeping useless things for years and years. Others use the garage and leave the car outdoors. I'm talking about such items as the bird cage of a dead bird, broken video games, an empty fish tank, a broken battery-operated vacuum cleaner, a 220 volt brioche cooker, a dead black and white console TV, the clothing you wore when you had a 32-inch waist, a box of Christmas gifts people gave you that you don't like—and a large, framed picture of Joan Rivers!

A room in a house costs $10,000 or more. So does a garage. In an apartment, an extra room increases the rent by $50 to $350 per month. So it costs you $600 a year or more just to keep all this stuff—in rent, house payments, or interest lost. Have a yard sale and sell all you can, then donate the rest to charity—remembering to get a receipt and claim the charitable deduction on your taxes! Then you can put something worthwhile in the room you cleaned, such as a home office to start an Internet business. Or you could rent out the garage or move to a better smaller place and save lots of money

Look Before You Leap

We can also lose when we buy too cheap an item to save money and it proves to be worthless and we have to buy a better one later. Dad, feeling sorry for my mother washing clothes by hand during the Depression, came home with a used table-top washing machine he found somewhere. It never was any good so he lost the few dollars he put into it. Sometimes it is wasteful to buy new things too early—like one of the first digital watches back in the 1970s for $200. It takes willpower to resist the latest invention when it is announced. Neither the store nor the advertisers will give you any reasons *not* to buy. You must think of all these reasons yourself to be a balanced person and get out of the "Shop Till you Drop" frame of mind.

Why Do People Work So Hard For Nothing?

It is silly for people to wreck their health and move heaven and earth to make a little more money. They take two jobs, put the wife to work, do all sorts of things. Then when they get the money, they spend it without thought—for instance, buying a $3,000 set of drapes for the living room or buying an expensive new car on impulse with $5,000 of unnecessary accessories. Or maybe they buy and finance a $25,000 motorboat that uses $20 worth of gas per hour, will cost $150 a month to store at the marina, and that will be used only two or three times a year. Most people, even upscale people, are nothing but a channel, a tube for money to run right through them—as if they had taken a dose of salts. Don't let it happen to you.

Don't Be One of the "Apparently Wealthy"

I know some people who bought a big house of more than 2,500 square feet, with a large lawn and garden. They like to entertain and have dinners and drop-ins frequently. They are of moderate means and have no servants, so they have to do all the work themselves. Housecleaning, yard work, gardening, cooking, waiting on guests, and making frequent repairs take most of their time. They also have a summer home. They take a kit of carpenter's tools and a lawnmower when they leave for the weekend and spend all weekend working on the summer house. Their boat demands constant work, and they are always fixing things for their grown-up kids and lazy son-in-law. They never have time to enjoy life.

Big houses and summer homes are luxuries for people with real money who can hire a maid to cook and serve, a yardman and gardener to take care of the outside of the house, and another caretaker for the summer place.

You don't gain any real status by owning these things. When people see you sitting on your red Snapper mower looking like Forrest Gump, chugging back and forth on your one-acre lawn, and then they see your wife in old clothes bent over double pulling up weeds, then all your status is gone. They will know you are not really wealthy people but just pretenders. Why do these things? Why live expensively? It is just foolishness. The term "the apparently wealthy" was coined by salespeople who sell yachts, airplanes, condominiums, and other expensive luxuries. They can waste a lot of time canvassing people who have no real money, but just look prosperous.

Note well: It is dangerous to own a vacation house or camp in a deserted area with no close neighbors, or neighbors who look out only for themselves. Sooner or later it will be broken into, vandalized, or burned down. You *must* get a live-in caretaker, and that will be very expensive.

Our friends, Winston Alden Cunningham and his wife Emily, had to sell a big, beautiful, shingled oceanfront home on Cape Cod, Massachusetts, after it was repeatedly broken into. It had been in the family for years. The last straw was the time vandals built a fire on the living room floor and left it to burn through the floor and fall into the cellar before snuffing out. The Cunninghams gave up and the house was sold. The problem was our friends could get no help. No one cared. They paid a man $3,000 a year to watch the property and make repairs, but he never saw anything until too late. Whenever something happened he made them drive down from Boston to assess the damage and approve the repair before he'd do it—even for as small a thing as a broken window.

The Cunninghams were so afraid of burglars that every time they left for home they packed everything of any value in the back seat of their big, old Olds 98. Radios, answering machine, TV, toaster, mixer, microwave, silverware, clocks, and even the vacuum cleaner—anything good had to go home. They left the house nearly bare when they were away. The furniture was old oak and the beds were of iron. It was nothing that most people would want, but the vandals enjoyed destroying it anyway. They even burned up the cabana for a bonfire on the beach. The police never saw anything. Problems like these are why nowadays many people prefer a condo, a camping trailer, or a motor home to a vacation home.

1. Hollingshead, A., *Elmstown's Youth*, New York: John Wiley & Sons, 1949.

Chapter 2

A Day of Cheap Living

A LOW-COST LIFESTYLE

I wouldn't be much of an author if I did not practice what I preach. I actually live in a small town. Although I am far from poor now, I still love to live cheaply. It reminds me of the good old days and of my mother and father. And I can use the money we save.

Personal Possessions

I awaken to the sound of a battery-powered alarm clock I bought in a flea market. It is not digital and does not have to be programmed. I hate digital things. I try to get up at sunrise to minimize use of electric light. As I dress, my pants are mail-order Wearguard work pants. They are washed, not dry-cleaned, and do not have to be pressed. My wife made my short-sleeved shirt from a worn out long-sleeved dress shirt that I used to wear to weddings and funerals.

My watch is a cheap Timex. My wallet is from a flea market and cost a dollar. Shoes are either generic athletic sneakers bought in the flea market or expensive Florsheim dress shoes bought in 1990 and now twice-resoled and too scuffed to wear to church.

I shower with low-cost, natural gas-heated hot water. The shower nozzle is specially made to conserve water. Sometimes I get clean by swimming in the lake with a cake of soap instead and we can turn off the hot-water heater. I shave with flea-market blades—about 3 cents each—or an old secondhand electric razor. I use ordinary soap instead of shaving cream. I now use toothpaste but I have often brushed with table salt instead and I am known to use ordinary white string for dental floss.

An attic fan made from a $15 Kmart room fan and run in the morning to save air conditioning cools the old house. We have a swamp cooler, or evaporative system, instead of the costly conventional air conditioner. In winter we heat with natural gas and we have several space heaters so we do not run the furnace for only one room. The little gas heaters came from the Salvation Army and a used-furniture place.

Breakfast

Breakfast is frozen orange juice and one cup of coffee—my only cup for the day. I eat oatmeal cooked from cheap oats with dry skim milk, which is also used in the coffee. It is cooked with natural gas on a secondhand range. However, we do allow ourselves to enjoy a real luxury—cane syrup from Cairo, Georgia. We buy this syrup by the case from the factory when we drive through Cairo to Florida.

Mornings

I walk to the post office two blocks away since my old V8 car eats a lot of gas. I always look in the trash and sometimes find a free magazine or newspaper someone threw away, which saves me from buying it. I open the mail in the post office and throw away junk mail. Sheets of paper written on only one side are saved to write on. My briefcase that I carry the mail home in cost $5 at a yard sale. I answer all possible letters on the letter itself with pen, and note on a calendar what I said, if it is important. These days I make much more use of e-mail than the postal service. I do not return long-distance calls unless urgent, since the person is sure to write or phone again. Stationery is plain copy-machine paper hit with a rubber address stamp. Envelopes are cheapest from Wal-Mart or Office Max and I use a rubber stamp for the return address. I work right at home on my computer so we pay no commuting cost.

Lunch

Lunch is the big meal for us. We have a can of tuna fish, bought in great quantity at Sam's Wholesale Club, mixed with Sam's canned peas and mayonnaise to make a salad. There are also free tomatoes and summer squash from our garden. Our drink is water and for dessert there is a two-day old banana with soft parts cut away.

Supper

Supper will be a can of New England clam chowder with the extra crackers they give us when we eat salads in restaurants on trips. We save them in a basket. There will be a salad of homegrown lettuce and a sliced tomato. Dessert will be cinnamon toast made from stale bread from the surplus bread store, cinnamon from the Hazen flea market, and sugar. No candy, no cigarettes.

Recreation

I may read an old book bought for 25 cents at the library discard sale or from a flea market. I recently finished Axel Munthe's, *Story of San Michele*, an autobiography of a famous doctor and Renaissance man who lived on Capri. We seldom watch TV. Our small TV set is 12 years old and has no cable. We enjoy listening to a classical music station on a big old Marantz stereo we bought for $35 at the Kiwanis flea market. We also get international shortwave on a 10-year-old Sony portable radio. The computer is our biggest recreation. We get fun and games and news from all over the world. This costs us $21 a month for Internet fees. There's more about computers in Chapter 6. We may exercise by walking on an abandoned railroad trail or along the river. I never wear a jogging costume; I couldn't afford it. I used to play volleyball at the church but I'm getting rather old for that.

Fellowship

We have lots of local visitors, fine people, and we keep a nice living room with Victorian antiques for them to sit in. Some items came from our parents, and those pieces of furniture we bought came from Black Mountain, North Carolina, where antiques are very cheap. They cost less than new furniture from stores such as Sears and should last a hundred years or more, unlike the cheap, particle-board furniture of today.

We belong to various social clubs. There we enjoy a covered-dish supper where each family brings a casserole or a pie. We get to eat a whole lot of different food and it costs no more than staying at home.

Evenings

There is usually a program or entertainment of some kind. The local people are very talented. They like to play our piano and sing nice, old tunes, and even classical music. The piano was my grandmother's and costs nothing except for repairs and tuning.

****

So that is how we live and I wouldn't have it any other way. We think we are all right and the world is all mixed up. Maybe that is something to think about.

Chapter 3

Save Up to $37,500 a Year and Live on $12,000 a Year

It is a terrible feeling to be earning $25,000 a year and spending $35,000. It is like being in a sinking boat that is filling up faster than you can bail it out. People have committed suicide due to such stress. Here are some good ways to cut down on your spending. These figures are for the savings for a couple for one year. Bigger families will have bigger savings.

HOW TO SAVE UP TO $37,500 A YEAR

1. Cut out smoking. Two people each smoking one pack a day, at a little more than $2 a pack, saves $1,500

2. Sell your medium-priced late-model car (such as a Ford Taurus, Honda Accord, or equivalent) that you drive 15,000 miles per year and trade every three years. Replace with a carefully selected 10-year-old car such as Plymouth Sundance, Honda Civic, Toyota Tercel or Corolla. Drive 60 miles or less per week or use a moped or bicycle or walk to save at least $4,000

3. Drop all country clubs, golf clubs, gyms, and professional societies. Savings vary greatly but should be at least $1,000

4. Stop going to fancy restaurants with tablecloths, china, liquor, and waiters or waitresses. Occasionally you may substitute a pizza, barbecue, or seafood restaurant, or a low-cost steakhouse such as Western Steer, Ryan's, or Ponderosa, but mostly you should eat covered-dish suppers and picnic. Save $2,000

5. Stop all credit cards and charge accounts and save at least $500

6. Stop all newspapers and magazines. Read in a library and you will save $500

7. Don't buy beer or liquor for home use. Don't drink cold drinks except Kool-Aid, lemonade, or ginger switchel (see Chapter 8). Limit yourself to one cup of coffee daily. The saving will be at least . . .$500

8. Stop getting haircuts, tints, sets, shampoos, and manicures at the barber shop or beautician's. Men should shave with a straight razor and stick soap, or grow a beard. All hair should be cut, washed, and set at home. No cosmetics. You save $1,500

Now add this all up and you will find we have already saved $11,500. If we make some more changes, we can save even more.

9. Don't pay for movies, stage shows, or athletic events. Watch TV or read $1,000

10. Cut out the phone. Use a $25 used citizens band radio for emergencies $1,000

11. No more hired yard work or snow shoveling. Do it yourself . .$1,000

12. All clothes except underwear, shoes, and socks should be bought used from flea market or thrift shop. No more dry cleaning or starched shirts $4,000

13. Sell your $250,000 house and rent at $300 a month. Invest the difference, save on taxes and insurance $15,000

14. Cut out luxury foods, raise a garden, cook and bake (See food chapter) $1,000

15. Cut out electric power, water, gas, and oil. Heat with wood, burn trash in a wood stove for heat, use solar hot water, maybe 12-volt power $1,000

16. Stop spending weekends and vacations in resorts. Camp in state parks instead $2,000

Total savings	$37,500

Note well that if these columns are totaled, the grand total is $37,500, which is more than most people earn! The figures are in 2001 dollars and the savings will be greater with more inflation. You simply have to cut down expenses. When you get used to the changes, you will probably enjoy your new low-cost lifestyle much more than being a big spender. Details of making all these changes to save a lot of money are covered in the next chapters.

HOW TO LIVE ON $12,000 A YEAR

You can live quite well on very little. It all depends how well you plan, how careful you are to get the best buys and how well you take care of your possessions and avoid accidents. Health care is the big worry. You simply cannot take chances with accidents or disease. You must be very careful of your health.

This list covers food, clothing, and shelter. You need a budget and an expense book to keep track of how you spend money. Many people waste their money on little things they really do not need.

The biggest savings are in housing, cars, and clothing. A friend who built his own masonry house 40 years ago, drives old cars, and wears flea-market clothing tells me the savings over a lifetime of secondhand living add up to at least a million dollars! He is now actually a millionaire because he invested the money he saved in good businesses. The specifics of how you keep each budget item so low are explained in the following chapters of this book.

Budget For Two People

- *Food:* $3,500 (about $70 a week). See Chapter 8. Avoid frozen convenience foods, bake your own bread or buy day-old bread, and eat lots of vegetables.
- *Rent:* $3,600 (about $300 a month in a smaller city or town).
- *Utilities:* $1,200. No phone or cable TV.
- *Clothes (used):* $500 a year.
- *Transportation:* $1,200 using an older car, limiting mileage. Spend even less by using a bicycle, moped, bus, or walking.

This leaves $2,000 for personal items, gifts, donations, and medical care. It can be done. You can live much better on $15,000.

Chapter 4

Some Ways to Live on No Money at All

We'll give the easier ways first, since some of the others are rather austere.

LIVING FOR FREE

Be a Caretaker of a Wealthy Person's Summer Home or Estate

Our cousin, Wilder Tenney, lived better than most any of us long ago. He was caretaker for a millionaire's summer estate near Deering, New Hampshire. It was a giant New England farmhouse dating from the 1600s with dark wood and four giant fireplaces clustered around a great big chimney. Wilder lived in an apartment in the back with his wife and two kids. The rent was free and he had a salary as well. The wealthy owner had several other houses and was seldom there.

When he was away, the Tenney family and guests had the run of the whole place. The owner would leave groceries after he left and my cousins were supposed to eat it all and buy fresh groceries for the next time the big man arrived. Cousin Wilder mowed the lawn, cleaned the place, and did small repairs. It took very little of his time. He was able to save enough to get into mink farming and later he bought a small local telephone company in Weare, New Hampshire, which he owned and ran for the rest of his life.

If you are known as a reliable person and are handy with tools, you can get a similar job. One way to get one is to place want ads in local weekly newspapers and shoppers or upscale regional magazines such as *Yankee, New Hampshire Profiles, Southern Living,* or *Vermont Life* that have classified ad sections. Be ready to move and be prepared to produce good references. You can also ask around locally and write owners of vacation homes to offer your services (their mail is forwarded in winter). You can make money around a resort caring for many summer homes, but the problem then is, where can you afford to live? A motor home, perhaps, if you can find a place to park it.

Rent Your Home in Summer

Dad's friend Wayne Tuttle built a nice home on a lake in New Hampshire. The Tuttle family lives in it 10 months of the year and rents it by the week in July and August for about $1,000 a week. All the tourism and rental activity is crowded into these two months in the North. During that time they live in a camp in the woods. The weekly rental in summer covers the entire cost of the house for the year and pays it off quickly.

The Florida panhandle, surprisingly, is a summer resort area. You could have your nice home there and escape to the Smokies or to the North in the summer months and camp or live in a small cabin or trailer. If you live near ski areas you can rent your house to skiers in the winter months and go south.

Buy or Build a Duplex

Live in one side, rent the other. The rent from one side pays for the whole house. See Chapter 10 on shelter.

Living Free in the Inner City

An intelligent reader wrote me that he believes this is possible. There are many abandoned buildings where you can live, he says. Food is obtained from Dumpsters outside grocery stores and most other items you need from other Dumpsters. You get in with some friends who are not gang members or druggies and you help each other.

He told about standing in a window and aiming a laser pointer at some drug dealers gathered on the street below. It scared them when they saw the mysterious spot of red light on their bodies and they moved on. I have no experience with any of this; you are on your own.

Be a Companion To a Sick Person

You get room and board free and usually a small legacy after the person dies. If you like the work you could upgrade yourself by taking LPN (Licensed Practical Nurse) training at your community college. With this certificate you will be greatly in demand and the pay is quite good.

We know a lady of 75 years of age still doing this work and enjoying it. She enrolled for her LPN after forced retirement from an insurance job due to her age. She is a real blessing to the sick people she helps. This work can also be done by men, but the openings are fewer.

LIVING OFF THE LAND

I knew of some Vietnam veterans who lived in the midst of a giant swamp in one of the gulf states. They seldom came out, and their provisions and supplies were brought in to them by a guide with a flat-bottom boat with tunnel propellers. Their house was camouflaged and built on tree roots and trunks a few feet above the swampy water, a bit like a tree house. They fished and hunted about as they pleased. As you can guess, these men were very angry for the way they were treated after they returned from Vietnam. This is one of the few modern successful retreats from the world I know of.

Living off the land in the North is much harder due to the snow and cold. Those few who do it generally break into hunting camps and steal, sometimes sleeping in the vacant camp to survive in winter. Their morality is compromised and their existence becomes nothing one can respect. I have heard of homeless people in the country keeping warm by hiding themselves in the crawl spaces of typical small ranch houses. They get water from the pipes and bury wastes in the dirt floor. They enter at night and leave before daybreak and stay very quiet.

It is possible to sleep outdoors in the winter snow at below-zero temperatures. You simply get two Kmart-type sleeping bags and put one inside the other. Have an old plastic shower curtain or a tarpaulin underneath to keep out dampness. I have done this and I am not extremely hardy. But that was for only one night. After weeks of it, one would get very uncomfortable. Southern states—including the Carolinas, Tennessee, Virginia, Arkansas, Georgia, and Alabama—are much better states if you want to live outdoors all year long. It is also possible in the Southwest if you are careful.

Squatting on land is becoming popular. Why buy land any more, many libertarians and populists argue, when each year the government has more control over your rights to use it? And how can you escape Big Brother if your name is on a deed in the courthouse? They feel that government land such as the national parks and forests belongs to the people and not to the tiny elite that manages it.

The government's land holdings are vast and poorly supervised. Crashed airplanes have been lost for decades in national forests. If they are sophisticated in woods lore, survivalists can easily live for several years in a primitive hut in a national forest and never be discovered. Some of the people living in forests are engaged in illegal activities. You either have to avoid them or show them you are not a threat. If squatters are discovered, the authorities merely put them off the land with their belongings, and their shacks or lean-tos are destroyed. Others rent woodland for a small sum and some make deals to watch a piece of land.

To get sophisticated in woods lore, read Francis H. Buzzacott's 1905 *Complete Campers Manual.* "Buzzacott," as he called himself, always with quotation marks, was a famous 19th century woodsman, hunter, guide, and philosopher. He was a real pioneer himself and knew the ways of people like Kit Carson and Daniel Boone, so the book is much better than later books for a person without money who must do without. Bigger libraries carry it and a book search service could locate a used copy.

Another fine book with the lore of the pioneers is Horace Kephart's, *Camping and Woodcraft.* Kephart was an eccentric and highly educated man who spent much of his life hiding from his estranged wife in the Great Smoky Mountains. He started about 1900, so he was able to learn from real old pioneers and from the wisdom of the old Indians. For long-term independent survival you need the knowledge in these old books too, because you must do without expensive modern conveniences. A reprint of this 1916 classic, sold in bookstores, is published by the University of Tennessee Press. It is fascinating reading. Kephart probably did some moonshining, too, so it is oriented to the person who wants to make a

Francis H. Buzzacott

clean break from civilization. I read it as a kid in the Boy Scouts. Old Boy Scout handbooks from the days of Dan Beard offer fine easy instruction.

Among modern writers on woodcraft and survival, Ragnar Benson is excellent. His books are published by Paladin Press, the publisher of this book.

I have had help from a professional trapper and several hunting guides, have been on civilian survival exercises, and learned a lot about survival in the army. Hiring a guide will help you in your woodcraft skills

Getting Away From It All

When I was a young boy, a weekend in the woods in a pup tent was my favorite recreation—and about the only weekend I could afford. I used these outdoor skills later to save money by avoiding motels and paid parks when I was young and poorly paid in the 1950s. We've traveled all over the United States and I've found it simple to drive off the road out of sight and set up camp. It was easy with high old cars that had 16-inch wheels. With a low modern car I find it is harder, but still possible. You have to get the car out of sight or it will be towed away. I also used a smaller motorcycle, first a 250cc Harley Sprint, now a 185cc Honda Twinstar (with a good, quiet muffler) that can be driven between the trees. It works out splendidly. I have never been discovered or put off the land in all my decades of doing this. You must respect fences, and "posted" signs, close all gates, and remember that picking apples or stealing garden produce in the country is considered a crime like shoplifting and severely punished.

"The hilltops are deserted. They only travel the road." I took this picture with a 1920s Vest Pocket Kodak that cost $12. Most of the pictures in the book were made with low-cost antique cameras I bought in flea markets.

The big secret is that the woods are empty of people except near rivers, waterfalls, high mountains, and natural attractions, and during hunting season. Astonishingly empty! People climb 6,000-foot Mt. Washington but never 700-foot Eagle Rock or 1,800-foot North Pack Monandnock. Also, they are lazy. They will not go cross-country. They must have a path. Any climbing or dense brush stops them cold. Just like a wild bird, you must look to hiding in dense brush as your protection.

You need to know that most people are scared to death of the woods at night. I made them run away with fake animal calls when I was a kid. These days they are even more scared of people they think might be what they call "mountain men." If you can move about easily without a flashlight as many of us learned in scouting or in the service, you can enter your hideout after dusk to sleep and leave just before daybreak. The risk is being seen entering and leaving the woods, but then we should ask, is it an impossible risk? It is not nearly as dangerous as a city slum at night.

People never look *up*. They do not like to climb upward. Pick a spot where the road goes through a valley with a brook, take your motorcycle or go on foot across the brook, and climb up about 200 feet above the road. There you make camp. I use a war-surplus olive drab pup tent and sometimes a jungle hammock, which is easier to put up on a slope than a tent. You cannot use orange, yellow, blue, or other bright-colored civilian camping gear. Tent or hammock, sleeping bag, poncho, and all clothes must be camouflage or drab colors or they will be spotted. Campmor is a large mail-order supplier of this outdoor equipment with a very complete catalog (but try to find this stuff used). Their address is P.O. Box 700, Saddle River, NJ, 17458-0700. Their Web site is www.campmor.com. All this survival living is more or less risky, and we take no responsibility if you try it. But, being in the woods is much nicer than being an urban homeless person or a bag lady.

Let me tell you what I used to do as a teenager. It does not reflect much credit on me and I hope your kids are more honest (as I am now), but it did work and it shows what you can get away with. I had a little girlfriend in a town about 35 miles away. I used to hitchhike over to see her and I would return very late, as late as 3 A.M. if the hitchhiking was bad. My parents would never have approved of that. What I did was tell them I was going to sleep out in the woods to improve my scouting skills. This they would approve. I would hike about a mile into the woods with pack, tent, and all the works. Then I would climb a tree where I had a suit of Sunday clothes hidden in a surplus waterproof bag. I would dress for my date, then put the camping outfit in the bag and raise it in the tree. Then I would hike to the highway and hitchhike to my girlfriend's town.

Coming back I always had myself let off near some house to prevent suspicion. I would hike back along the highway, then cut out through the woods to my tall tree with the pack. I walked all of this in pitch darkness without the flashlight. I'd get the pack down, put my civilian clothes back in the bag, raise the tent, and go to sleep. This went on for some time and never was I caught. Was the girl worth it? Yes, until she joined the Jehovah's Witnesses. But that is another story.

Hiding Things

Once when I was driving to Canada, I forgot I had a .22 target pistol under my car seat. I had a legal permit for the United States, but there would be trouble if the Canadians at the border found it. Going through a valley I stopped the car, opened the hood to make it look like a breakdown (always wise), and climbed quickly up the side of the hill between approaching cars until I was some distance up. I hid the pistol in a plastic bag in the crotch of a tree, carefully marked it with stones and bent

HIDING YOUR CAMP. If you are living primitively, you won't have any security unless your camp cannot be seen from the road. You cannot enter and leave a camp repeatedly without making a path that is obvious to anyone who looks—even if you try to come and go a different way each time. One thing to do is to use a streambed as the trail leading to your camp for a while, and then cut off cross-country. You leave the stream at a different place every time so as not to burn a path. The different paths look something like a river delta in shape and converge to one trail then leading to your camp. You can also use rocky places if your camp is on high ground, as I prefer. See the map below.

Note dense woods (A) and high cliffs (B) protecting your camp (C). Note delta shape (D) of different paths you take. Note streambed (E) you follow from road. (F)

twigs, and resumed my trip. When I returned it was fine. Always mark carefully where something is hidden. I once spent half a day hunting for a cache. If you leave food you have to hide it so bears, coons and other animals will not get it. The usual way is to bag it and suspend it from a tree limb on a rope too high for bears to jump and reach it. If you bury anything, you cannot dig it up after the ground freezes. People forget this. (Read Kephart on caches.)

These skills would be useful in a scenario where the government ran out of money for payroll, welfare, and Social Security, the banks closed and checks could not be cashed, and the people were rioting and looting—which historically is the end to a spendthrift government, although it may not happen here for 50 years, if ever. But woods living does provide free housing, which is a boon. Supposedly you can kill animals and eat berries and mushrooms for food. I have eaten such a meal with a group of people on a survival exercise. A regional civil defense director who was good at survival gathered and prepared the food. It was quite tasty. I even ate a coon once, when I was a bureaucrat. I had to, because it was cooked by a member of the state legislature.

The amount of food in the woods could never support a large number of people. At best, living off the land is a full-time job. You could spend 12 hours a day just getting food and you'd still lose weight. American Indians had famines and starved, you remember, in spite of all their great hunting skills.

Does it really pay to be totally self-sufficient, to live like Robinson Crusoe or the pioneers and make everything yourself—yarn from sheep's wool, clothes from woven cloth, shoes from hides, tools and furniture from trees you cut down? To raise your own livestock—chickens, pigs, cows, and bees for honey and candle wax—make butter, cheese, and soap, and do everything yourself? Definitely not. It takes ages to get your homestead going and your family will all work 15 hours a day and make about 40 cents an hour. My great-grandfather on my mother's side tried it on a homestead near Yarmouth, Maine, in the last century and they all were poor and bitter as long as they lived there, as old letters revealed. Uncle John, his son, tried subsistence farming on 80 acres in New Hampshire until about 1922. But in an emergency, or to keep your freedom or your religious faith, you might have to do these things someday—so they are good to know.

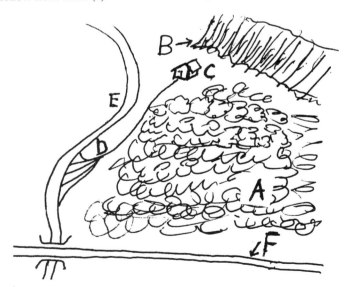

Your Equipment

You will need warm wool clothing for the North, good boots, wool socks, a sleeping bag, knapsack, a waterproof poncho, long knife, compass, emergency waterproof matchbox, canteen, and hatchet. You'll need mosquito repellent and netting when it is warm.

BIC or Zippo lighters are an unromantic way to make a fire, but unlike matches they are waterproof. Matches must be the type that will strike on anything, not just on the specially treated paper on the box that will soon rot out. Waterproof matches are handy as long as your striking surface doesn't get soggy; then they are as useless as any wet matches.

You need a shelter, which can be made of brush as shown in our pictures. Sheets of plastic or old, discarded shower curtains help the waterproofing. Or you could make a lean-to or an A-frame from branches and bark of trees. To stay a while, pack in boards and tools enough to make a neat little hut as shown in Chapter 10.

A hatchet will make a loud noise that carries a long distance. A saw is better for cutting up lots of wood—never use a chain saw. You cannot carry in heavy, expensive things like folding chairs, a camp cot, air mattresses, and a camp icebox in a squatter's camp. With time you make all these things—tools, cutlery, a pine-bough bed, rustic chairs and tables, and a food cooler sunk in a brook or spring.

One reason few people are found on the tops of hills is because there often is no water. Sometimes, however, a good spring is far up a hill. Otherwise you have to pack water in.

You need to be way out—where the hermit thrush still sings. This is very different from camping in a state park. Fires must be very small to avoid detection. Avoid burning green brush and leaves, which smoke. Remember camouflage so you cannot be seen from the air.

Some people find it more convenient when traveling to push a large outfit in a wheelbarrow, much as the urban poor use shopping carts. Sometimes two people carry a large outfit on a stretcher-like device made of two poles, or balanced on a bicycle. Or you can make several trips.

Survival Gear vs. Ordinary Sporting Gear

Survival gear cannot have fastenings made of Velcro; mud or ice will soon ruin them. Zippers, unless very large and tough, will not last long either. You need snaps or buttons as a backup to zippers, like those on an Army field jacket. If wetted, down-filled coats, sleeping bags, and parkas become dismally soggy and dangerously uncomfortable. Many plastics become brittle and useless in real cold. Most civilian camping items such as packs or tents are too light-duty to last long, if used steadily. Polypropylene rope or straps deteriorate rapidly and become dangerously weak. Bright colors or chrome or polished brass items must be avoided. Often military surplus equipment is best to get for your outfit.

Learning More

There is much more you need to know that cannot be included here, or this chapter would be too long to suit most people. So read the old woodsmen's books and more recent military survival manuals and try living out in the woods nearer to home, before you take the final plunge. It is worth hiring

WHY UNCLE JOHN QUIT FARMING. Uncle John had a farm with about a dozen cows. One hot day in July one of the cows drank a gallon of green paint and died. There were no backhoes then so he and his son, Lothrop, had to dig a giant hole and bury the cow. The more they dug, the hotter they got, the more they sweated, and the angrier they became. Uncle John, being a Congregational deacon, could not let himself swear, and that made him even angrier. After the cow was buried he declared, "Any animal that will drink a gallon of green paint is too stupid an animal for me to keep! I'm getting out of the farming business!"

The next day a cattle dealer came and led off all the rest of the cows in a long line. Uncle John then went into the antiques business and was successful from then on. He even sold some antiques to Henry Ford.

Subsistence farming may not be as pleasant as some people today dream it is.

Camp furniture you can make: a board-back chair and log table and benches.

Tricks of Woodcraft.

Things That Can Be Made In Camp.

1—Blanket Tent.

17—Brush Tent.

2—Spoon   3—Knife   4—Fork

5—Camp Shovel

8—Bark Plate.

11—A "Game Spit"

6—Pot Hook and Poker

13—Camp Sun Clock Dial

16—Bark Shanty

12—Tomato Can Candestick

10—Camp Broom.

7—Tomato Can Cup.

9—Camp Fire Tongs.

14—Brush Lean to Teepee.

15—Camp Fire Place.

a guide for a hunting or fishing trip, as I have done, to learn all he knows. Keep him talking!

Many people who live this life have a gun. A 12-gauge shotgun will give good protection against a dangerous animal or person, and shoot birds, but the shells in quantity are expensive and heavy. A .22 pistol or rifle and 1,000 rounds or more of ammunition is a popular choice. Even if your shack is on rented land or you are caretaking the land, you want to be very private about its existence. There are bad guys who might bother you, or steal your possessions and vandalize it while you are away.

You can test the safety of land you may want to use by leaving a sealed package where it can be easily seen. Any passers-by would certainly open it out of curiosity if it was about the size of a stack of bills. None of these packages I have left in high country were ever disturbed. You need to check your own land because conditions change. I once set up a camp late at night deep in the woods (so I thought) when I was very tired. Next morning at sunrise I discovered our tent was only about 250 feet from a house that had people in it. We got out of there fast. I was young then.

You can also hide out in caves and limestone quarries, but I have no long-term experience doing it—only a weekend stay 600 feet underground in a marble quarry. No problem, with a good sleeping bag.

WOMEN. In the woods or in any unusual circumstance, women should conceal pretty hair with a hood or bandanna and wear shapeless, drab clothing. I never heard of any ladies hiding out by themselves in the woods, but several years ago I gave a ride to two middle-aged ladies who were hitchhiking home. They both lived in a junk Cadillac nine-passenger limousine abandoned way out in a field in rural western North Carolina. I took them to it and had a look at it. How they earned a living was a mystery. Maybe it was alimony. They looked too poor to be on welfare.

Women can thrive in the outdoors. Note neat brush lean-to.

Desert Survival

Desert survival is not as difficult or unpleasant as people think. Most of the American Southwest is not a total desert like the Sahara. Many animals and birds live in it. It is cool and often moist at night and early morning. You seldom need any waterproof shelter. Often you can take shelter in a cave or under a rocky shelf if it should rain. Various plants hold water and it is usually not far beneath the surface in dry streambeds. It can get deathly hot in the daytime and you need plenty of shade and two gallons or more of water a day. Talk with people in the Southwest who know the desert well before you try it.

Conclusion

The survival lifestyle costs nothing for shelter, utilities, and taxes. You will get your meat by killing animals and fish but you will probably need to supplement the game, which is extremely lean, with lard and suet. You will have to buy some staples: flour, lard, oatmeal, dried peas, beans, sugar, salt, and powdered milk, as well as soap, lighter fluid, matches, bug powder, ammunition, and antiseptic. These provisions will cost about $500 a year for two people if you must buy them all. But most of the food items are available from the government surplus food program if you are really strapped for money.

The happiest memories of my life are of living in the woods in a survival lifestyle. My wife loves it, too. Camping in national parks where they provide a tent platform, a fireplace, toilets and showers, trash removal, and a protective (if somewhat nosy) park ranger is no equivalent in pleasure to outdoor living by yourself in a real wilderness. You need to get this experience before you are too old. Go for it.

Chapter 5

A New Career or Business for You

Many careers are dead end. If you have not found a job yet, maybe you never will. There are too many middle-management people, too many middle-aged workers, and too many people whose training is obsolete. If you are an electronics engineer or technician and know only tubes and transistors, not digital circuits and chips, you are finished. If you work in accounting, bookkeeping, graphic arts, or journalism and know nothing of computers, you are finished. If you are a computer person and only know Fortran, COBOL, DOS, or the Mac Operating System, you are finished, too. Things change fast.

STARTING OVER

If you really want to move to an attractive rural area where there is no technology, you need to learn an occupation you can practice there. Maybe you can do business by mail or over the Internet. If you want to own your own business, you need to learn a new occupation, in most cases. Here are successful new careers that actual people I know have used to make new beginnings. I hope one of them is suited to you.

What to Avoid

Avoid working in luxury- or hobby-related businesses in hard times such as yachts, general aviation, interior decorating, or arts and crafts such as ceramics. My dad told me he made a big mistake to try to become a photographer after he lost his job in the Great Depression. The poor people did not need any pictures and they had no money to pay for them. He had a dismal time until he finally found a good job again.

Today one meets people who want to open boutiques, or decorate cakes, teach bow and arrow, scuba diving, or guitar. These businesses cannot succeed in a recession. People buy only necessities. Remember, if a business is great fun, everyone will want to try it and you should avoid it. Repairing forklifts or office copiers or rebuilding pallets are less exciting jobs that should make much more money.

Manual Labor

If I lost my job, I would buy a cheap old station wagon or van and get a lot of ladders, scaffolds, and paint brushes and go door to door wearing white coveralls asking to paint people's houses and do home improvements. I'd hire extra help from men hanging around the employment office for each job and pay them by the hour. I'd make the homeowner pay for paint in advance so there would be no overhead.

My good friend Bill Kallio told me about a very profitable way to paint houses. You become an actual paint contractor—you dress well and carry a clipboard when you call on the prospective customer. You rent a high-pressure washer and spray the house first, getting all the flaked paint off. Then you rent the Sherwin Williams airless liquid paint-spraying machine and buy their high-gloss white paint. Do not offer to paint the house any color but gloss white. It always looks the best. Also refuse to do the window frames or mullions, which are very time-consuming. If the people demand it, find a guy to do it and pay him well. You do mask the windows down to the glass on the outside. The house will come out looking beautiful. You will earn at least $100 an hour and do a house in about two days.

But that is only the beginning. For additional money, you offer to spray their lawn with weed killer and fertilizer and to dye the grass bright green with your power spray equipment. And you arrange deals with other workers to sell gutter shields, new guttering, pavement, skylights, low-voltage lawn lighting, carports, and many other contracting jobs for which you get an override commission.

Cleaning corporate offices, washing windows, or offering lawn mowing on a contractual basis are equally good businesses. Big industrial lawn mowers, bought used, don't cost much more than small residential ones. Snowplowing in winter with a 4WD truck or Jeep, or even shoveling snow by hand, are good ways to make money. Another good business is moving people's households. You rent the truck and everything from U-Haul for each move and hire people by the hour, so you have no overhead. Advertise in the classified pages. We always hire this kind of mover in preference to the big nationally advertised movers, who are too costly. You can also use a pickup to take away trash for people. Often they give you valuable items that you can sell for additional profit.

Manual labor is one of the best opportunities around, but modern young people want no part of it so you have little competition. Laborers seldom save enough money to go into business in competition with you. In a lifetime they seem unable to learn even how to measure a house and estimate how many gallons of paint it will take to paint it.

Gypsy Cabs and Buses

Clever people use their cars or vans as unlicensed cabs and take people to airports, welfare offices, and bus stations for a reasonable price. One Gypsy bus, the Great Speckled Bird, operates between Los Angeles and San Francisco. The same idea might work with a van between Baltimore and Washington, D.C., or Dallas and Fort Worth, or between any airport and another up to 100 miles apart if you were discreet and astute at avoiding red tape. Such a service is badly needed to take people in towns along the Rio Grande valley into the airports at Albuquerque and El Paso.

The all-time master of the people's bus is a libertarian teacher I know who bought an old Winnebago motor home from a GI in England. He got it very cheaply because the GI was shipping out. He registered it in South Carolina by mail and insured it for the minimum, just as if it were a camper located in the States. He put the South Carolina plate on the back, added extra seats, and proceeded to tour all of Europe with the Winnebago packed full with a dozen or more American tourists who paid a good sum of money for the tour. He cooked meals in it and served them and sold drinks. The tourists used the Winnebago toilet, but slept in cheap inns, *gasthouses, pousadas,* and pensions at night. He had quite a struggle driving the clumsy vehicle on Swiss mountain roads and through the narrow streets of medieval towns. European border guards and traffic officials seeing the big South Carolina license plate and all the clean, well-dressed, smiling Americans looking out just waved him on. They never checked his papers or looked for an inspection sticker, since a South Carolina vehicle was out of their domain of responsibility.

If you ever went through all the red tape and expense to register a car in Europe, you'll love this story. The point is, the man had no money or property, nothing to attach, so he could get away with it. If you are discreet and have nothing to lose either, such opportunities are good.

Learn the Welding Trade

Take a short course at your community college or technical institute. Then mount an electrical and a gas welding outfit on the back of an old truck and travel around welding broken farm implements, autos and trucks, factory machinery—whatever job you find. Cost is about $6,000 with mostly used equipment. MIG/MAG weld-

ing and the skills of welding cast iron and aluminum are well worth learning and are particularly lucrative. There are new welding helmets that darken only for milliseconds when the weld is being made. Welding pays better than most jobs requiring a college degree. There is little competition because welding is low status and people fear being shocked or burned.

My son, who can do this work, warns that many bigger welding firms have quit the business because of the risk of legal liability if a weld breaks. If you are poor and have no big luxury house that the lawyers can seize in a judgment, this might be a good opportunity for you.

Be a Mobile Mechanic

Learn auto repair and how to tune-up later-model computerized cars at a local tech school. Get the handheld devices that can read modern automobile computers. Equip an old station wagon, van, or truck with a generator, tools, parts, jacks, and spare batteries. You do the work in the customer's driveway. You can do tune-ups, start cars with dead batteries, replace starters, alternators, and fuel and water pumps. Advertise in the classified section of the newspaper and add Yellow Pages advertising when you are successful. A person at home can take calls for you and forward the message using your cell phone or pager, saving much unnecessary travel. About $6,000 will get you going, less if you already have plenty of tools.

Own Your Own Junkyard

There is good money in junkyards. One can do well by scrapping a popular make of car or motorcycle and selling the parts by mail, as well as selling to the crusher. Mustangs, Nash Metropolitans, Cadillacs, Corvettes, '55-'57 Chevrolets, Corvairs, Jeeps, VW Beetles, MGs, and even the German Ford Capri have mail-order and Internet used-parts specialists. You can also recycle copper, aluminum, brass, lead, and many other metals. I have never seen a poor junk dealer!

Motorcycle Repair and Sales

Motorcycles are luxuries in boom times and necessities in recessions or when gasoline is prohibitively costly. If gas increases greatly in price, they could become much more popular again, and this opportunity might become a good one. Brands and styles of motorcycles are cyclical. Once British bikes such as Triumph Bonneville were in great demand, then they passed their peak. People once liked small Honda 50s and 90s. "You meet the nicest people on a Honda," went the ads. At that time you could buy surplus police Harley-Davidsons for very little money. In 1966 I bought a 45 cubic inch Harley WLA for $150 to sell at a profit later. Since the 1990s big Harleys are trendy among yuppies, and most cost $15,000 or more used. Take advantage of these fashion trends. Meet people's needs. Motorcycle repair is harder than auto mechanics. You need to take factory training, enroll in a motorcycle school, or work under an experienced repair person.

Tax Preparation, Payroll, Record Keeping, and Bookkeeping Services

People with business training, bookkeeping experience, and computer skills do well with these services. There is no need for a costly franchise. Do your own ads and keep all the profit yourself. The second year will be better than the first. In a nice location, you may well make more money than you made on your salary back at the old sweatshop. You may need state licenses—better check. Producing documents and forms on your personal computer with a design program and a low-cost laser printer is another possibility. Writing and printing résumés is good, too.

Tutoring Kids

Kids have trouble learning in school today for a variety of reasons. Tutors must have college degrees and are paid quite well, often $12 an hour or more. See what the local economy will stand and do not sell yourself too cheaply. You will teach the kids, either in your own home or in their homes. These may be grade-school, high-school, or even college students, if you know these subjects at college level.

Engineers, even retired ones, are highly in demand to teach remedial math, chemistry, and physics to students. An uncle of mine, a retired civil engineer, did a lot of tutoring in algebra and geometry and liked it very much. He did not need the money. The young housewife who drew the pictures for this book also tutors kids in art.

If you have any experience or a certification teaching reading, even a very old certification, you will be much in demand by the parents of the kids who cannot read. It is not all that technical to teach reading. The kids need a little sympathy and encouragement, personal attention to be sure they are making progress, and some emphasis on phonics. See how the "Hooked on Phonics" program works. Read some books and take a course or two in reading if you are rusty. Advertise your services in classified ads, on bulletin boards (both real and on the Internet) and by word of mouth. Successful students lead to happy parents who give you many more referrals. In time, if you are sincere, they may come to think of you as some sort of miracle worker.

Taking Care of Kids, Sick People, or Prisoners

The women do very well in these fields. Child care is well known, so there is little to add here. Taking care of sick people is good, too, and can give you room and board as well as pay. The LPN practical nursing certificate is good to get, but you can work without it, sitting and watching sick people who cannot manage for themselves. Study for the LPN at your community college. Guards are also needed for the almost two million prisoners these days. Prisons are a growth field. Qualifications are minimal.

Occupations If You Are Desperate For Money Right Now

Try well-known fast-food places like McDonald's. They are always hiring. They train you, and the management is professional and less frictional than some entrepreneurs. Also try washing dishes in any restaurant. They may give you a meal and you'll learn restaurant work. Maybe you can even gain enough experience to fix up a van or trailer to serve hot dogs, burgers, and soda at public events.

Sometimes you can get a chance at a job by offering to work for nothing on approval. Many people have gotten really good jobs by working as volunteers in hospitals, schools, libraries, and social-work agencies. (This is a good way to transcend a poor résumé.) Management soon notices they are efficient and finds them good full-time jobs in the organization.

Also try to find work with temporary services like Kelly and Manpower. Often it is the temp who is hired full-time in preference to the person who answered a help-wanted ad. Actually, help-wanted ads are often placed after the job is filled, simply to fulfill a regulation that the position be advertised. You have no chance at all answering such a dummy ad. You will just get hurt by the rejection.

Homeowners need lawns mowed, leaves raked, and trees and bushes trimmed. Modern kids don't do yard work any more, so there is little competition. Go house to house and offer to do this work. If one person says no, do not be upset—you know you are good and honest. Keep on

Darius D. Robinson (son of the well-known New England auctioneer Darius E. Robinson) tells this story about life in the 1930s. At that time, many people were out of work. Two men stopped at his family's New Hampshire house and offered to paint it free for room and board if the owner supplied the paint. His dad took them up on the offer.

and probably at one of the next doors you knock on, you will be given work. Some of these people ask for and get as much as $100 a day in prosperous urban areas. Keep your appearance neat and clean and try to look happy and competent even when discouraged. Women will find work easily cleaning motels, offices, and homes. It is not such bad work. You'll have a little money very soon. Then save it to try one of the better small businesses.

Most cities have a street corner where men who want work by the day hang out. Bosses and foremen drive by early in the morning and pick them up. You'll do things such as picking apples, raking leaves, or painting. Payment is minimum wage or better, sometimes in cash. Many of these people have lost their licenses from DUI and cannot drive. Another opportunity is all-night gas stations and convenience stores. They are desperate for people to work in them. Little happens at night and often you will have time there to read and study for a better job

Employment Agencies

Walter McCaffrey owned a dry-cleaning plant, which he cleverly sold at the right time. However, he soon found that dry-cleaning plant owners were not regarded as qualified for many other jobs. So he took a job in a private employment agency helping other people find jobs. He resolved that when a really good job listing came along he would take it. In time this happened and he was well pleased.

Be a Flea Market or Antiques Dealer, or
Buy Out Estates or Abandoned Mini-Storage Warehouse Units

This takes at least $12,000 to start and you need an income while the business gets going. Contact owners of all mini-warehouses near you. Contact lawyers, undertakers, and bank-trust officials to tell them you appraise antiques and buy estates. (Check to see if a certification is needed, as it is in some states.) Learn values from the many antiques price

Flea Markets are a good low-risk way to start in antiques or in retail sales.

guides sold at newsstands and flea markets. Go to sales and auctions and learn about the market yourself. Advertise economically with cards on bulletin boards, a computer Web site, small classified ads in shoppers, and perhaps a sign on your car, truck, or place of business. You can work this without a truck. Simply buy or rent cargo trailers as needed. For a big load you rent a truck. There are many clever things to do. Some of these guys always send a sympathy card to the heirs of people they read about in the obituary column. They put in their business card with it.

The principle is, you buy the entire contents of a house for a very small sum, like $1,000. Get it all out of there quickly before the heirs strip it for souvenirs. The heirs are more generous and are less likely to quarrel right after the funeral than later on. Then you sort your load and discard the absolute junk in a Dumpster somewhere. Keep the rest in your garage, barn, or in a mini-warehouse until it is sold. You sell each valuable item with ads on the Internet (try eBay or Yahoo! auction sites), in trade publications, or to specialist dealers. One dealer gets the oil lamps, another the guns, and another the coins and stamps. Rugs, books, china, dolls, old toys, cameras, radios and other valuables go to other specialist dealers. You take the low-value items to flea markets or sell them to a flea-market vendor. There are antique supermarkets where you can rent a booth and the management will do the sales clerking for a commission while you sit at home. The higher levels of flea markets include auction galleries and trade fairs for valuable items. These are usually held in auditoriums or conference centers. Booths can cost $50 or more, but the return is great. There are antiques programs on television that will help you learn about valuable pieces.

You need to be a real horse trader, but if you act too greedy or cheat people with fakes, you will soon be finished. I would give a widow who appreciated the deceased husband a good price, but if the heirs are greedy people who only want the money quickly and think their relative was an old fool, I really use all my wits to buy the estate dirt cheap.

Always check the pockets and linings of old clothing carefully. People hide wads of bills in them. They also hide coins, guns, and jewelry inside mattresses, in attic insulation, and in many strange places. I have used metal detectors to find them.

The hints I give you in this book are real secrets that are seldom given out to the public. They are closely held by families in the antiques business. I hope you appreciate them.

Getting Antiques Free

A way to get goods free is to place classified ads in newspapers and shoppers offering a trucking service to clean out attics, garages, and vacant houses. The people will actually PAY you to cart off the stuff. Some of it is quite valuable. These ads work best in wealthy areas and upscale neighborhoods. City trash removal and dump personnel are good people to know and can lead you to some good deals.

Business Strategies

I once worked for the old White Elephant Shop, then the largest antiques store in the world. It was a whole abandoned factory in New Hampshire full of old things.

The owner told me he usually bought for 10 percent of his selling price. He would try to pick up a truckload of goods and sell one item for what he had paid for the whole load; that way the rest of the goods cost him nothing.

It is bad business to like the goods you sell too much. You'll charge too much so you won't sell anything, and you'll pay too much and keep back your best goods. The business becomes merely a vanity hobby rather than a real business. A lot of so-called dealers do this. I am thoroughly sick of most of the things I sell on the Internet, and sometimes call them "junk" within the family. So I still make money.

If you trade, always get money to boot, no matter how unequal the value. I've heard about a New England Yankee who, starting with a jack knife, swapped and swapped one item for another, each being a little better, until, after a number of trades, he ended up with a car.

Uncle John, who sold antiques in Hillsboro, bought a table for $10 and sold it for $50. The person who bought it from him for $50 sold it for $1,000. So it sometimes goes.

Redneck Economics vs. Millionaire Economics

It is a great and popular misconception that big profits are made by keeping valuable goods for many years before selling for a final big appreciation. That is NOT true. High volume and rapid turnover of your stock is the real secret to making money. If you sell everything you buy for an average profit of 50 percent after expenses and roll over your entire stock each year, your gain after 10 years will be astronomical. For example, if you started with a stock-in-trade of $1,000 and rolled it over every year at 50 percent profit, its worth in 10 years would be over $56,000. Do the math yourself. This is how the really big fortunes are made.

By staying in business year after year, as the good stuff all sells, your shop will become filled with junk that nobody buys. The thing to do then, say the experts, is to sell the shop and start over. This principle applies to most businesses, not just to antiques.

The way rednecks think is entirely different. For example, take the man who bought a commemorative Winchester lever action rifle 10 years ago for $500. Today he finds it is worth $1,000. He thinks he is a brilliant investor. He is not, because if he had instead invested wisely in stocks, in 10 years his $500 would be $5,000 or more. If he had put it in a supply of goods he rolled over every year at 50 percent profit his $500 investment would be worth $28,000! A serious businessman would laugh at only doubling his money every 10 years.

Here is another example. A rich man buy two E Jaguar cars for $10,000 each in 1975—one to keep and one to drive. In 2000 he gets the unused one out and finds it is worth $30,000. He thinks he has made a killing. Actually he is only breaking even. Here's why: Let us assume he earned $20,000 a year in 1975. His $10,000 Jag cost him 6 months' work. In the year 2000 his $30,000 1975 Jag still is worth 6 months' work at the

$60,000 a year a similar job would be paying now. He hasn't allowed for inflation. That is redneck economics. The principle here is that there is no profit in buying something cheap with cheap money and keeping it a while and then selling it for expensive money. Learn this principle and always apply it and you will know something only very few people know and be on your way to making really big money.

The know-how of rich people is really kept secret by general agreement. It is only passed down in families or told to favored employees selected for rapid promotion. College won't teach it to you. I took economics in college. The professor told me a lot about how bad capitalism was, and how it was destroying the environment and how we had to have big government spending programs to regulate the economy (Keynesian economics). I learned nothing about the stock market in college, nothing I could use to make any money. *This book is one of very few that actually reveals the secrets of wealthy families. I hope you appreciate this.*

Yesterday's Trash Is Today's Treasure

I am amazed when I look in a flea market and see that items I had as a kid and lost or discarded or sold cheaply are now for sale at huge prices. Old Superman and Tom Mix comics, Boy Scout insignias, cereal premiums, art deco plastic radios, toys like the Marx electric train I sold for $30 as a kid—these are now worth big bucks. What will be the future valuables? Do you know? Maybe Barbie dolls and Dale Earnhart souvenirs. But it is redneck economics to think you can support yourself by stashing things like this away for 20 years or more. You will make more money doing something else.

But if you are going to buy something anyway, it might be better to buy a future classic. I have a tentative belief that very early Mac computers such as the SE and IIsi and some PC computers may have some value later. So will old pocket calculators, microphones, and vacuum-tube hi-fis. I love early manual typewriters of the 1920-'45 period because I used them for years. I've bought a lot of them at $10 or so. But they are worth little more today. I suspect that books that are not politically correct may be valuable later, as will Clinton memorabilia (because most of it will be discarded).

People today show real love for the Saturn car, the Mazda Miata, and the Datsun 280Z. The 450SL Mercedes convertibles are cherished and may have some appreciation. The Chrysler PT Cruiser, Plymouth Prowler, and Dodge Viper look like winners. I'm not sure that any of these items I have mentioned will go up greatly in value, but I doubt they will drop much. What do you believe will be tomorrow's antiques? Think about this. Try to find out.

Yard Sales

Yard sales can have amazing bargains. A customer told me he bought a $2,000 Hasselblad camera for $5. I bought the first 1888 Kodak camera for $50 and then sold it to a museum for $2,000. I regularly buy high-grade Japanese cameras such as Nikons for $35 and sell them for $150 or so on the Internet.

Many people still do not know values in spite of the many antiques price guides available. Some dealers in rural areas will buy locally and sell nationally. These people are called "bird dogs." Yard sales and thrift stores in upscale areas and areas where there are a lot of senior citizens are particularly good. I found those in Falmouth, Massachusetts, and Tryon, North Carolina, had many valuable treasures at low cost. Antique shops in some newly settled areas have to import their antiques, sometimes in containers from Europe.

Now that so many people collect, much of the business is selling established collections of people who give up their homes or die. In the antique business, they say the goods stay the same and the customers change. In most businesses, like groceries, the goods change and the customers stay the same. These days now that old things are widely believed to be better than newer things and people often cannot afford new, the secondhand and antiques trades are particularly promising. You might do better with antiques than in anything else you could find. It is great fun, too!

Become an Auctioneer

If you have a quick eye and a gift with words, you might make a good auctioneer. It is a lucrative little-known trade that gives you an inside to all kinds of good deals. I knew Darius E. Robinson, the best and most colorful of the old-time New England auctioneers and traders. He made a good living at it and was greatly respected. Go for a few weeks to one of the auctioneers schools advertised in the antiques collecting magazines found in libraries and on newsstands. That is the way it is learned.

Become a Part-Time Photographer

Dad almost starved when he tried to be a photographer during the Great Depression. The field does poorly in hard times. But today it might work as a part-time occupation since most pictures are taken evenings and weekends. To make money and not lose a lot, here are some cautions.

1. Do not take a college photography course. They are oriented to making you a "fine arts" photographer or a war-zone-type "photojournalist." The world is full of these and almost none of them make any money. The professors have an absolute disdain for the profitable aspects of photography, such taking photos of weddings, babies, groups, and industrial and architectural shots. To learn right you should read good books on photography, or work for a photographer and carry his bags for nothing. Or seek out correspondence schools (sometimes called distance learning). The New York Institute of Photography (NYIP) Correspondence School course in photography is excellent. You learn various trade secrets so your pictures will no longer look like amateur snapshots. The instructors write you long letters critiquing your pictures.

   It mystifies me why people will spend $2,000-$3,000 or more for a camera outfit and then refuse to get any training at all. Their pictures continue to look like snapshots, even with the fancy camera. If you think the cost is too great you may be able to find a secondhand NYIP course.

2.   Do not believe newsstand photo magazines such as *Popular Photography, Petersen's,* or *Shutterbug.* Their articles are simply infomercials designed to hype expensive new cameras and lenses that you do not need. There are many consumer problems with the New York mail-order stores advertising in them. *The Rangefinder* is a pro magazine. Philip Greenspun's Photo.Net (www.photo.net) is the best Internet photo resource.

3.   Do not spend a lot of money for fancy cameras unless you are really big time and making fabulous money. You can do fine work with a used 35mm Pentax Spotmatic or K1000; Minolta SRT101; Olympus OM-1; Canon FTb or AE-1; or the Nikon FE, FM or FG. These cameras can be bought in yard sales in the more affluent suburbs in the $35 range. Sometimes they are given away. I was given a fine Nikon FG. Avoid autofocus. You need a big flash, such as the Vivitar 283. Photographers tend to go equipment-crazy and spend all their profits on new cameras. Cameras last a long time. Many of them 30 or even 50 years old are not obsolete. I use older cameras including the Kodak 35RF, Flash Bantam, and various bellows-folding models; Nikon FG, and Leica IIIa for the pictures in my books because I enjoy using them so much.

4.   You don't need a darkroom any more, though they are fun. You can have 35mm negatives developed and proofed by Wal-Mart, then

It is very profitable shooting big group photos like this one that I took. Each person buys a picture for $10 each.

print them professionally on your computer on glossy photo paper. Or use a mail-order lab dealing with professional photographers such as Garrett & Lane Professional Imaging, 1017 Virginia Street, Columbus, Georgia, 31901. A modern color copier, or inkjet computer printer, will make big prints good enough to sell.

Here is what you *should* do to make money with your camera. Big groups are excellent. Taking photos for class reunions, church homecomings, and clubs and organizations provides good money. I can sell 100 prints of a group of 100 people for $10 each. The prints cost me $2.40 each. Nice money. I use a Mamiya C330 medium-format camera for groups over 50 people and a 35mm for smaller groups. The Yashicamat 124, about $150 used in stores, maybe $35 in yard sales, is fine too. A Kodak Monitor for about $25 will do the job, but you will have to mail order the 620 film. Use a flash, shoot several pictures in case someone blinks, and arrange the people like bricks on a wall so they are not directly behind each other, but each one is looking out between two people. Or get up on a ladder or shoot out a window at the people looking up at you.

Weddings are pretty good money, and fun too. Get paid by credit card and take a deposit. Work closely with your professional lab on these. (Some pros still keep a camera in the car all the time for accidents and spot news but if that's what you're looking for you will make more money with video that you can sell to the TV networks.) It is very hard to compete with the chain studios for portraits. You may make more money copying and restoring old photos, or using a camera to illustrate your own articles and books as I have been doing for years. There is a wedding photographer who uses a digital camera, does retouching on the computer, and displays his proofs on the Internet.

Airbrush Work

A person who is artistic should try this. You set up in a flea market or mall, or work out of a van or motor home. You paint T-shirts, auto front license plates, motorcycles, and maybe cars and vans. You paint kid's faces (with nontoxic, washable paint, of course.) Some people travel the country doing it and seem to make money.

Franchises and Other Opportunities

Many of them are hopeless, but some are worthwhile. People have made money applying tints to window glass, fixing broken windshields with a special process, applying a dye to make faded lawns look green, selling frozen foods to housewives from a refrigerated truck, installing aluminum windows, gutter shields, vinyl siding and spraying stucco on houses. There must be some franchise like these now that is new. You need to look for it and be very careful. Things like hats with solar-operated propeller fans have not done so well.

Mail-Order Business

We've done mail-order business for more than 30 years. It works well and supports us anywhere we want to live. Books sell well by mail. So do smaller antiques and specialized items like high-fashion novelties or high-tech parts and hobby supplies. I have been selling lots of goods by mail since the 1960s and by now I use the Internet almost exclusively. In the 1960s I sold high-grade cameras to collectors and professional photographers. My ex-wife sold antique quilts. She had a group of rural women making them in North Carolina and we sold them with small classified ads in *New York* magazine. We had no catalog, simply took color slides of them and sent the color slides to the customer on approval. It worked unusually well until the farm women discovered how much the quilts were really worth and doubled their prices.

What I do now is to sell technical books on how to repair cameras and radios by mail. We have been doing this since the 1970s. I wrote most of them myself. Please don't feel obligated to buy any; this is not a gratuitous sales pitch, but what we discovered can help you with your own telemarketing business. You have to figure out something else to sell that would be good today, perhaps used music CDs, baseball cards, health items, something for computers . . . who knows?

I learned the trade of camera repair from military manuals and with some help from a retired camera repairman. I discovered there were no new books on repairing cameras. So I wrote a 24-page pamphlet which we had printed by the *Mother Earth* people. We sold them for $8 in 1975. It had a catchy title, *Trade Secrets of Camera Repair*.

The books didn't sell well with classified ads, but when I put a $100 display ad in *Petersen's Photographic Magazine* the sales really boomed. We kept revising and expanded the book to more than 130 pages, raised the price gradually to $39, added other books, and even put in a stock of small tools to repair cameras. We knew the business would soon peak out, so we were careful to invest very little money in it and keep inventories low. The money we took out of the business we put into our retirement savings account. It is lucky we did this.

We succeeded because our book had a catchy title, the ads were hard-hitting (Fix Your Own Camera), and we ran lots of them. The ad budget in national magazines was as much as 40 percent of our gross—much more than we spent for the book itself. The big ads used to cost $4,500 each. We ran into violent opposition from most camera repair shops and camera stores who didn't want amateurs fixing cameras. They felt it would depress the market. We were able to turn this opposition to our advantage by saying in effect, "If the dealers don't want you to fix your camera, it surely must be a good idea."

This is now an overly mature business and it is declining. I don't care, because I want to retire, which is why I am telling you about it. But you can take some other product, some other book in a different field, or something else and market it exactly as we did. As the business declined, we found we could not sell enough books to have a thousand copies printed by a print shop any more. If we'd continued to use commercial printers we would have gone out of business. But by then, 1989, we discovered that a Mac computer and a laser printer could produce an excellent camera-ready book. Even photos could be screened wonderfully in the Mac. So now we did not have to pay for expensive commercial printing. And big office copiers by then were good enough to print a book from our master that looked like offset litho work, collate the pages automatically and make the books fairly rapidly—50 pages a minute. We purchased a big Canon 6600 copier. It printed all our books and also made a pretty good black-and-white four-page illustrated catalog on a single sheet of folded 11 x 17 paper.

We never had any full-time employees, just temps whenever we were very busy. My wife Sara took phone orders and kept the records and often ran the copier. Most of the office furniture was cheap surplus stuff. Desks were made of doors on cement blocks or old two-drawer file cabinets. The business is kept in a garage. We store the books in a portable building in the yard. No locks or high security are needed with books. Bad people can't read. Space in a house costs less than space in an office building.

The next problem with the business came in the early 1990s. By then the ads cost a huge sum of money compared to our reduced sales. The smallest one-inch display ad in *Pop Photo* cost $600, and I had to run them all year long to get any results.

Then in 1995 we got on the Internet. I designed a Web site, www.edromney.com, something like my catalog, with a lot of pretty color photos I took with a $100 1936 Leica and a $10 Agfa Karat. This Web site immediately became a winner. The site outsold the magazine ads so greatly that we stopped advertising in magazines entirely. So the Internet saved our business!

I urge you to try this format with some other product. It should be very successful. More information about the Internet is in Chapter 6.

Fun and Problems of Mail-Order Businesses

The fun of a mail-order business is you can work in a cellar, garage, or temporary steel building way out in the country. You don't have to dress up or have a fancy office. Success is almost entirely the result of your own ability and ambition. But it is a risky business. Never use borrowed money. Many mail-order firms have failed recently because they were mailing too many unsolicited catalogs and direct-mail letters. We never send a catalog unless it is ordered. It keeps costs down to design and typeset your own ads on a personal computer and submit them camera ready, which entitles you to a 15 percent ad agency professional discount. The Internet is the best ad media of all.

Starting a Factory on Practically Nothing

My son Edward, now age 38, is quite bright, but two years of college was all he could stand. He knocked around for a few years being a disk jockey and doing various things at near minimum wage. At a factory where he worked he met a man who was recycling pallets. This man got them for free, knocked the nails out of them, and reassembled them with new pieces of wood where needed. They were then about as good as a new pallet. He would take them around in an old GMC truck and sell them. He was getting sick of the work and offered my son the whole business for $2,000.

My son bought it with money from his mother and soon was selling so many pallets he quit his factory job. The old truck was replaced with a discarded Ford U-Haul 24-foot van. He removed the body from it and made it a pallet truck. By then he was hiring employees. He has unusual personal skills and was able to work with unskilled laborers who had many problems. (Many had lost driving licenses due to DUI.) He used to drive around and pick them up for work. The work was all done out of doors and in an open shed regardless of weather, which can be done in North Carolina.

I didn't bankroll him or give him advice; I think I have only given him about $2,500. I don't know anything about pallets, and very little about running a factory.

He built Ed's Pallet World himself entirely out of earnings, added automatic machinery, bought a big, new International diesel truck and now, 12 years later, has five trailer trucks—all Macks and Freightways—35 semi-trailers, 40 employees, a giant wood-chip grinder, and a 100x150-foot steel factory. Last year he grossed $1.5 million. He says it is great fun, like a hobby, owning and maintaining big trailer trucks, a bulldozer, tractors, and forklifts. That is something to think about.

He still drives around town in old working clothes in a very old Chevy pickup. I remember he got seriously interested in business after he read Ayn Rand. My son says you can still start a small pallet business for a few thousand dollars using an old pickup truck and working out-doors, and succeed and grow. That is the point of this story. Go for it!

Build a Power Company on Practically Nothing

Some years ago an intense, unusual man came out of the woods of Canada. He looked something like Abraham Lincoln and his name was Leonard Rodenhiser. He had a mission—to bring electric power to the town of Sherbrooke, Nova Scotia. This was during the Great Depression, so no investors would give him funding. So he took up a subscription from the town's people and started to build—with boundless energy. He built a giant dam of logs with the help of friends. From abandoned mines and factories he found the huge pipe to take the water to his tur-bine. His turbine and generator were discarded surplus too. He chopped

Ed's Pallet World then and now.

his own trees and set power poles and strung wire all by himself. And there was his power company and it lighted the town, just as he promised. It provided electricity to about a hundred houses and lighted the streetlights, too. And he built it all himself!

It was easier to do things like this in the Depression, when surplus was practically given away. But it still can be done, and is being done. The United States is in an industrial depression right now in the Rust Belt of Pennsylvania and the Midwest. The textile industry is depressed in the South, and in New England where the textile mills are being abandoned rapidly. Large generators and turbines are still available from these mills for about the value of the metal in them. I wasn't fortunate enough to know Leonard Rodenhiser, but I do know Lt. Col. Warren H. Taylor, who has done the same thing recently.

Col. Taylor built three power plants in New Hampshire, Massachusetts, and New York. He started by buying the old abandoned Mascoma Mills in Enfield, New Hampshire, for a very low price. He and his son, Tim, doing most of the work, raised and improved the dam and installed the generator that they bought surplus for practically nothing. The mill they fixed up as an industrial park. It is rented to various fine small businesses, including a pipe-organ factory, and used to store boats, cars, and motor homes against the New England winter. The power is sold back to the power company. This is the way it is done these days. Taylor built two more power plants like this one. They run unattended—controlled by a computer over the phone lines. This can be quite a lucrative business when the waters above the dam are high. Taylor mentioned casually that one of his power stations had been earning $1,000 a day!

Maybe the greatest success secret I ever learned came from the Colonel. It is never to let oneself be intimidated by something new.

In the early days of television, before he got into generating power, Colonel Taylor built a whole cable TV system to bring the first TV to a village deep in a valley in Vermont from a mountaintop antenna. It used homemade vacuum-tube boosters and twin lead in place of coaxial cable.

Next he started a tabloid classified-ad shopper called the *Bargain Buster*. It used two big old sheet-fed litho presses he rebuilt. He built his own plate-making camera out of an old metal TV cabinet with a metal wastebasket telescoping into it like a camera bellows holding the lens. It was driven by rollers and strings on spools and worked well for many years. To assemble the paper, he made his own collating machine with long wooden arms that swooped down on the paper sheets and grabbed them in little clips and set them in piles on a conveyer belt driven by an old washing-machine transmission. The arms were pivoted on bearings made from old roller skates. Taylor's experience in printing was nil. His collator and camera were unlike any I had ever seen, but they worked well. And he made money and did a lot of good with his fine, patriotic editorials in the shopper—which is what really counts. Now the Colonel is working on a new type of steam engine to bring low-cost power to farmers and woodsmen. Taylor does not have a college degree. He is a correspondence school graduate and rose from the enlisted ranks to be an officer.

The Shoe Factory That Could

A deal like this is big bucks. I used to drive past a shoe factory in northern New England on other business. It was doing well then, but a few years back it nearly failed. Here is the story they told me.

When the factory was going down fast, but still running, a very good salesman who needed a job called on them—direct approach, cold turkey. He saw the shoes were good but they were not selling because the present salesmen were just taking orders. They only did business with those stores they had supplied for years. They did not look for new business. They never contacted the newer discount department stores that were buying shoes in large quantities or the mail-order catalog firms.

So this guy took over the sales department. He worked day and night, wore out a car every year, was always leaving on the plane, meeting with customers, talking with them, phoning them, setting up new accounts and following up sales. This man knew nothing of the shoe business. He just knew how to sell. He saved the company!

Honest selling is seeing and meeting a need. It is communication. They say in sales meetings that if there were no salesmen (and women) in the world, people would still be living in houses with dirt floors, chopping firewood, and carrying water from the well. It is the salespeople who get people going, make people want new things, who create enough of a demand so the goods can be sold cheaply. Maybe you would like to make a BIG comeback and do something like this.

Chapter 6

Low-Cost Computers for Fun, Profit, and Education

You don't need to be a whiz at science to use a computer. Most of it is like driving a car, just press the keys and work the mouse and see what happens. Computers are not expensive. Lots of older ones are on the market now for a few hundred dollars or less. I bought a working Mac IIx for $25 in 2000. Older computers may be easily upgraded with more memory and modern features. Macs are much more user-friendly than Windows and are low cost used, but may be getting obsolete. Windows has more programs for business and is better to learn today. You really begin to learn only when you actually get behind your own computer.

Here are some of the opportunities for you to make money in computers.

- Show new users how to work their computers in their own homes. People buy computers from discount stores like Kmart and get no support and no training. Many experts who understand computers can't explain them to others; they make it too complicated. If you can explain computers simply, you will make lots of money instructing people.
- Deal in old computers. Buy them cheap, buy surplus ones, assemble them from parts, upgrade them, sell them, and sell used programs. This can be lucrative.
- Get a home sales business on the World Wide Web. You can live anywhere. My own Web site developer lives in Japan. My own Web site promoter lives in California. My publisher for this book is in Colorado. I buy programs and computer supplies on the Internet, too. I have sold unusual things easily on the computer bulletin boards, including an accordion, a 1923 radio, and many professional cameras with no advertising cost. I buy mail-order books and many other products from Internet Web sites. You are not handicapped in any way if you live in the country. There are free e-mail services such as Juno.com and Yahoo.com and free Web sites available at www.geocities.com. but you have to put up with advertising. You can use computers free at many libraries, until you buy yours.

These opportunities are fabulous! There is far more potential than we can cover here, more than you can imagine now. Good luck!

Everyone knows that computer are big time today. But they are widely misunderstood. You do not have to be very young or incredibly brilliant to use one. I have worked on a charity that gives computers to senior citizens and disabled people. Most of the old-timers do very well with them after some sympathetic instruction. Too many computer professionals use complicated words and concepts that make them excessively difficult to understand. But you can use a computer much as you use a radio or a tape recorder without understanding where all the electrons go and what the chips do. That is how most people use them.

The Macintosh computers are simpler to use than Windows. Many highly creative people prefer them. Rush Limbaugh uses Mac. So does Paladin Press. I have used the Mackintosh exclusively with great success for more than 10 years. I have never had a breakdown on a Mac. Programs have crashed but I have been able to reinstall them or make some changes and get the computer going again. These days used Macs are very cheap, often less than $100, but most computers are of the Windows variety and Mac programs are hard to get locally, so Windows is probably the better choice.

There is a myth that computers become rapidly obsolete and only the latest, most powerful, most expensive one is of any use to the consumer. This is not true. They do not change that fast. In our mail-order business we used our first Mac, the IIsi for five years. In 1995 we replaced it with a Power Macintosh. It is in use now in 2001 and I am composing this book manuscript on it. It produces my Web site, too. I see no reason for me to trade since I know it well. I just bought another 7200/120 Power Mac for a backup for $164 from Herb Johnson on the Internet. Visit his Web site at http://njcc.com/~hjohnson/ or e-mail him at hjohnson@pluto.njcc.com

Computer fans brag about the speed and memory capacity of their favorite computers much as auto enthusiasts brag about the horsepower and rpm of their muscle cars. It makes no sense for serious users; you don't need a Jaguar to run a taxi business. The slowness of the Internet puts a speed limit on computers much as heavy traffic forces a powerful car to move slowly on a trip through town. Cable modems and new faster systems such as DSL do help. But if you do not have a cable modem, you do not need a fast computer—don't let the salesmen fool you. A specific example: I do not type fast—about 45 words per minute. I was able to out-type my old 16mhz Mac IIsi of 1990 so the words were delayed or it jammed. My Mac 7200 at 120mhz is impossible for me to out type. So why do I need a 500mhz computer?

It is possible to upgrade older computers with larger hard drives and more RAM (memory) so they work better and store more data. Bigger hard drives and RAM chips are low cost from specialty firms on the Internet selling surplus or used parts.

We cannot teach computers in one chapter, obviously. You need to buy a book from the popular *Macs for Dummies* or *Windows for Dummies* series. Public libraries have computers the public can use, usually Windows, and their people can help you learn them.

Many computer courses in colleges are taught by people who feel they are very brilliant. Perhaps they are, but nobody can understand them. They talk about bits and bytes and parity and databases and PPP, TCP, and TCP/IP until you are thoroughly confused. Unless you hear from students who have taken it that a certain college computer course is excellent, do not enroll in it.

SOME OF THE THINGS YOU CAN DO WITH A COMPUTER

Computers are good for getting the news at any time. Reuters News Service from www.yahoo.com is more objective and unbiased than the mass-media news. The Drudge Report at www.drudgereport.com gives you exclusive news stories you will read nowhere else. Yahoo! has good financial and business news and will give the value of your stocks at any time. Yahoo! and other services, such as www.weather.com give you the weather anywhere.

These sites are good for doing research—looking up information and finding obscure books and articles. Type in what you want to find in www.yahoo.com or other similar search engines such as Excite, Google, Lycos, or Alta Vista and you will get a long list of Web sites to go to. You can buy an Encyclopedia Brittanica on a compact disk for $125, much less than the $1,250 you would pay for a new Brittanica as a set of books. The computer will print out detailed road maps of anywhere you might want to drive in the United States, and it can find most anyone's address and phone number.

Computers are good for buying things. Type in whatever you want in Yahoo! or other search engines and you will get a list of dealers selling it. I have looked up British motorcycles, Wurlitzer organ parts, and Mamiya cameras in the last few days—with success. People make travel plans, buy tickets, and sell cars, boats, and real estate on the Internet. We sold our old sailboat easily.

The Internet is good for fun and games, for social activities, and making new friends. Myst is a wonderful computer game. The Usenet newsgroups have friends who meet and discuss almost any topic you can imagine—from buttered scones to frugal living and Dumpster diving. Many cities and states have regional newsgroups to put you in touch with local activities and help you make friends in a new area. AOL has chat rooms where you can converse with people who share similar interests and make new friends. With a computer, you can live most anywhere and stay in touch and not feel lonely. They work worldwide, not just in the States, and it costs no more to send an e-mail to Japan than it does to talk locally.

The computer can print photographs and enhance them. You can retouch and restore old photos with a program called Photoshop. The LE version of Photoshop is lower cost, sometimes even free, and is quite adequate. I prefer a 35mm scanner to a digital camera. Polaroid SprintScan is best. A flat-bed scanner, about $100, will put photo prints into your computer where you can work on them. The laser printer produces black-and-white documents that look like commercial printing.

If you travel a lot you can keep in touch with a laptop or use the computers in libraries and computer cafés. AOL and some other services provide call-in numbers all over the country. Services like hotmail.com permit you to use library computers anywhere to access your email.

I buy most things for the computer over the Internet. I download new programs, many of which are free, and instruction and repair manuals, buy laser toner, upgrade RAM chips, and buy accessories such as modems. Computer newsgroups help with problems, sell me used Mac programs and accessories, and give me good advice.

The computer is wonderful for business. It can keep your payroll and tax records, control your inventory, do most of your correspondence and advertise your business better than any other media world wide. You can trade stocks online. The cost is very low. A commercial Web site costs about $50 a month. Simple Internet service is about $20 a month for unlimited use. Juno.com is free for Windows users.

WHY MANY DOT.COMS FAILED

Many Web sites, unfortunately, are of terrible quality—even those of big companies. The trouble is the pages are very slow to load, they're too complicated, and they keep you clicking your choice and waiting, much like one of those irritating Merlin automatic telephone systems. For example "If you live in America click one; if you live in Mexico, click 2; if you are going to spend over $100 click one; if over $200 click 2; etc., etc., etc." Computer pros will give you a slow, boring Web site if you let them, because they know nothing about people. They make the graphics much too big and slow to load and use too much Java. Separate windows are confusing, as are moving cartoons. You can tell how good a Web site is by how long it takes to load and how many times you have to click and wait before you get your data. A good Web site is www.paladin-press.com. My own Web site, www.edromney.com, seems to work. I try to make the people keep on reading and not interrupt them by making them click on choice boxes all the time. Many Web sites do not make money because the owners do not promote them and link them to other pages (www.submitit.com is a service that will do this for you).

Internet security worries some people. I feel the computer-fraud problem is greatly exaggerated. We never had a customer report a stolen credit-card number from our site. I think most Internet credit thefts are simply dishonest employees in the mail-order firm copying off credit card numbers the old-fashioned way by hand, and not computer-related at all. There are risks in meeting strangers of course and you and your family must be very careful.

If you don't want life to pass you by, I urge you seriously, sacrifice if need be and make yourself a part of this fascinating new computer environment.

Whether, Where, and How to Relocate

You need to relocate if you have lost your job and cannot find another, if it costs too much to live where you are, if you have to escape a troublesome ex-wife or husband, or if the government puts a low-income housing project right next to your residential neighborhood.

THE INS AND OUTS OF RELOCATION

You can relocate if you have to. The pioneers relocated with success. The only risk in moving is finding the same or worse problems in the next place.

Some people take their problems with them. Are you one of them? You have to check your own motives and first carefully research the place to where you want to move. A new location often means you have to learn a new career or retire and live on a small income. Can you do it?

Getting Money To Relocate

In places like Los Angeles, San Francisco, the D.C. area, Connecticut, Westchester, northern New Jersey, Long Island, and others, ordinary houses are $350,000 to $750,000 or more. If you live in one of these high-cost areas, simply sell your house and move to one of the many low-cost places described in this chapter. There you buy a house or a doublewide for between $40,000 and $75,000 and invest the difference and live on the interest using the money-saving methods in this book.

Growth Area or Low-Cost Living?

If you want work or you plan to start a local business, it is best to move to an area that is prosperous and growing. On the other hand, if you plan to retire or want to live on a small income, you will be best off in a place with a low cost of living, usually a depressed area where your fixed income goes a long way. Most of these are in the East or Midwest. You can start businesses in depressed areas, however, if the products are

All authorities agree that you can live better on a small sum of money in the country or in a small city than in a big one. The problem is, you will also find it harder to get work and you will be paid less. But most people find quality of life and freedom from crime and being hassled a big plus for the country. If you live in the city in a condo or apartment in a high building with a doorman, travel everywhere in taxis, and work in a high-rise office building where you never see the streets, city life can be quite nice. Otherwise it is often horrible.

People in cities are hassled by police, mugged by criminals, and must play games with a large hostile government bureaucracy to get their checks, food stamps, and other benefits. City welfare benefits are usually much higher than those in the country, but living off the government is a degrading existence.

sold elsewhere. You must decide if you are looking for a job or a safe haven before you can pick a place where you will relocate.

WHERE TO RELOCATE

Surveys report that the places most people want to move to are Vermont, Florida, and the Southwest. California is now too expensive and crowded. Florida still has great possibilities but Vermont is hardly a low-cost place to live. We will discuss other places to settle that may be better for you, some with unique opportunities. A good Internet site for finding basic information on various cities is www.2chambers.com. This site links to the chambers of commerce for cities in every state in the nation. Be aware: these sites will probably only list the positive sides of each city.

I will talk a lot about lifestyles and values because they are so important to a person relocating. I've traveled all these states, sold goods in them, and visited neighborhood coffee shops to gather information for you. A lot of people have provided the data here. I've tried to be as fair as possible and apologize to any I have offended.

Maine

The coast is costly and somewhat unfriendly, but Aroostook and Washington counties in the northern part are outstanding places to live for those who are not seeking work. This is lumber country. The potatoes are doing poorly. Several industries have failed and the area has seen better years. Closing of the Loring SAC bomber base hurt the Aroostook County economy badly. All this means low-cost housing and opportunity for the newcomer with a little money. The climate is severe with autumn leaves falling in early September and snow often lasting on the ground until May. See www.houlton.com for information about the region.

Aroostook and Washington counties have beautiful small cities and towns including Island Falls, Houlton, Presque Isle, Caribou, Mars Hill, Danforth, and Fort Kent. Danforth has exceptional real-estate opportunities and is near Grand Lake, a giant lake unsurpassed for boating and fishing, with many beautiful camps along its winding shores. Land in northern Maine can be bought for around $1,000 an acre. Farms are less than $100,000 and smaller homes and camps are as low as $15,000 in 2001 dollars.

There are beautiful museum-grade Victorian homes in cities like Houlton for around $75,000 that would be $500,000 in Connecticut. Rents are quite low due to the declining population, and plenty of apartments are available for about $300 a month plus utilities and heat. There is a unique bed and breakfast in Danforth, Maine, where teachers, government employees, retirees, and some seasonal hunters and fishermen have lived together happily for years. Calais (pronounced "Kal'us") is an interesting, quite international city on the Canadian border near colorful Eastport and Canadian St. Stephen, New Brunswick. These are fascinating low-cost places you will enjoy. Look them over.

The Maine people are very intelligent, about an equal mix of Catholic French Canadians and Protestants. The girls are beautiful even when conservatively dressed. Aroostook people remind you more of Southerners than other New Englanders. They are quite religious. They have camp meetings and revivals. A lot of antiques and fine antique cars can be found in barns. I bought half a dozen antique cars when I lived there. Old lever-action hunting rifles and double-barreled shotguns were quite cheap, too. There is a lot to do socially in northern Maine in the winter, many clubs, meetings, concerts, plays, evening classes, bingo, auctions, and fish and game club dinners of salmon, venison, and even bear meat, so you really do not mind all that snow and cold. None of this fun costs a lot. Crime is virtually nil. The men do a wonderful job of keeping the roads clear in the winter. You'll have no problem getting stuck unless you live on a dirt road. You do not need a Jeep, just drive a smaller car with front-wheel drive. But the DUI rate is high in Aroostock County—give these people plenty of room.

A typical northern New England house, about 100 years old, is very desirable. Note the sheds between barn and house so you do not have to go outdoors in blizzards to get to the barn. With cozy bedrooms under the eaves, the house is worth about $100,000 in northern New Hampshire and Vermont, and about $50,000 in northern Maine.

If you move to any place like rural Maine, you must have an explanation for why you are relocating so the local people will accept you. Never criticize them or call them quaint. Never gossip among them since you may be badmouthing their cousin or nephew! If you have a local relative or a friend living nearby it helps a lot. If you buy a home from a prominent person, that person can be of great help. We have been helped this way. It helps if you are not competing for local jobs or for their welfare checks. Retirement is pretty well understood and they accept a person who loves to hunt, fish, canoe, and camp. It helps to join their clubs, which are easy to get in if you seem sincere. But as for finding a job in northern Maine, forget it. With that exception, Maine is well worth exploring.

New Hampshire

New Hampshire is a unique and most successful state. Its political climate is fairly conservative, almost libertarian—no sales tax, no income tax, limited state government, excellent for starting small businesses if you can sell the products elsewhere. New Hampshire is the Switzerland of America, very beautiful and independent, with the people perhaps not too friendly, unless you need help. Then you will be astonished what they will do. They like to mind their business and they do not talk a lot. This is because the intense winter cold hurts their teeth like eating an ice cream cone when they open their mouths. Few people know this.

New Hampshire is to liberal Massachusetts what West Germany was to East Germany during the Cold War. Little love is lost between the two

Milford is typical of neat New Hampshire towns.

states. To see the immense contrast and prove in your own mind what limited government and low taxes will do, you must drive from Rindge, New Hampshire, to Ashby, Massachusetts, right across the border. Note the neat, restored colonial homes worth hundreds of thousands of dollars in prosperous New Hampshire, without paint, neglected, and left to rot in deteriorated Massachusetts, all because Massachusetts taxes are too high and the owners are impoverished. Recently New Hampshire has become much more liberal as people from Massachusetts, New York, and New Jersey move there.

New Hampshire is not a cheap state in which to live. Houses that would be $60,000 in northern Maine or Pennsylvania are more than $150,000 in New Hampshire. You can not buy even a minimum lower-middle or working-class home in good repair under $120,000 in southern New Hampshire. Quality Cape Cod-style houses are a quarter of a million dollars or more. Small camps on crowded, cold Lake Winnipesaukee are $250,000. Apartments in New Hampshire are $500 to $900 a month for two bedrooms, unlike the usual $300 for good apartments in the country elsewhere. Fuel is very expensive, and will go up more, so it is important a house be small, well insulated, and equipped with double-glazed windows. But living in New Hampshire may be worth the high cost. New Hampshire schools are the best in the nation by test scores. The people are very intelligent and everything is very well run. It would be a good state to start a business to make products to be sold elsewhere. The work force is honest, capable, and hard working.

New Hampshire is quite densely populated in the southern half. I like Nashua, Wilton, and Peterborough. The northern half and the part toward Vermont are more the way New Hampshire used to look 50 years ago. It is lower-cost. The New Hampshire people are not particularly religious, and Protestant church attendance is poor. Their state motto is "Live Free or Die," which says a lot about the state. The Manchester Union, a most unusual crusading newspaper with many interesting classified ads, is essential to understanding New Hampshire thinking. Get some copies before going there. Back issues of it are even more fascinating. If you think the way they do, it is worth what it takes to live in New Hampshire.

Vermont

Vermont is quite different from New Hampshire, both culturally and politically. Geographically it is similar, but it rains much more. It is extremely liberal. The one congressman is a self-proclaimed socialist. State government is unusually large with many opportunities to work in it. Welfare is munificent. Taxes are very high and small businesses are over-regulated and heavily taxed. Gays are allowed to marry each other, and drug users are well tolerated. It is the least religious of any state. I asked why they did not have church in Wheelock. "The kids broke in and wrecked it and they took the organ apart and threw all the pipes out in the snow," came the reply. No one seemed to care. In isolated Island Pond, kids harassed the town's only doctor, recently recruited from out of state, with practical jokes and fake emergencies until he left in despair. Vermont still has a lot of very liberal people, communes, and small progressive colleges such as Goddard and Bennington. These people are quite interesting and unusual, even though you may disagree with them.

There have been some regrettable human rights violations in Vermont, which the Vermonters strangely seem to tolerate. In Bethel, in 1955, 50-year-old Lucille Miller was put in the federal insane asylum for protesting the draft. She was not crazy. You can read about little-known cases such as this in the files of newspapers in the state library when you visit the beautiful capitol at Montpelier.

Vermont, like New Hampshire, is a beautiful state. It has fine hunting, fishing, hiking, and skiing. It is not a cheap place to live and costs more than New Hampshire. You can buy land and then find environmental regulations prevent you from living on it. Water access can be a severe problem. It can be difficult or illegal to place a septic tank in the rocky soil. Check water and sewerage regulations before you buy land. Before you start a business you must have an environmental survey made, which can cost $100,000. The northeast part of the state from St. Johnsbury to Derby Line, called the Northeast Kingdom, is less of a tourist trap than the southern part. It costs less, too. Many people in Vermont are homeless squatters. Houses are extremely expensive in most of Vermont and so is fuel to heat them. I saw an old, worn-out trailer on a small lot near Killington for $65,000 ten years ago with no view. Prices are higher now.

The Midwest

People seeking unspoiled small cities and rural areas will do very well in the Midwest Rust Belt. This is an area ranging from Iowa to Pennsylvania and including as far north as Wisconsin, Michigan, and Minnesota and south to the Kentucky border. Many larger cities, including Chicago, Cleveland, and Detroit, and even smaller ones like Youngstown, Ohio, have serious urban problems. The country and the smaller cities are still unspoiled, low cost, and have a high quality of life. Towns 40 or 50 miles from the better large cities such as Pittsburgh and Cincinnati have low, rural costs and offer easy commuting to the city for concerts and educational and cultural affairs. Thousands of people enjoy baseball and football games in giant modern stadiums.

Tough Labor

Many workers from the Rust Belt are hostile to management and prone to strike. They have driven out new companies, including Volkswagen, which tried to locate a factory in Pittsburgh. In the Rust Belt, this attitude is known as *tough labor* or *labor-union mentality*. If you are a self-employed person, tough labor need not concern you, and may even be a boon. Service in restaurants and stores is poor in the Rust Belt. Mechanics, carpenters, and yard workers are slow and apathetic. Printers run their presses with headphones in their ears and the books come out with missing pages. This apathy of Rust-Belt labor presents opportunities for you. If you can run a better restaurant with clean forks and warm, tasty food, or fix a car without scratching the hood and getting grease all over the upholstery, or print a book without a bad page, or weld steel so it does not crack, you can get a lot of business. The local working men are quite pleasant and friendly. You will like them if you are not employing them. Surprisingly, their politics are not particularly liberal.

Smaller Cities and Towns

Southern Illinois is vastly different and more pleasant than around Chicago. Peoria is a nice, small city. Monroe, Michigan, and way up north in the Upper Peninsula are much nicer than Detroit. Typically, in all these smaller Rust-Belt cities, you get apartments in good neighborhoods for about $350 a month, smaller bungalows and story and a half homes for $50,000 or less, and heating costs of about $600 a year with low-cost natural gas in the suburbs (natural gas lines do not run out in the country). In the cities further north you may have a climate cool enough in summer so you only need an occasional room air conditioner.

Hunting for a New Home

There are a great many fine places to live in the Rust Belt, more than we can tell about here. The best way to find them is to take a car and a detailed road map and drive around on older two-lane roads. A safe town will have more churches than beer joints; count them. Buy local newspapers and read them carefully. Study the Yellow Pages: If you see escort services, video gambling places, massage parlors, and adult bookstores in the phone book, organized crime has a foothold. Listen to local radio call-in talk shows. Ask local people in restaurants, stores, and gas stations about their town. Buy them a coffee in the local coffee shop. You'll find all you need to know. Is real estate low cost because a local factory is closing and thousands of people are leaving the area? If the government has stepped in with housing projects and poverty programs, you cannot live there. It will be just like a New York City slum with drugs, crime, and political corruption.

Local Culture

See what nationality the local people are and go to their churches and clubs to really know them. If you are of Polish, Hungarian, Swedish, Italian, Serbian, French, or German extraction you will find it great fun to move in with your own kind of people. They do not speak the language or remember the old country any more, but they are people you will like and enjoy. The people of Lake Wobegone still live in the Midwest and they are very nice people to live with, kinder people than many New Englanders. Iowa is a pleasant state with declining population and many opportunities for new settlers. Northern Michigan, Wisconsin, and Minnesota offer low-cost living as well as hunting and fishing to rival Maine. Ohio has many smaller cities where living is cheap.

Pennsylvania

Pennsylvania is a big state, Rust Belt in the west, highly developed in the east. It has very beautiful hills and mountains and resembles New England, but is low cost. Pennsylvania has large expanses of wilderness in the northern half from around Warren and Kane and extending to Troy where one could vanish into the woods completely. There are big lakes, and good boating and fishing, too. The Allegheny River has been cleaned up. It is a beautiful river that resembles the Rhine. You can swim in it. People build low-cost summer camps along it and enjoy them more than a lakeshore camp. They cost a quarter the price of a camp on a lake, $35,000 to $75,000. You can take your outboard motor boat or canoe from Brady's Bend, Pennsylvania, to New Orleans if you have the time. Beautiful big Victorian houses are common in Pennsylvania and usually sell for $70,000 or less for a real showplace. Small mill houses are very cheap. I was offered a livable one for $8,000 in 1989.

Two Pennsylvania houses. The one on the left was offered at $15,000, with a nice interior and an elevator. The luxurious, restored-brick Victorian house below with central air conditioning sold for $55,000 in Parker, Pennsylvania, a few years back.

Appalachia—Better than People Think It Is

West Virginia is a beautiful, unspoiled state, similar to the way the rest of America was 50 years ago. It is one of the cheapest in which to live. The climate is warmer and heating costs are much less than in the North. Food is inexpensive and you can raise wonderful gardens. Low-cost houses without cellars are quite comfortable. Fly over West Virginia in a plane and you will see that all the civilization is along the valleys, rivers, and streams. There are no roads—nothing but trees—in the mountains, which make up most of the state. In many valleys, you need a costly satellite dish to get any TV. Here is a splendid place for you to really get away from it all! Travel the local roads without route numbers to really see West Virginia.

But the local people may be difficult. One family I know, teachers with degrees, failed in their attempt to settle on a small farm near Rich Creek, West Virginia, because they could not get along with the people. They talked down to the local people, which was a bad mistake.

A good low-cost way to get to know the state and get acquainted with local people who vacation there is to camp in the various state parks. Often these campers live only a few towns away. The wife and children stay at the park weekdays while the husband commutes to work. He joins them on weekends. A West Virginia relative or acquaintance will be a big help in meeting people and finding your way around the new place. The state is part of the political empire of the Rockefeller family, which is one reason it is a poor state, but locals do not pay much attention to them. West Virginia citizens are good people but not particularly law-abiding and they regulate themselves with fences and guns. You will be saved endless trouble with forms, paperwork, permits and building codes if you do as they do.

You can rent a nice house or apartment for $350 a month or less, which is advisable before you settle permanently. A house costing $60,000 in West Virginia will be a mansion showplace. If you want to work for the government, there are a lot of opportunities in federal programs that are particularly active in Appalachia, or if you feel more deserving than most, you might go after the benefits of these programs. The eastern area of West Virginia nearest Washington, D.C., has great growth opportunities. The rest is lower-cost. Jobs are available and you can start a good small business. West Virginia has many advantages over other rural states. Look into it!

In undeveloped parts of Kentucky and Tennessee, conditions are very similar to West Virginia. But these states have a better business climate and a dedicated, trained, highly motivated labor force. You find new automobile plants—some for Japanese cars—and a lot of jobs, prosperity, and economic growth in many parts of Kentucky and Tennessee. The giant blue lakes in Western Kentucky and the area around Paducah are attractive.

Virginia

Virginia is highly urban in the parts nearer Washington and Richmond, stylish and expensive like Connecticut around Williamsburg and in many other parts. The areas around Roanoke and along I-81 and I-77 are particularly interesting for future growth. (Since I wrote this sentence in the first edition 10 years ago there *has* been a lot of growth. This book works.) Hillsville and Galax are attractive cities without crime or racial problems. Wytheville, Arcadia, Buchanan, Lexington, and many other smaller cities and the rural area around them are delightful places to live. Virginia is more modern, less isolated, and friendlier than West Virginia. Costs for land, housing, and other living expenses are somewhat greater, but so are opportunities. The Winchester and Front Royal areas are sophisticated, cultured, expensive, but very desirable. It is a state well worth looking at.

West Virginia and Virginia are renowned for their famous hot mineral springs with healing waters. Sweet Chalybeate Springs on Route 311 near the border of the two states is Victorian and unspoiled.

The Carolinas and Georgia

North and South Carolina and Georgia are Appalachian in the western parts and offer a Deep-South lifestyle in the coastal part. The upstate is preferable. Cities such as Greenville, Spartanburg, and Columbia are noted for high crime, but they do have nice, smaller towns around them. For example, Chesnee, Converse, and Cowpens, South Carolina, near Spartanburg are still fine places to live. Eat old-fashioned country food at low cost at Turner's restaurant in Chesnee for about $5 a meal. Get a fine breakfast for $2.50 with eggs, bacon, grits, and coffee at Dolline's friendly restaurant in Clifton. Enjoy the beautiful Pacolet river and the abandoned factories along it (which could be bought and used again as the Amoskeag Mills in Manchester, New Hampshire, were). Rural areas of North and South Carolina offer good little houses with all utilities and a bath for $40,000 or less—sometimes much less. Rentals start at perhaps $300 a month. Are South Carolina people very conservative like Jesse Helms or Bob Jones? No, most of them think more like Jimmy Carter or Ernest Hollings. They love federal funds.

Southern Advantages

It is cheaper to build a Southern house because you have no cellar, only a crawl space, and the roof does not have to be heavily built to stand up to deep snow like those in the North. Heating costs are very low. Older people in the country go without central air conditioning, perhaps just an attic fan or a window air conditioner. Many small "mill houses" were built by the mill owners long ago in such towns as Drayton, Converse, or Pacolet, South Carolina. They are quite attractive, in a Victorian way, and are available very cheaply, usually by a private sale. A lady we know sold a group of them for between $18,000 and $40,000 each. Many people are fixing up

You will enjoy the beautiful names of smaller Carolina towns. Traveling north from Chesnee, you go through Henrietta, Caroleen, Ellenboro, Hopewell, Sunshine Community, and Golden Valley. By the names, you can tell the people there are happy and would not live anywhere else.

mill houses. Look into it. Many sales and rentals are not advertised in newspapers. You get them word of mouth and again you need local sponsorship, church affiliation, and appreciation of the local lifestyle to gain acceptance and friends. Join the Grange. In the South you will find wonderful barbecues, low-cost fish restaurants, square dances, country music, auto races and revivals. Attending these events in person is much more fun than seeing them in the movies or on TV!

Hickory, North Carolina, is the world's furniture-making center. Skilled woodworking and refinishing specialists work there and they also moonlight at refinishing antiques and repainting cars. When you get to the Carolinas, you have reached the real South. It still is a low-cost area but it is growing fast. There are lots of jobs and lots of new industry, including a giant BMW plant in Greer on I-85 that pays $50,000 per year for ordinary labor. Recent recessions have not seemed to affect these states. They have fairly low taxes, a willing labor force trained in local two-year technical colleges, and state governments that are expert in attracting new industry. If you need a job, these are good states to move to. If you start a small service business, it should grow as rapidly as the population grows. Rent first and look around before settling permanently.

Mountainous western North Carolina around Asheville is a resort and tourist area. Columbus, Saluda, Brevard, Tryon, Black Mountain, Bryson City, Murphy, and Boone are nice places to live. You can disappear into the woods in the Great Smoky Mountains and live a long time. It does snow and it costs more to live in the mountains than most places in the Carolinas. Lake Hartwell, Wylie, Norman, and other man-made lakes are very nice for boating and swimming. The water is warm like a bath tub in summer. You can buy homes overlooking the water at prices that are surprisingly reasonable for lakeshore property.

Well-built Carolina row mill-houses are becoming popular again. People restore them.

Atlanta and South Georgia

Atlanta is a world-class city like New York or London in its attractions and sophistication. Except for traffic congestion on the beltways and inner-city crime, it is recommended.

Look at the towns around the periphery such as Decatur, Druid Hills, Doraville, Chamblee, Roswell, Norcross, and particularly conservative Kennesaw, with its low crime rate. Kennesaw has passed a law that every head of a household MUST own a gun! Job prospects, even at high levels, and opportunities for starting a business are excellent around Atlanta, even in recessions. The part of Georgia next to Florida has a climate like Florida and is low cost. Try Cairo, Georgia, which has a lot of community spirit. You can eat delicious chicken at the famous Mr. Chick restaurant there and hear all the news from the friendly local people and from Wayne Hadden, the fire chief who runs it. He often drives a 1922 Nash car on the quiet local streets!

Florida

Florida is still good, though most of the east coast of the state is dangerous and unpleasant except for places too expensive to be in this book. The central portion and the west coast of Florida are still quite desirable. The panhandle, which many people consider too cold in winter since it has a climate like Georgia, is quite low cost and unspoiled. The lake area around attractive, well-run Mount Dora, Lakeland, and Winter Haven has fine retirement communities. Ocala is nice, but becoming crowded. Lake Wales is cultured, but low cost. Babson Park is very fine. You will love the beautiful Bok Singing Tower with its carillon of bells in the park with the flowers and the reflecting pool. Jobs are virtually unavailable for senior citizens in Florida because there are so many of them seeking work, but living costs and taxes are still quite low.

Florida Houses

The typical retirement or lower-middle-class Florida home is a single-story cement block, two- or three-bedroom home built on a concrete slab with carpet laid right over the cement for flooring. Cement blocks show inside and out and are painted. It will have a carport. The roof is low, windows are casement, and a heat pump in the wall or ceiling both heats and cools the house. These homes can be quite attractively styled, decorated, and landscaped. They have much lower maintenance expenses than wood homes, which rot and become bug-infested in the hot, damp climate. Many of these houses are still under $70,000, so retiring in Florida is still within reach of moderate incomes. Be sure you have some orange or grapefruit trees in the yard out back. The fruits are delicious freshly picked.

Low-cost housing in Florida is a trailer or so-called mobile home with a large, attached screen porch known as a Florida room. The trailers are never moved—they are bought and sold with the lot. Older people often wind up in nursing homes, so there is a good market in their old trailers that you should look into. If carefully bought, these homes cost as little as $50,000 with ownership of the lot. In many parks you own the

SOUTHERN LIVING. The South is one of the cheapest places in the world to live. When I first came to know the South, I was amazed at how easy it is to live simply and well. You do not have to bother with snow and ice and you can do almost anything out of doors all year long—cook meals outdoors on a wood stove, change engines in cars with a hoist hung from a tree, store things under a pole building with a tin roof, run a computer, do office work, write a book, or sell at roadside stands.

Winter is the most delightful time, like October in New England. You can use a bicycle or a motorcycle all year long; there is no need for a car. With warm, Northern-style clothing you can live and work outdoors all day, even in January. Southerners do not dress warmly enough and really do not appreciate their climate as much as they should.

Construction is so easy in the southern states. You can bury water pipes and wiring only six inches deep, support a building on a simple foundation of treated wood posts, or make a garage or porch floor by pouring a few inches of concrete on the ground. Roofs can be made from low-cost trusses and chipboard, and valuable goods can be stored in cheap, portable buildings. Cars never rust from snow and salt exposure and can be left outdoors all year. It is wonderful to be able to do so much for so little money.

A house trailer is not confining in the rural South. They cost about $4,000 used retail without lot, cheaper if you fix up an older one. The lot costs a little more than that. You may cook, bathe, and sleep in the trailer, but most of the

Continued on page 67.

trailer but lease the lot. This costs much less but may be ill-advised. Lot rental is subject to inflation and if you own a really old mobile home and have to move you may find it hard to find another trailer park, since many of them do not accept the older models.

Trailers are found close together in numerous developments in places like Zephyrhills and have clubhouses, pools, and social programs. Many people like this lifestyle. Others do not enjoy it and soon return home to the north. To prevent an expensive disaster, do not sell your home and move everything at first. Instead, rent out your northern home while you rent a furnished place in Florida for a year to be sure you like it.

Condominiums and high-rises present great financial risk to the buyer. It is far better to rent a condominium than to buy one. Maybe you can get a remarkable buy if you are clever at checking out these deals and spotting scams. Condo rents are readily available, sometimes even by the day. I paid only $40 a night for a fine condo near the ocean on Cedar Key some years ago. The condo had been for sale for $65,000, but they couldn't sell it. The real estate market in Florida is quite cyclical; try to buy when it is down. This condo was a nice place, but think what the other owners felt when they saw this exclusive development becoming little more than a motel! They must have been furious.

Costs for food, utilities, and most everything else are surprisingly reasonable for what Florida offers. Socially it is exciting, with something going on every night for the older folks. Younger persons might not like it as well and kids howl that there is nothing to do. Florida residents claim it is no hotter there in summer than many other places. I miss the four-season climate and love Florida only in winter. Many clever people have a Florida residence but stay in the mountains of North Carolina or around Gatlinburg, Tennessee, in summer. Taxes in Florida are much lower than in North Carolina, so they are ahead money-wise. There is a lot of high-tech and electronics industry in cities such as Tampa, with plenty of good job openings. Tampa has an inner city with high crime, as does St. Petersburg. Traffic on Route 19 is extremely congested. The older people drive poorly and cause many accidents. The cost of renting or buying a home is remarkably low in older non-resort residential sections in cities like Tampa. Disney World, near Orlando, is a large employer where many people like to work. Florida has a lot of opportunities.

Arkansas and the Ozarks

Arkansas and the Ozarks have opportunities similar to western North Carolina. Eureka Springs is a fascinating resort and retirement city with fairly reasonable housing around it and many job opportunities in the hospitality and entertainment fields. Many survivalists live in the rural parts of northern Arkansas. Harrison is interesting.

The Arkansas climate is reasonable all year. The central part of Arkansas is virtually deserted and the landscape often looks like pictures from the 19th century. We stopped at a country restaurant and what drove up next but a Model T Ford Beach Wagon with a nice older couple in it! Arkansas is a fascinating state to explore by car and you should look into it. Growth prospects are fairly good. Nearby parts of Missouri are similar to Arkansas.

The Southwest and West

California is not recommended except for the arid central portions, which are similar to Arizona but more expensive. Arizona has many attractive low-cost areas. Jerome is a colorful former copper-mining town high on a mountain. Houses were for sale there for a few thousand dollars until quite recently. Now it is beginning to catch on as a resort and costs are rising. You will like nearby Clarksdale and Cottonwood. Small houses there start at about $60,000. Trailers sell for less. Sedona, further north on Route 89A, is a high-status resort with fine stores and art galleries in a beautiful canyon. Oatman is a real ghost town, now being turned into a resort. You will also like Globe, Arizona. Other ghost towns in Arizona and New Mexico remain to be discovered. Seek them out!

New Mexico is cheaper than Arizona. Much desert land is unclaimed and unoccupied. You could put a converted school bus, motor home, or small trailer out there and live as a squatter without difficulty. We have seen many people doing it, some in small colonies. Trailers are the most common low-cost housing in the desert since it would cost a lot of money to feed, transport, and house carpenters, plumbers, electricians, and masons in the desert while they built a conventional house. People I have met living in trailers in the Southwest have no complaints.

Water may be easier to find in the desert than you might imagine. A retired man with a small ranch told me that if you sink a well 30 or 40 feet deep near a streambed you will often find plenty of water. The desert is beautifully flowered in spring, cool and pleasant at night, and generally much nicer than you might expect it to be.

In southern New Mexico the government sells land quite reasonably at times. Write your congressional representative for details of land sales or watch local newspapers. Real estate developers buy it up and sell the same land for $10,000 an acre for a five-acre "ranchette." Watch out for

time you are living outdoors. Give your trailer a big screen porch on front. You can clean yourself in the creek most of the year with a cake of soap, so you will not miss modern plumbing if you lack it.

You can raise wonderful gardens with crops almost all year long—from April to November. Harvest peas and radishes in April, lettuce in early May, cabbages, tomatoes and summer squash by June, corn and shiny eggplants so beautiful you wish you could save them forever by July. In hot weather, you harvest okra and watermelons. Then in the fall you pick giant winter squashes and pumpkins and harvest collard greens until the end of the season in November. You grow these crops successively on the same plot of land. Local people plant too late and raise too few crops. With a little study and work you can show them a garden that will surprise them. This land is too good for tobacco! You can raise peanuts, figs, and peaches if you wish. The rural South is one of the cheapest places in the world to live. You will never be short of food if you have the slightest ambition. I would rather live in a one-room cabin on a five-acre plot of land in the rural Carolinas than in the Trump Plaza in New York.

This very old school-bus conversion parked in a shady oasis offers low-cost housing. School buses like this can be bought outright for less than the cost of a year's apartment rental. Note the big evaporative cooler on the side to keep it cool and comfortable. This is a permanent location. It would be difficult to move this bus.

them! It takes a great many acres of desert land to feed a herd of cattle. The "small" rancher I talked to owned 3,000 acres! In New Mexico, towns such as Deming, Hillsboro, and Truth or Consequences, with its mineral hot spring baths, present great retirement possibilities. Attractive small houses with town water and power are $60,000 or less. Cement block, stucco, or adobe construction has many advantages. Decent small apartments range from $250 to $400 a month in Truth or Consequences. Fairly good older motel rooms are as low as $25 a night there. Some retirees go to colder places such as Colorado for the summer, but many stay all year. New Mexico has a dry heat that is seldom uncomfortable in summer.

Job opportunities are about nil, but businesses that cater to retirees can succeed. We met a man who sold his used bookstore in San Diego after being robbed and beaten. He moved his entire stock-in-trade to Truth or Consequences in three U-Haul trucks. He loves it there. You see lots of single, unemployed young men roaming the streets and seeking work around Truth or Consequences; local people tell me they are harmless. It might be possible to put them to work fixing up an old house you bought. But remember, you need a pension, a mail-order business, or some kind of outside income to live in places like this.

There are many Indians in Arizona and New Mexico who have extensive tribal land holdings. I have found them interesting and enjoyable people.

You can buy high-quality fresh fruit and produce in local grocery stores at low cost. Some of it is imported from Mexico and some is grown locally on irrigated land. You can travel to Mexican border towns for low-cost dental work, prescription drugs, auto bodywork, and upholstery. Many air bases in the Southwest are closing now that the Cold War has ended—making vacant homes for civilian and military personnel near them sell at very low cost. Clever readers will look for them. The Southwest has fascinating possibilities. Rent before buying there.

Make friends with local people who will help you become "desert-smart." It could be extremely dangerous otherwise—you could die in a day if your car broke down and you were without water. Illegal immigrants are often bitten by rattlesnakes when they hide in caves to escape the Border Patrol, local people tell me. You must have four-wheel drive if you want to drive on rangeland, dry streambeds, or off-road; the sand can be soft and difficult to drive on. However, there are no tornadoes in Arizona and most of New Mexico. By taking sensible precautions the Southwest is as safe as any other part of the country.

Attractive, low-cost apartments for retirees in Truth or Consequences, New Mexico.

Texas resembles New Mexico in some parts, but is more like Dixie in others. Alpine, Texas, is a nice town to live in. The Dakotas have a terrible climate but the people are so nice you may want to live there anyway. Oregon and Washington are expensive, partly because they are populated by people from California. Oregon is the Vermont of the West. Montana and Idaho still have real wilderness, and are nice places to live. I have visited Cheyenne to see my friend, Charles Bristol, vice president of a bank there. It is a fine, friendly town and cultured, too.

New Mexico dirt roads go for miles. Your car must be in good repair for secondary New Mexico roads. There are no gas stations for more than 100 miles on some roads. This 1988 Plymouth Sundance hatchback is very reliable. Front-wheel drive gives fairly good traction in dirt.

Alaska

There are many opportunities in Alaska. Consider the port town of Whittier, which has just been opened up with a road going to it. Before you could only get there by boat or rail. For years most of the people in town have lived in a giant high-rise ex-government building. Everything is in it—stores, restaurant, church, movie theater, post office, doctor's office, etc., so you do not have to go outdoors when the snow is 12 feet deep! Most of the residents are men who work on fishing boats, with a few sportsmen and retirees. But what a beautiful, exciting place! Visit it.

Where Eligible Men Are Plentiful

In Anchorage we went to the Presbyterian church—a modern, brick, A-shaped building similar to many churches in the lower 48 states, but

This giant hi-rise building in Whittier, Alaska, has most everything you'd ever need. It was built by the government during World War II.

with one surprising difference. The men greatly outnumber the woman in the Sunday School and at the services. These were fine, decent, single men with good jobs, among them engineers, biologists, foresters, geologists, and pilots. What an opportunity for a woman who wants to get married! The men greatly outnumber the women throughout Alaska. Until you get north of Fairbanks, bigger Alaska towns have most city amenities. We spent several weeks in Alaska and loved it, drove all around in a small rental car. It is not cheap, but the opportunities are great. It is a fun place

and it might be well worth all the expense and trouble of living there. We like Homer down on the Kenai Peninsula and the Matanuska Valley country around Palmer.

Overseas

With the declining dollar, relocating overseas is no longer the bargain it used to be. Mexico, Costa Rica, Greece, and Portugal may be slightly cheaper than the United States. Some like the area around Lake Chapala in central Mexico. Wealthy Americans of Portuguese extraction retire to the Azores and Madeira and love it. We still love to visit Lisbon, which is a beautiful city like Paris, cultured and elegant, yet low cost. Many Italians enjoy Sicily, and Greeks like Greece. But for me, receiving English reading matter, running a computer, flying back and forth and keeping up with my business, would eat up any saving in living cost. So I always return home. There must be a reason all the world wants to live in America!

WHEN TO MOVE

If you lose your job and then wait too long and spend all your money, you will not have enough left to afford to move. To sell a house, start high and cut the price weekly or monthly until it is gone. If you begin cheap, you may sell it for less than you could have gotten. You can rent it if you are in a bind, but I have had trouble with tenants and do not advise it. We sold an impractical house in Wheelock, Vermont, without a real estate agent with small ads in *National Review, Saturday Review,* and *The Wall Street Journal.* Today you can even sell a house over the Internet.

If you are going to a smaller house or apartment from a big house, you will not have room for all your belongings. Nothing looks tackier than a person who has moved all the furniture of a house into a small apartment. Anyone is reminded instantly that they have come down in the world. Have a yard sale or auction and get rid of most of the junk. You can buy replacements at a yard sale or thrift shop where you are going for about the same price you received for your old junk. So why worry? Grandfather's oak desk or Mother's rocking chair you keep, of course. But the rest, who needs it? Accessories like brooms, cleaning materials, tools, hardware, and small appliances are very expensive if you must buy all of them at once. They are exceptions. It is better to take them along.

MOVING

The cheapest way to move is with a rental trailer or truck. The trailers designed to be hauled by a small front-wheel drive car only hold a room full of furniture, while those towed with a full-size car or pickup truck can carry the contents of a smaller house. The trucks you rent carry giant loads and will tow your car behind as well. Get moving boxes free from grocery or liquor stores—never buy them.

There are local movers at each end who can be hired to pack and unpack at low cost if you wish. Look for their ads in the classified section of your newspaper. The large nationwide movers are so expensive that only corporations can afford them.

A borrowed pickup truck or van can move a shorter distance with several trips. If you have very little to move, a car will do. You may want to rent an enclosed roof rack for greater capacity.

There is considerable danger of your rental truck or trailer being broken into outside a motel room. It is better to get permission to park at an all-night gas station and sleep in the cab or in back on top of the load. Better still, put the truck or trailer in a state park and camp beside it. You do not need a tent. Simply stretch a tarpaulin or a piece of plastic on ropes. I move a lot of real antiques and I camp in parks whenever possible. It also saves money to camp in a state park while you hunt for a house or apartment. A month of motel rooms really costs. I hope these hints help you have a good move.

Checking Out Motels

Good locally owned motels are even cheaper than economy chains like Econolodge or Motel 6.

When choosing a motel, look at the cars parked outside the rooms. If they have in-state license plates, the place is used for parties, not for sleeping. If the guests have macho or vanity cars such as Camaros or pickups with big wheels you may be bothered with noise and fights. A bar or restaurant on the premises or next door is a bad omen. So are hookers, of course. A neat clean pool with children is a good sign. A well-run motel with construction workers paying by the week can be OK. Conservative middle-class four-door sedans such as Toyota Camrys or Buick LeSabres are a good sign. Word of mouth can help you. There is a place called the College Inn in downtown Spartanburg, South Carolina, that is heavily used by state police, judges, and courtroom people when court is in session that is pleasant and low cost—with a free Southern breakfast. We always stay there. It has a chain link fence around it to keep out criminals—essential here. You would never find it just traveling through.

Asking around will find you similar good motels in cities and towns all over the country. Most lower-cost Florida motels seem to be good. Many lower-priced, smaller motels all over the United States have been bought up by families of immigrants. The whole family works there. Sometimes these motels look old, but they seem to be safe and rooms cost in the $25-$35 range. Avoid any place with no private toilet and only a washbasin in the room—old men urinate in them. Avoid places housing welfare people; the owners are often politically connected and indifferent to providing service. Often you can make a deal to rent a motel room for a week for no more than two or three days' rent.

BUYING LAND

Buying land requires considerable skill and experience and has many pitfalls. Edward Preston's book *How to Buy Land Cheap* (ISBN O-9666932-7-2 published by Breakout Productions, Box 1643, Port Townsend, WA

From the old days, here is Mr. Buzzacott's advice to the traveler packing for a trip by rail or boat . . .

> *And now be ye wise,*
> *And take ye from ye olde garret,*
> *Ye olde trunk that ye near forgot,*
> *And put ye all thy party has got therein carefully,*
> *Shoulde ye locks and handles be off, cord it well;*
> *And when the Packet comes and goes,*
> *Where ye will go, it goeth with thee;*
> *And they asketh not its fare neither way.*

98368) explains how to buy land sold by government agencies for unpaid taxes or abandonment by the owners. This land is found by contacting county and state governments. He reports how one reader bought eight building lots in Montana for a total of $25 and another bought a fix-up home for $750. I have heard of other people getting amazing buys like this. Preston's methods really work if you have some time and are willing to do some letter writing and paperwork. Get help with titles, right of way, and government regulations. Land prices vary greatly, but land costs much less when it is bought in large quantities than as house lots.

Hilltop land with no access by road, no electric power, telephone lines, water, or sewer is almost impossible to sell. It is still very cheap to buy— maybe a few hundred dollars an acre. If you are willing to live without phone and power and build a road, you can save a lot of money. Tracts advertised by real estate agents and developers are usually too expensive. These days a failed resort development might be a buy. Check notices in the courthouse and classified ads for land sales and auctions.

Ask your congressman to notify you of federal land sales near you. Do not pay for this information.

Many tracts of land are too large for the average individual to afford. It takes a nest egg of cash. But the rewards can be great. My friend Nicholas Economou, after fighting successively both the Nazis and the Communists in the underground in his native Greece in World War II, was fed up with Europolitics. He moved to Vermont in the 1950s and purchased 300 acres of forest land near a ski area on which he built a fine one-room log cabin in which to live. It was a very smart move. Most people would have bought a luxury house on a small lot for the same money instead. Incidentally, Nick was pretty smart about cars, too. He drove a battered old Corvette made of fiberglass that the Vermont road salt could not rust. He was a fine man and he always helped his family and the old people in Greece after he became successful.

Chapter 8

Save Money on Food

It is difficult to design a low-cost diet that will suit everyone. Most people will not eat really low-cost food such as beans and greens, so we have to give you some alternative diets.

The traditional old-time diet of poor people in the South used to consist of pinto beans cooked from dried beans, corn bread, collard greens and other greens, maybe an onion sliced into the beans and some pork and maybe molasses, and watermelon for dessert. Nowadays they have more money so the modern Southern diet is less healthy. Now they can afford to eat more ham, chicken, sausage, and other fried foods.

Today, the Southern diet is different. Nearly everything they eat is fried. Meat is more than 50 percent of the modern Southern diet by weight. Hardee's restaurant sausage biscuits and Kentucky Fried Chicken are pretty much what most Southern food is like, although real Southern cooks make the chicken tastier. This is an expensive and unhealthy diet. The Carolinas have the highest rate of stroke and heart attack in the United States. Still, most people love the high-fat diet. The old timers—both black and white— who ate pinto beans and greens were much healthier, studies show. Many of them lived to over 80 years of age. Maybe we all should eat cheaper food.

If you need to save money and want to be healthy, I urge you to eat the "old-time Southern soul food"—lots of pinto beans, corn bread, greens, onions, watermelon if you can raise it, and molasses. Still, most of our readers will not eat it, and I seldom eat it, so we have to give you other foods to compromise. The real economy is in the dried beans, which cost about 45 cents a pound. (But this is a dried food and when you soak them overnight before cooking, which you must, they more than double in weight. So they cost less than 25 cents a pound ready to eat—a wonderful food buy.) Beans are a meat substitute. They contain the same proteins as meat without the harmful saturated fat. They are noisy unless you eat spinach and greens at the same time to quiet them down. Northern people like beans, too, but theirs are cooked differently. The traditional Boston baked beans contain a lot of molasses and sugar. This sweetening of food is demanded by soldiers and lumber-jacks who do a lot of hard work in winter and may consume 3,500 to 4,500 calories a day, the woodsman Kephart reports. They can eat this much and not gain weight working hard outdoors. The Northern-style beans are delicious, but fattening unless you get a lot more exercise than most people. We have reprinted authentic healthy old-time recipes for pinto beans, Johnny Cake, biscuits, fish chowder, hash, and other good things at the back of this chapter, hoping you will try them.

SEVEN WAYS TO SAVE ON FOOD

1. Buy food cheaper. Buy it in quantity at discount markets like Sam's Wholesale Club rather than 24-hour convenience stores. Buy older bread from bread thrift stores. Buy cheaper varieties of food, larger size packages. Avoid TV dinners, frozen convenience foods, and salty baby food in jars. Avoid advertised name brands of food; they tend to cost more. Buy generic food. Avoid bacon and similar foods that are mainly grease, which is then left in the pan. Avoid eggs unless they are very cheap. Buy foods requiring more home processing: flour for baking, rolled oats for cereal, dried peas and beans, and dried skim milk instead of whole bottled milk.
2. Raise food—Have a garden, fruit trees, a berry patch, grapevines, a rhubarb patch, bees, chickens, or a pig.
3. Get food free by hunting or fishing. Forage for greens—dandelion greens are everywhere. Get restaurants to give you free food; ask at the back door. Ask caterers or go to soup kitchens. Look for govern-ment-surplus food discarded in housing projects. Many of the people there are too lazy to cook things like flour and oats and they sneer at the government cheese and Spam. You will also find often surpris-ingly good food in Dumpsters.
4. Lose weight. Each pound you lose is equal to buying and eating 4,000 calories. Free food inside your paunch!
5. Try not to waste food. Cook just enough and see it is all eaten. Know how long food lasts and do not let any spoil. You can tolerate a fair amount of grease if you exercise a lot, avoid eggs, whole milk, and cheese, and do not put butter on food. Save your frying pan grease in jars for baking, as my mother did in the Depression. Keep fish grease separate. It tastes fishy.
6. Avoid restaurant take-out food. A quarter-pound Big Mac or a Whopper costs $2.09. With hamburger at $1.79 a pound, that much

meat costs 45 cents in the grocery store. With roll, tomato slice, lettuce, and dressing the Big Mac is worth perhaps 70 cents. If you paid as much for your hamburger meat as McDonald's sells it for, it would cost $8.00 a pound! Other fast food restaurants have similar prices. The same ratios hold for other restaurants serving fried fish, chicken, and most other fast food.

7. Avoid tokenism in food. Bullion cubes are supposed to equal meat but they are little more than flavor and salt. Deviled ham spread thinly on bread as poor people do, is a token food too. There is little food value in a half ounce of any food, no matter how rich.

THE CHEAPEST FOODS

The following table lists the prices of a variety of foods by weight. To save money you need to study it. Note that the cheapest foods are flour, potatoes, beans, dried milk, and things like that sold in bulk that you have to cook. If you have a wood stove burning all the time or low-cost natural gas, it will really pay off to make beans, bread, and other things you cook or bake for hours. The old timers in Central Europe kept a pot of stew simmering all the time and added meat and vegetables whenever it got a bit low. It took the place of refrigeration, since the cooking kept it from spoiling. A pressure cooker from a yard sale or flea market will speed up all the cooking and save energy. Old-time Southern people of style had a cookhouse separated from the main house by a porch so as not to heat up the house. You can cook and bake out of doors over a wood fire yourself. Avoid charcoal for fires. Dry wood is much better.

Note in the food table that the meat poor people buy in small cans is the most costly food of all. Deviled ham tops the list at $5.37 a pound! Corned beef, a better food favored by old soldiers, is only $2.96 a pound. Baked goods and finger foods are expensive, too. Chocolate chip cookies are $3.50 a pound. Ritz crackers, $3.40 a pound. Cheerios cereal is $4.08 a pound whereas cooked oatmeal is about 68 cents a pound. Potato chips are $2.10 a pound, whereas potatoes are 30 cents a pound. The poor really spend more money. Chicken is only $1.20 a pound, although some is wasted in cooking. See why it really pays to bake bread and cookies, and roast or broil meat at home. We eat a lot of chicken today.

PRICE OF FOOD IN THE SOUTHEAST IN FALL 2000 BY WEIGHT

Tuna	$3.20/lb.
Hamburger	$1.79/lb.
Cube Steak	$2.56/lb.
Chicken	$1.20/lb.
Flour	$0.32/lb.
Hot Dogs	$1.60/lb.
Spam	$2.30/lb.
Sirloin Tip	$2.72/lb.
Corn Beef	$3.99/lb.
Chicken Patties	$2.16/lb.
Frozen Chicken Pie	$3.49/lb.

Stew Beef	$2.59/lb.
Fish and Chips TV Dinner	$3.50/lb.
Large Canned Ham	$4.00/lb.
Deviled Ham Underwood	$5.30/lb.
Ritz Crackers	$3.41/lb.
Navy or Pinto Beans	$0.43/lb.
Dried Skim Milk	$1.64/gal.
Potatoes	$0.30/lb.
Potato Chips	$2.05/lb.
Bread: day old	$0.64/lb
Chocolate Chip Cookies	$3.50/lb.
Cheerios	$4.08/lb.
Sliced Process Cheese	$2.50/lb.
Peanut Butter	$1.63/lb.
Popcorn kernels	$0.72/lb.

Applying all these ideas to buying food can save a couple $600 a year or more. You may not notice your savings right off, since it only comes out to about $11 a week, but in time it really adds up. Here are more foods that save money:

- We drink skim milk made from powder, which is much healthier than fatty whole milk. It costs less than $2.00 a gallon. You have to get used to it; try mixing it half and half with your usual milk at first.
- Oatmeal is a fine low-cost cooked cereal. Buy the oats in a large paper drum, not in little packages.
- You can make syrup in large quantities as we did in the army by adding a small amount of imitation maple flavor to heated sugar and water. The real thing is better, but very expensive.
- Molasses is delicious and healthy. It is not as low cost as it used to be now that the health food people have caught on to it. Brown sugar is the best substitute.
- Apples are delicious fruit. You should have some trees or know someone who does. Make applesauce and apple butter from older ground apples and apple cider from the worst apples.
- Popcorn made from the kernels you pop yourself is much cheaper than potato chips or Fritos.

Try to buy all your bread, cake, pies, and rolls at surplus bakery thrift shops. These are affectionately called "Dead Bread Stores." Old bread is actually better than the new product—it is less spongy, sticky, and has a better texture. I would think it would cost more than new bread the way cheese or brandy that has been aged does! Day-old bread is a great bargain. An even greater bargain is when they sell the older bread in the surplus bread store for $2 for a shopping cart full. It is actually intended for pig food. Sometimes it is moldy, but often it is very good. Dunkin' Donut shops throw away day-old doughnuts. Make friends with an employee and get some for yourself. Or, if really brave, look in the Dumpster out back.

Bismark and Napoleon liked canned herring and sardines and they went a long way with them. Maybe you can, too. They are good to eat in the woods for a lunch, or warm over toast for an English breakfast, or in a salad where the oil from them becomes the salad oil, saving money. Sardines are good to serve on a sailboat and when you eat in your car. The favorite woodsman's noon meal of long ago, which really gives energy, is a big chocolate bar, half of a pack of raisins, an apple, or perhaps some sweetened reconstituted lemon juice to add to water. The necessity to eat meat for strength is greatly exaggerated today. The meat-eating urge is probably a form of primitive magic, in which we believe we get the strength of the bull from eating him. Perhaps we get his short life span instead. Some meat is OK but not a lot. If you try to live on wild game the problem is too much lean and not enough fat. Suet and lard are highly recommended as supplements. If you live a vigorous outdoor life, cholesterol is not a serious problem.

RAISING A GARDEN

Gardening saves money if you do not buy too much equipment. To save buying a tiller or tractor, trade something with a neighbor who in return will plow your garden. Lettuce, tomatoes, and squash are the easiest vegetables to raise and even come up in northern Maine. Greens are important to your diet. Try to plant crops at different times and buy different varieties of vegetables so they do not all come to harvest at once. Try to avoid freezing and canning produce, which is expensive and time-consuming. Jams, jellies, preserves, pickles, relishes, and chutneys are the canned items that are easiest to sell. Try to raise expensive perishable vegetables instead of those lower-cost vegetables like potatoes. Eat what is in season.

HUNTING AND FISHING

A deer or an antelope can supply as much as a hundred pounds of meat. Sometimes every member of a country family shoots one. I hate killing, but hunting is no more cruel than the slaughterhouse where we get our hamburger. But do not waste meat and never kill for the fun of it.

A single-barreled 12-gauge shotgun loaded with buckshot or a slug will kill a deer. (It can also defend your home.) Loaded with bird shot, the shotgun is used to bag turkeys, partridges, and pheasants. Such shotguns cost $60 or less used. Someone may give you one. A .22 rifle is better for small game. You are not supposed to shoot a deer with one, but it is done. They are about $75 used for a single shot, more if auto or repeater, maybe $100 in flea markets. Bought privately from individuals they could be much cheaper.

Deer Rifles

For longer-range deer hunting, you need a high-powered rifle. Converted military rifles such as the British Lee Enfield, the SKS, or even the Mannlicher Carcano, are $75 to $125 used, more with scope. They are

I really believe that people do not appreciate low-cost food as they should. For example, if all the peanut crops were destroyed by a terrible blight (God forbid) as the elm and chestnut trees were some years ago, and the price of peanut butter rose to the price of caviar, I feel sure people would pay the high price. Then they would come to regard peanut butter as a rare delicacy for special occasions, equal to caviar, because it is so good. It is better than caviar in my opinion. So are day-old bananas! In the good old days, Russell H. Conwell, who founded Temple University, gave a wonderful speech on this topic, that the best things in life are seldom noticed. It was called Acres of Diamonds. Dr. Conwell went all around the country by steam train giving his great speech over and over again in lyceums and at the old Chatauquas. Get a copy of Acres of Diamonds from the library, or free from Temple University in Philadelphia. Or read the text online at http://www.temple.edu/about/temples_founder/acres_text.html.

the least expensive rifles that are still adequate for hunting deer. The Lee Enfield has the longest range and is the most powerful of the three.

All lever-action U.S. deer rifles, including Winchester, Marlin, and Savage, are very fine, but expensive, and will become heirlooms to keep forever. Bolt-action rifles with higher power cartridges like 270, 30-06, 308, or 8mm Mauser are preferred for long-range shooting. They cost more.

Guns last 100 years easily; never sell one. Pistols should be kept as heirlooms and for home defense, too, but it is difficult to hunt with them. The Ruger .22 automatic pistol is good. War souvenir P38s and Lugers are around and are worth having if low priced or a gift. They are costly in a gun store.

Never carry a pistol when you can carry a rifle or shotgun. Have plenty of ammunition and keep it in a cool, dry place. Older ammunition is uncertain after about 35 years, and you may have an occasional misfire. Unless your father taught you to shoot, as mine did, take a hunter safety course from the NRA. Check your local gun store for information, but don't let them sell you anything expensive. The best guns were made before 1964 and can be bought privately at low prices.

Fishing

Fishing is successful in many places if you have plenty of time. Bring a book to study while you fish. I have caught fish with worms and a line

A friend shot this fine antelope. It is in his freezer now and will provide meat for months.

only, no rod and reel. You do not need a lot of expensive equipment or a fast, loud motor boat.

TASTY LOW-PRICED DRINKS

Only drink one cup of coffee daily at breakfast. Iced or hot tea is good and fairly reasonable. Kool-Aid is a classic that kids love. Avoid Coke, Pepsi, and other sodas. They are expensive and harmful. Lemonade and cider are OK.

The old-timers made switchel. It is vinegar and molasses in about equal quantities flavored with a touch of ginger. It should be very weak, about like maple tree sap from your sugar bush. Try one teaspoon of molasses and one of vinegar and a pinch of ginger to two quarts of water. If you do not like it, it may be too strong. You can make it sweeter with honey or saccharine tablets if you wish. *This stuff costs less than five cents a quart, tastes good, and is good for you!*

You can make root beer from an extract sold in country stores, and by the Lehman people by mail at Box 41, Kidron, OH 44636. My parents used to make root beer. We always keep an old army canteen full of water in the car so we never have to buy anything if we get thirsty. In the deserts of the Southwest, we also keep several plastic one-gallon jugs of water.

RESTAURANT FOOD BUYS AND FOOD WHILE TRAVELING

Drinks and desserts are the big moneymakers at restaurants. Avoid them and drink water and you save a lot. If you go to Wendy's, get the $1 chili or burger and take it to the car and eat it with iced tea you made, some homemade coleslaw, and cookies and you get to eat out for a dollar! Low-cost areas sometimes have fine local restaurants. Visit Dolline's in Clifton, South Carolina. Note her low menu prices. Another good reason to live in the country!

All-you-can-eat buffets at Wendy's and steakhouses like Ponderosa

Dolline's Restaurant.

ONCE AROUND THE WORLD. Kermit York was a very saving man. When he retired and went with his wife on a trip around the world, he realized he would only pass through all these countries once. So he never tipped any of the waiters or hotel people in all of the 25,000 miles. Although I could not do it myself, after so many rude foreigners have overcharged me on trips abroad, I laugh when I think of the global circle of outraged waiters.

Dolline's menu in the year 2000.

are good for people with big appetites on pay day. A pizza is more reasonable than a meal in tablecloth restaurants where you have to tip. Hospital cafeterias open to the public are often cheaper than any other restaurant in town. Look for them.

You can cook canned goods on a car motor top. Find a place where the engine is very hot but not boiling; an oven thermometer may help you do this. Hold the cans in place with a coat hanger, handle them with pliers or heat-protecting gloves. The can will take a lot of pressure and, by the time it cools enough to handle, it won't blow. Still, watch for burns and scalding when you open the can.

An aluminum canteen will heat water for tea or coffee. Buy only Stanley all-steel thermos bottles. The glass kind break so often that they cost a lot more in the long run. Our flea-market Stanley thermos bottle lasted 20 years.

EAT ON $3,500 A YEAR

This is for a couple. The following menu is a typical menu for a week of low-cost eating. Two people can eat this food for under $70 a week. We eat all this stuff. So do many other people, including some who could afford much more expensive food. This menu tries not to be unusual. We left out those healthy low-cost foods liver and spinach, which most people will not eat. This diet does require considerable cooking and baking. If you eat more soul food—pintos, cornbread, and greens—your food will cost even less than the food on this list. This menu was not prepared by a dietitian, but it is a low-fat diet of good, but not rich food. We know a lot of very fine country people who eat this way and they are still healthy and happy at more than 80 years of age.

Sunday

Breakfast: Oatmeal with molasses, syrup, or brown sugar, margarine, and skim milk on it; orange juice; one cup of coffee with sugar or sweetener and skim milk.

Lunch: Roast chicken; dressing from stale bread; homemade cole slaw; cooked carrots; biscuit; margarine; iced tea; canned pineapple (pulp).

Supper: Peanut butter and jelly sandwiches; apple; skim milk; homemade cookies.

Monday

Breakfast: Toast from day-old surplus bread with margarine and homemade apple butter; orange juice.

Lunch: Quarter-pound hamburger, broiled, maybe outdoors on fire (save the grease); baked potato with margarine; cooked, dry lima beans; tomato juice; water.

Supper: Chicken soup from Sunday's chicken; bread croutons from old bread; skim milk; apple sauce; sugar or syrup.

Tuesday

Breakfast: Biscuit with margarine; orange juice; coffee with sugar and skim milk.

Lunch: Chicken salad from the same chicken, made with canned or fresh peas and mayonnaise; bread and margarine; Kool-Aid; sliced bananas in skim milk with sugar or syrup.

Supper: Grilled cheese sandwich; homemade dried pea soup; Jell-o; skim milk; tea with sugar.

Wednesday

Breakfast: Oatmeal with margarine, brown sugar, raisins, and skim milk; orange juice; coffee with skim milk and sugar

Lunch: Homemade spaghetti with hamburger meat; tossed salad with cucumbers and tomatoes; water; applesauce.

Supper: Lettuce and tomato sandwich; skim milk; chicken soup; gingerbread; popcorn from kernels with margarine.

Thursday

Breakfast: Pancakes with homemade imitation maple syrup and margarine; orange juice; coffee with sugar and skim milk

Lunch; Tunafish salad with lettuce, peas, and mayonnaise; bread and margarine; canned pulped pineapple; water.

Supper: Fish Chowder (Buzzacott's recipe); tomato juice; tea; cinnamon toast from old bread.

Friday

Breakfast: Buzzacott's fried corn Johnny cake fried in saved hamburger grease; orange juice; coffee with sugar and skim milk.

Lunch: Sardine salad with lettuce and beets; tomato juice; bread with margarine.

Supper: Big Eat Out at Wendy's: 99-cent burger; iced tea from home; cole slaw from home; Wendy's soft ice cream, all eaten in the car.

Saturday

Breakfast: Oatmeal with skim milk and imitation maple syrup; orange juice; coffee with sugar and skim milk.

Lunch: Buzzacott's corned beef hash (see our recipe) with ketchup; carrots or beets; lemonade; cookie.

Supper: Homemade chili beans from boiled dry beans with hamburger meat and pork; biscuits with margarine; cole slaw; tea; apple dumpling.

RECIPES

We are only giving those old-time recipes that are hard to find these days, now that most everyone cooks from a mix.

Buzzacott's Corn or Johnny Cake

1 pint corn meal
1 pint flour
2 teaspoons baking powder
Salt, sugar to suit

Mix not as stiff as biscuit dough, fry in lard, bacon or hamburger fat. Mr. Buzzacott really knew how to cook wholesome food.

Buzzacott's Camp Biscuits

1 quart self-rising flour*
1 pinch of salt
1 tablespoon shortening

Make the dough soft with cold water and stir with a spoon, just enough to make a fairly stiff dough. Do not knead or stir too much or you get heavy biscuits. Drop from spoon into well-greased pan (this saves a cookie cutter) and bake 15 minutes, or until done. These are also called drop biscuits. If you make them as a single loaf, they are camp bread.

*The great woodsman made them with self-rising flour. If you use regular flour, add 1 tablespoon baking powder per quart of flour.

Buzzacott's Gingerbread

3 cups flour
1 cup molasses
1/2 cup shortening
2 teaspoons ginger
1 teaspoon baking soda
Add water to make a thick batter; bake in a hot oven.

These really go like hot cakes, so if you wonder where that expression came from, these are the real thing. My wife made them for an event with her church ladies and I almost ate them all up myself before she could pack them, they were so good.

Buzzacott's Camp Cookies or Hot Cakes

1 quart flour
1 tablespoon baking powder
1 cup currants or chopped dried fruit*
1 cup syrup or sugar
1 teaspoon cinnamon
2 tablespoons shortening

Mr. Buzzacott says to take the flour and baking powder, mix well, then add the rest of the ingredients. Mix with water to make a thick batter. Roll out and cut cookies with a cookie cutter or a tin can and bake 15 minutes in a quick oven. Or you can make drop cookies by simply pouring gobs of the dough in a greased pan. Everything this great outdoor gentleman suggests in his book is successful.

*We like dates.

Darlene Velzy's Barley Bread

2 cups barley flakes
3 teaspoons salt
4 cups boiling water
3 tablespoons lard
2 packages dry yeast
9 cups flour
3/4 cup lukewarm water
1 cup molasses
1 tablespoon cinnamon, or to taste.

Combine barley flakes and boiling water, cover and let stand for one hour. Soften yeast in lukewarm water. Add to barley flakes with molasses, salt, and melted lard. Add flour and cinnamon and mix well. Let rise. When light, knead. If the dough is sticky add a little more flour until it is the right consistency. Shape into loaves and place in greased bread pans. Let rise. Bake at 375 degrees for 45 minutes. Turn out onto cooling rack. Yields four loaves. This bread freezes well. Recipe by Darlene Velzy, New Mexico farm wife.

Kephart's Sourdough Bread

Mix a pail of batter from flour and water and hang it up in a warm place until it ferments. Then add a teaspoon of salt and a teaspoon of bicarbonate of soda (not baking powder) and one teaspoon sugar, thicken with flour to a smooth dough, knead thoroughly, form as loaves and bake. The advantage is you need buy no yeast, and yeast might be hard to get.

To taste as people like it today, corn bread needs eggs and must have wheat flour as well as corn meal.

Kephart's Corn Bread

1 pint corn meal
1 pint flour
3 tablespoons sugar
2 heaping tablespoons lard or margarine

3 teaspoons baking powder
1 teaspoon salt
2 eggs
1 pint of milk

Mix the shortening and sugar together. Add the beaten eggs, then add milk. Sift the salt and baking powder into the corn meal and flour. Pour the milk over the dry ingredients, beating well. Pour into a well-greased pan and bake 30 or 40 minutes in a moderately hot oven. This recipe also makes muffins, Kephart writes.

Note: You can buy bread and biscuits cheaper at your local "dead bread" store. The main reason to make these baked goods is to avoid the deadly chemicals in bought baked goods. Look at the ingredients on modern food labels. They read like the contents of Love Canal!

Lt. Col. Warren H. Taylor's Boiled Dinner

This man is a genuine war hero. After his wife died, he did all the cooking himself. The Colonel's boiled dinner consists of fresh potatoes and carrots boiled, with a can of mushroom soup poured over them. It tastes wonderful.

Boiled Beans

Always soak beans overnight, changing water twice. They swell double their weight. A cup of dried beans feeds a family of four. Boil after soaking and add, while boiling, a teaspoon of baking soda. Boil until well done, about three hours (or half an hour in a pressure cooker). Season and flavor with salt, pepper, spices, and a piece of pork to suit. Add hamburger for chili, or season for Mexican food to suit. Good for Navy, pinto or Lima beans.

Baked Beans

The favorite of Northern outdoor people who need a lot of calories. Soak a cup of beans overnight, boil a half hour, add a teaspoon of baking soda while boiling. Add pork or bacon, molasses, or brown sugar to suit. These ratios are not critical since there is no chemical reaction, unlike bread. Bake all day in a bean pot in a hot oven. It is too wasteful of fuel to cook them unless your stove is also used for heating the house.

Buzzacott's Fish Chowder

Cut small slices of bacon. Fry them in the bottom of a kettle. Put in a layer of fish, then a layer of onions and then potatoes and biscuits. Season each layer, cover with water and stew slowly for half an hour. Today we mix with an equal quantity of milk before serving.

Buzzacott Corned Beef Hash

Buy corned beef in square cans, usually from Argentina, mix with an equal quantity of cooked potato, salt if you must. Add chopped onion and fry. If you add beets, it is called Red Flannel Hash because of its red color. It has much better ingredients and tastes better than canned hash. Fish cakes are made the same way but with mashed up fish. Ratio is two parts potato to one part fish. You can substitute bread crumbs for half the potato.

Ginger Switchel

1 teaspoon molasses
1 teaspoon vinegar
A pinch of ginger

Mix thoroughly in two quarts water. If you want it sweeter add six saccharine tablets or honey. Old-timers would cringe at the saccharine. This may be better even more diluted. Serve ice cold.

Apple Butter

It is dense, very sweet applesauce with brown sugar or molasses added until it shows a very dark color and tastes good. Season with cinnamon to taste.

Chapter 9

Save on Clothing

When I left my salaried job and went into freelance writing, I continued to go into town and to the post office wearing a good suit and tie. Then I thought, what an idiot I was! I have no customers in town I have to impress. My readers are scattered all over the country. What good did it do to impress post office clerks and salespeople in stores?

I began wearing old work clothes and sweaters to town and it never made a bit of difference. If you are no longer running with a pack of executives, you can downgrade your clothing, too. Here are other ways to save on clothing to cut your clothing budget to as low as $600 a year for a couple. We'll outline them first, then go back over them in detail.

My wife bought the 100 percent camel's hair coat she is wearing for under $10 at the DAV thrift shop in Roanoke, Virginia. The denim dress is like those selling for $150 in good stores. She bought it for 98 cents at the same place.

SAVING ON CLOTHES

Buy Most of Your Clothing Secondhand

This is the greatest saving of all. Go to the Salvation Army, St. Vincent DePaul, Morgan Memorial, Goodwill stores, flea markets, yard sales, and private thrift shops. You'll find men's pants and ladies slacks for a dollar, nice dresses and sweaters about the same, suits for $10 and luxury fake furs for $15 and leather coats that originally cost $300 to $400 for about $35. Much of the clothing is high-grade, high-fashion name brands. The top brands cost only a few dollars more than cheap brands. You will be able, with a little care, to pick out items that look like new. It does not deprive the poor to buy Salvation Army clothes. They have a great surplus. Do not be bashful. We know people making more than $50,000 a year who love old clothes.

Get Clothing Free

Look in dumpsters outside shopping malls, on college campuses at the end of the semester and behind thrift shops. Much clothing is thrown away.

Get Socks, Underwear, and Shoes New

If you buy anything new, concentrate on buying durable work clothes, underwear, socks, and shoes. UPS delivery people, service technicians, and working people wear the most durable clothing. Much of it is purchased mail-order from firms like WearGuard (order a catalog by writing WearGuard, Box 9105, Hingham, MA 02043-9105 or visit their Web site: www.wearguard.com). Get the pants in gray, navy, or brown—never forest green—and they will not look like work clothes. The mail-order firms have women's work clothing, too. Buy good new underwear by name brands such as Haynes or Fruit of the Loom. You cannot save on underwear without being miserable. All socks should be the same color to avoid odd socks when one of them is lost or ruined.

Wear as Little Clothing as Possible

In summer, wear bathing trunks only. Women can wear shorts and a bathing suit top around the house. Go barefoot. You will need a hat for protection from the dangerous rays of the sun. Totally worn-out white dress shirts are good to wear over a bathing suit. Take them to the beach and wear them in your boat. Wear them to bed instead of pajamas.

Repair Clothing to Make It Last

Sew up rips and holes. Cut down worn-out long-sleeved shirts to make short-sleeved shirts. Make shorts out of pants with worn cuffs. Patch bad knees and elbows with heavy cloth, leather, or plastic. If you can't sew, you can often cement on a patch. Maybe make entire suits and outfits on the sewing machine. Learn how to do this by taking an adult class at night in your nearest adult education center, or inquire at your local fabric store. Protect valuable woolens from moth holes with moth balls and proper storage. Make attractive elbow patches for sweaters and jackets from leather cut from old leather coats, boots, or car upholstery. Resole shoes yourself with soles cut from tire tread, or take them to a shoe cobbler to be repaired. My mother used to cut worn bed sheets in half down the middle. They always wore out in the center first. Then she would put the worn part on the outside and sew them together on the machine again. I would have to sleep on a seam.

Invest In Clothing That Is Classic and Will Not Go Out of Fashion

Disregard high fashions, which are temporary. Old men's suits are the biggest clothing bargain, since few people wear suits any more. Often they are in fine shape for $10 or less in thrift stores. Avoid special outfits for jogging, designer jeans, designer sneakers like Nikes, and fancy materials like Gore-Tex unless bought used very cheaply. Work shoes or Wal-Mart shoes are just as good as fancy shoes.

Avoid Dry Cleaning

Buy clothing that does not need dry cleaning, except perhaps a good suit for funerals and weddings and a fine dress for the ladies. In situations where a man is expected to wear an expensive suit, he can save by wearing a tweed or corduroy sport coat with a turtleneck or flannel sport shirt and tie, and blue jeans or work pants. Keep your weight constant so you do not have to discard clothes that are now too small for you. Most thrift shop clothing probably got there because the original owners ate too much food! Very old suits have wide lapels like today and are worth buying. Newer used suits may have lapels too narrow to be stylish now, but they will come back.

Alternatives for Women

Women should wear as much men's clothing as possible. It is made better because manufacturers believe men expect their clothes to last longer. War surplus can be very good. Select a few colors that coordinate so that all your clothing will go together.

Cold Weather and Outdoor Clothing

You will probably be outdoors more now, and you may move to a northern state, or live in the wilderness. In the South, if you wear Northern-style warm clothing, you can live and work and have fun outdoors all winter long, unlike the local people who button up and go indoors after Labor Day.

To save on transportation, you will be walking more, or maybe riding a bicycle or a small motorcycle, which can be chilly. A coat that is warm enough to wear walking to the car in the parking lot will not be adequate to stay outdoors all day in winter, you will find. And staying at home in winter with warm clothing you do not have to make the fire so hot. So you need good, warm clothing. Hats are essential when it is below freezing.

Overcoats are never worn in the woods and are not good for manual labor, but are fine for street wear. In thrift shops you find plenty of men's and sometimes women's gabardine raincoats with a woolly zip-in liner for winter for $15 or so. These take the place of a raincoat, a spring and fall topcoat, and a winter coat down to perhaps 25 degrees. They are recommended over wool tweed or loose-weave coats, which are not as warm when there is wind chill. Charles Lindbergh toured the world wearing such a coat in his later life with only a briefcase for luggage.

You find lots of secondhand quilted ski-parka style coats and car coats, particularly in the spring, at big savings. They can be over $150 new. Avoid bright colors and choose dull tones since it is more discreet not to be seen in many places in the woods. Some of these are filled with down feathers and others with synthetics. The down is terribly soggy when it gets wet. There are long storm coats of down, and sheepskin fleece-lined coats that may be found used. The sheepskin coats are very warm and durable, but heavy. Women's sheepskin fur coats, called "mouton," are warm and durable but, of course, the sheep must die to make any sheepskin coat. I will not buy any fur but a synthetic. The animals are my friends.

Long underwear, either one or two piece suits, are the best way to keep warm in really cold weather. Both men and women love them. The type with an inside layer of cotton and an outside layer of wool is best. Buy mail-order from firms like Campmor or perhaps from the expensive L.L. Bean. There also are inner suits of quilted Dacron that are very good.

Workers who climb power poles wear them. Try Wal-Mart and Army-Navy stores to find the quilted suits. An outfit of long johns, a heavy, wool plaid shirt, work pants or jeans and a cap keep you warm working outdoors down to about 25 degrees for hours on end. If it gets colder you add a parka or surplus field jacket. If you expect to get wet from snow, wool pants are best.

Snowmobile suits cost over $150 new and are quite warm—often too warm. They are scarce used, but I saw one for $20 in a yard sale recently. The trouble with a one-piece outfit is you cannot take anything off to cool down without undressing completely. They have all the problems of a kid's snowsuit. You have to unbutton clothes when you exercise in cold or you will get all sweaty.

Make Your Own Footwear

Make your own sandals and resole shoes yourself. Take a sharp knife or saw and cut a sole from the tread of a well-worn tire. To make sandals, cut holes in the sole and thread a cord or a thong through it to tie as a sandal ties. See picture.

To resole a nice old shoe or boot you hate to throw away, get some heavy contact cement and glue the new sole on over the old. Clamp it in a vise until it dries and if you lack a vise, drive a wheel of your car on top of it. (We're really cheap!)

You can treat the heel in several ways. If it's not worn, remove it and glue it back on, leaving the nails in. Or make a heel with one or more layers of tire. You can try nailing your shoe, hitting the nail into a stone inside the shoe to turn it over or with a nail set, but it may not be successful.

Homemade sandals.

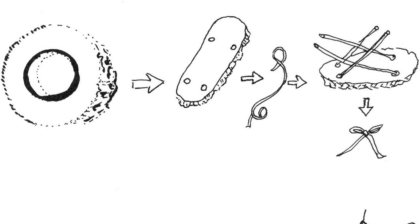

Cotton vs. Wool

Cotton is fine at home, but feels miserable and clammy outdoors in cold. It holds the damp. Wool is the only fiber that is still warm even if wetted through and through.

A Maine fisherman in a dory off the coast wearing a wool sweater will be warm even if he's drenched by a wave. The traditional heavy, wool flannel plaid shirt in red and black, or green and black, costing about $50 from firms like Woolrich and L.L. Bean is the best thing for outdoor wear in cold. It lasts 10 years or more, so it may be worth its high price. Do not work on greasy or dirty things with it since it must be dry-cleaned.

You can buy pants of similar wool material that are very good, too. You are very fortunate to find any of this used. Women feel better and look better in ski pants and wool sweaters with a quilted inner suit or a suit of long johns underneath. They can wear a windbreaker, ski jacket, or parka over it. Hoods are very desirable. Sweaters of wool or synthetic fibers are always good and may be worn in layers and kept even if old and full of holes. Wear several arranged so the holes do not line up.

Leather

A leather coat ($10 to $45 in thrift shops, $350 new) is a wonderful windproof, warm, durable garment. Many people will not wear them because they think they make you look mean and fierce. They are ideal for riding a motorcycle or bicycle in cold or windy weather—they'll save your hide if you fall off! Wear sweaters, wool shirts, or long underwear underneath since these coats have little insulation. They are designed for wear up to 45 degrees or so. If you do not like leather, the Army field jacket with liner is almost as good. They come surplus or new from Army-Navy stores and sometimes are found in a thrift shop.

Boots

You need long, warm wool socks and boots in cold weather. L.L. Bean boots with rubber bottoms and leather tops are very fine. My three pairs of Bean boots have lasted me 40 years! Over the years I have had Bean repair them and put on new rubber bottoms several times. Maine businessmen even wear the Bean boots to Kiwanis and Rotary under a business suit. Other makes may be cheaper, but Bean boots are the greatest.

Army combat boots are durable and fairly cheap from Army-Navy surplus stores. I like zippers on mine, as I had in the army, to save time lacing, but they are colder and not as durable. There are lots of good, reasonably priced all-rubber insulated boots and workman boots of tan leather in stores like Wal-Mart. Avoid very expensive (more than $100) new boots with exotic insulation, waterproofing, and mountain-climbing soles unless you are too wealthy to be reading this book. Take care of boots, rubbing the leather with neat's-foot oil, avoid excess heat drying them, have them sewed and repaired promptly. Women and men should wear the same kind of boots.

How to Stay Warm If You Are Really Broke

Several layers of newspaper inside your pants and between your coat and shirt equals a pair of long underwear. If you get cold sleeping, a layer of newspapers is equal to another blanket. Change the newspapers for dry ones often. English working men used to wind a very long, thick, woolen scarf all around diagonally inside their suit coats from the neck down to save wearing an overcoat, which perhaps many could not afford. A down or Dacron-filled vest can turn a raincoat to an overcoat. Plastic bags or plastic film found in the trash, or old shower curtains from Dumpsters make improvised rain wear for very poor people and reduce wind chill effects.

Rain Clothing

Wool shirts and parkas are water-repellent in moderate rain and in any snowstorm. Winter snow, when the weather is below freezing, is not wet. For heavy rain, a surplus poncho, plastic film raincoat, or rain suit is necessary. The English and Australians make rain suits and storm coats by waxing canvas cloth. They are very fashionable now and cost $300 or more. There is no reason you cannot make such a coat yourself by rubbing a lot of hot candle wax into cloth as Kephart described long ago. Ordinary water-repellent cotton raincoat cloth soaks through in 10 to 15 minutes of heavy rain. If the repellent is washed out, you get drenched in about five minutes. Re-waterproof with spray silicone waterproofing sold for this purpose.

Try to keep raincoats clean and do not send them to the dry cleaner if you can help it, because it impairs the waterproofing. The best ponchos and rain suits are made of a rubber-coated textile, not just a plastic-like film. The rain suits sold to ocean fishermen in boating stores are particularly good. Men like the Sou'wester rain hat best. Wealthy people like Gore-Tex. Reeves Brothers, which makes London Fog clothing, has a factory store near Spartanburg, South Carolina, that is really cheap. It sells slightly imperfect windbreaker jackets, raincoats and overcoats for men and women. This is luxury clothing but lasts a long time. Mother kept a raincoat she bought from Burberry in London for 25 years. After it wore out, we used it to cover things we left outdoors, such as a Crosley car engine.

Used Children's Clothing

Used clothing for children is scarce in thrift shops, perhaps best left to the really poor. It is the most common item in yard sales. Some families make a deal to get all the clothing of a child of a friend or relative who is a few years older. It may be altered to make it smaller or made over on the sewing machine. Always pass on used kids clothing to another family after the kid has outgrown it. One thing we should never be cheap about is giving.

Everyday Clothing

Blue jeans are excellent for both sexes but should never be the bleached or stonewashed variety which have half their life taken right out of them by this process. Buy the regular dark blue color in nondesigner style. Some men's jeans are so fashionable they put the belt line half way between the belly button and the crotch. What man wants to go around looking as if he were about to burst? Even suspenders cannot hold up some jeans. They are actually made this way, not just for style, but because the maker is cheap on cloth. Jeans are good buys in places like Wal-Mart and are sometimes found used in thrift stores, usually in smaller sizes that people outgrew.

Both men and women like blue jeans. Bib-overall-type blue jeans fit older men better and save wear on shirts. For tops, knit sweatshirts, turtlenecks and T-shirts are cheap and need no pressing. Old neckties cost little or nothing. I keep all my old narrow ties. Eventually the style will change and they can be worn again. I'm wearing very old wide ties that I have kept for years that are now back in style. If you still live in a liberal city like Boston, New York, or Philadelphia, wear only clip-on ties or bow ties. If a mugger grabs your tie, it will come off in his hand and he cannot strangle you with it. Mechanics and shop teachers do not wear regular ties since machinery could snag them.

You will like the fatigue pants and tops from an Army-Navy store for doing heavy work. I wear fatigues to change a car motor. People ask if they were my uniform when I was in the army. Hardly—I had a 32-inch waist then. My wife wears my old fatigue shirt, too. It is like a smock on her, and keeps her skirt and blouse clean doing housework.

Better Bargains For Smaller People

Every year people eat more and get bigger. Women size 7 or smaller and men wearing size 36 and 38 suits get wonderful clothing bargains. It always seems to be smaller sizes that are surplus. If you are big, you may not think these thrift shops are so wonderful.

Bargains In Shoes

Thrift shops and flea markets have a lot of used men and women's dress shoes for about a dollar a pair. If they are your size and not rough and worn inside, they are worth buying. You can also buy worn uniform pants from uniform rental firms in flea markets for a dollar a pair. New shoes are getting quite expensive. Stores like Wal-Mart still have some reasonable loafers, and sneakers. Dress shoes are very expensive. Hopefully those you already own will last many years. Keep them polished. Have them resoled. Mason shoes, sold by agents or through the mail, are good. Get to be an agent and sell your friends and buy for yourself too.

If you can go barefoot without stepping on glass or cutting your feet it is a very good idea. Then your shoe expense will be zero. Teenagers have to wear those very expensive sneakers like Nikes because their feet get soft from never going barefoot. Going barefoot, you get good at moving quietly and quickly through the woods like an Indian. They wore moccasins all the time. Their moccasins had no hard soles. Craft books tell how to make them. You can find a lot of valuable leather for making moccasins, vests, coats, and other leathercraft from worn out leather coats, worn-out high women's dressy boots, and luxury leather car seats from junk Lincolns and Cadillacs. The back seats are best—less worn. Cousin George Bryne's father used to tell him as a boy to walk on the grass going to school so his shoes would last longer!

Women's Clothing

The thrift shops have even more good buys for women than men. There are many beautiful dresses and suits; denim dresses are particularly nice. They have nice, tailored wool suits, belts, handbags, and accessories. You can find expensive-looking camel's hair coats and beautiful fake furs if you look hard enough. They have dressy party dresses, clothing with flashy sequins suitable for performing on stage, country and western clothing, all sorts of things. Yard sales in affluent neighborhoods

THE TIME DAD OVERDID IT. Back in the '30s, Dad, Mother, and little me all went down to watch the Memorial Day Parade with the band and the soldiers, the DAR ladies, and all the floats. All of us were sold bright, red crepe-paper Buddy Poppies by the American Legion men. After the parade was over Dad said, "You give all of the poppies to me and we'll keep them and wear them next year." My mother looked at him and screamed, "Edward! You are *too* cheap!"

have surprising buys on women's clothing. Women buy great quantities of it, then get too fat or need room to buy new things so they get rid of it practically unused.

You should know that flea-market vendors get most of their used clothing from yard and thrift shops that set the prices too low. The yard-sale items are usually cheapest. We buy our high-fashion used clothing in thrift shops out of town, partly because people do not dress up much here, but also so the wife will not be seen wearing another woman's old dress to church or to a party. Clothing styles and amount of dress-up vary greatly from one place to another, particularly in women's clothing. A new person should be careful to copy closely to what local people wear.

My wife contributes this: "Panty hose usually get a run in one leg before the other. Wait until you have a pair with a bad left leg and another pair with a bad right leg. Cut off the bad legs and combine the two pairs. Wear one on top of the other."

Leggings, leotards, tights, and stretch pants are much more durable than panty hose. Appalachian mountain women still wear old print dresses or a pinafores over a pair of blue jeans and you can, too.

HOW TO GET CLOTHING FREE

Look in the Dumpster in back of a Salvation Army or any other big thrift shop after it closes and you will find lots of clothing and other items inside that are almost as good as what is sold in the store. Americans are still wasteful, extravagant people—they buy new clothes and discard them so fast the thrift shop has no room for them. No kidding. If you are a volunteer worker, you get first choice of discarded clothing and help a worthy cause, too. You can also travel around to better neighborhoods just before the trash pickup to find lots of clothing and other things discarded in the trash piles in front of each house.

A good way to get a whole wardrobe of clothing cheap is to find a person your size who died and buy it all from the widow or widower. Try to get suitcases, hangers, accessories, closet items, and all the rest. Pay very little, perhaps $25, certainly less than $100 for a giant wardrobe. Often it is a gift and will cost you nothing.

Bedding, Towels, and Other Cloth Items

We must have good sheets and towels; we would feel bad without them. We do not know how to get them cheaply, except possibly from the trash.

Surplus army blankets are pretty good bed covers. We pay $5 for a used one. For sanitary reasons, you must always wash or send this secondhand clothing and linen to the dry cleaner. A regular-sized double bed uses much cheaper bedding than a queen- or a king-sized bed. The way to stay really warm in bed is with a pair of sleeping bags that you can unzip and lay flat and use as a quilt. They are very warm, yet not heavy on top of you. You can let the house get to 50 degrees or colder at night. Avoid cotton blankets or quilts since they are damp and clammy unless you have good central heating. Electric blankets really work but we do not use them any more due to concern at being surrounded by the AC electric field.

My grandmother said in Florida about 1900, when there was no air conditioning, the servants would wet their people's bed sheets with water in summer when it was intolerably hot. The evaporation principle really works. You may need it if you have to live without air conditioning and we show you how in the chapter on utilities.

THE LAUNDRY

If you live way out in the country with a well and no power, you may not have a washer because gasoline motor-powered machines are noisy, quite expensive, and use a lot of water. There is no place for a washer in many apartments. Take your laundry to the coin-operated washers in town when you do your weekly shopping, but bring your own soap. The slot machine packages of soap cost too much.

Clothes can be washed in a brook and the dirt scrubbed out using a rock like a washboard. It is hard work and the clothes suffer—they are between a rock and a hard place, you see. The family can help out by not getting things so dirty—being careful of grease, paint, and messy things like that. New spot removers such as Spray 'n Wash Stain Stick are remarkable. If well water is limited, the old Easy Washer from the 1920s used very little water, and there are automatic washers that adjust to use little water. Wringers of hand or powered variety save energy drying, but are quite dangerous. These old non-automatic washers can still be found used. Cold-water detergent saves a lot of energy. Woolite is good, will wash many woolens, and removes spots used full strength.

Avoid Clothes Dryers

The dryer uses a tremendous amount of energy. It takes a lot of life out of the clothes and makes towels rough and scratchy like burlap. A natural-gas dryer is always cheaper than an electrical dryer. Avoid the dryer and have a whiter, better-smelling wash by hanging your clothes outdoors on a clothesline.

It is a taboo in many neighborhoods to have a clothesline visible. So you better hide your clothesline behind shrubs or lattice-work, or in the attic! Many houses get extremely hot in the attic up above the insulation. Up in the attic is a good place to dry clothes, my wife says. It is free energy.

BEAUTY AND COSMETICS

Men can have their hair cut free at barber schools. If no one is going to promote you, who cares how you look? Women can have their hair cut, tinted, and curled free at beautician schools. A neighbor had her hair done at the beauty college, but the students dyed her hair orange by mistake so they had to make her a blond to hide it all. So beware.

My wife buys flea-market perfume and cosmetics, but we suspect the perfume may be watered down. There is no qualitative difference between discount drug store generic cosmetics and fashionable name-brand lipstick and nail polish. Why pay for stupid TV ads? People who try to cover up acne with lotion, paint, powder, and cremes get the whole jar infected with skin bacteria and the infection then spreads to wherever they apply the salve. Notice a lady with complexion problems always has them worse in the places where she applies the most cosmetics—usually her cheeks. They never seem to catch on.

Soap and water and avoidance of dangerous sunlight give the smoothest skin. Sunbonnets like the ones in pictures in old Victorian children's stories may come back in style now that we know how much they are really needed.

Wonderful thrift shops have good buys in used clothing, appliances, surplus food, and many other things

Chapter 10

Save on Shelter

RENTAL HOUSES AND APARTMENTS

We will consider apartments and rental houses first because that is probably where you will go first when you relocate. Later you may buy a home. In sections of the country where population is declining, where there is no great prosperity to drive prices up, the basic two-bedroom apartment is about $350 a month. This includes most of the South, small towns in the Southwest, the Midwest, upstate Maine, and Appalachia. The same type of apartment in places people like to live, such as Vermont, New Hampshire, or Colorado, will rent for twice as much. In fashionable parts of cities and in resorts, rents will be astronomical—$1,200 a month or more for small apartments. We avoid these high-cost areas in this book.

This basic $350-a-month apartment will be clean and neat. It may be a duplex, a quad, or in a larger building. Often it is an older building that has been remodeled, often of wood construction with vinyl siding or clapboards. Floors are usually shag carpet, doors flush plywood, often there is wood-grain paneling in the living room and the rest is Sheetrock. It will have central heat, and it may have central air in warmer climates. Otherwise you will be expected to cool it with a fan or window air conditioner you supply. It will be unfurnished. Sometimes the tenant supplies refrigerator and cook stove, or they may come with the apartment. It probably does not have a dishwasher and it may lack a place to hitch a washer and dryer. The single bathroom is fairly modern, but small, with tub and shower and one small basin. You will park your car in the street or in the driveway, no garage.

Two-bedroom apartments are usually best. Larger apartments are bad business for landlords because they attract large families with many children or two or more families living together, who tend to mistreat the property. (If you were going to be a landlord, the two-bedroom is the size of apartment you would want to own, because it is easiest to rent. The rent is paid by the month with one month's deposit, which elimi-

This luxurious Pennsylvania house has been converted into three apartments.

Typical good country apartment house. Apartments in houses like this rent for $300 a month or less.

nates real down-and-out people who may strip the place or sublet bedrooms.) Be sure to find out if heat and hot water are included in the rent. If not, you must calculate their costs accurately. They can run higher in a poorly insulated apartment than for a small home.

Very cheap apartments have problems; you will not like them. Those with kerosene stoves for each apartment are unsafe. The tenants let them blow up. Furnished apartments and apartments rented by the week attract the kind of people who spend all their time drinking, fighting, and throwing things, and playing the TV and the stereo as loud as they can. These people love trouble the way I love pancakes and maple syrup. They actually are unable ever to save enough to pay a months' rent in advance or to keep any furniture. This goes on for their whole lives. Stay away from them. If you have to rent by the week, take a motel.

The landlord must be fair and easygoing, yet clever at picking good tenants and willing to evict bad ones. Landlords vary greatly. Some are grumpy and cheap. Others really seem to treat their tenants like family. You can find yourself with another uncle or aunt, which is very nice. Many lifelong friendships have been formed among people living in apartments. But the tenants can change rapidly—if you get one or two bad ones next door, the only thing to do is move. So never fix up an apartment too well. Landlords get fooled because a sweet little lady will go to rent the apartment, supposedly for herself, and then fill the place with a half dozen people who look like gorillas and act worse. It happens all the time.

Finding the Best Apartments

Landlords are deathly afraid of the federal government. If they advertise an apartment for rent and a convicted rapist and drug dealer wants it, and this person also happens to be a minority, and is refused, the landlord can be prosecuted for civil rights violations by a giant federal agency with teams of lawyers set up just for this purpose. It can cost them $100,000 or more in legal fees to settle the case. Often good apartments can be found only by networking, much as you find a job. Apartment owning is a bad business for an individual to be in these days. If you are a corporation with savings and loan money, rental shelter can be profitable and if not, the stockholders or the government pick up the loss—so who cares. But individual investors are running scared.

Therefore, landlords do not advertise the better low-priced apartments by signs or ads in the newspaper. They are rented by word of mouth and often have a waiting list of nice people. You sometimes find such a place by simply knocking on doors of many attractive-looking, modest apartment houses and asking if they have any vacancies.

Modern Apartment Complexes

The lower range of modern, professionally managed apartment complexes may be cheap enough for you. These have names like "Carriage House," but do not assume from the name that the the average tenant is carriage trade. He is just as likely to drive a beer truck!

Many are very attractive places. Rich and very clever people who could easily afford a condominium sometimes live in them. We knew a little old lady more than 80 years of age who had lived in a garden apartment for more than 20 years and loved it. She enjoyed swimming in the pool. And she knew more about investments than I did. When she finally died, in her mid 80s, she left $2 million to her favorite college—much to everyone's surprise! The rent on this particular apartment complex was actually less than the interest on the money to buy an equivalent condo and pay property taxes and fees. The risk to equity with a rental is nil. Now that real estate is not necessarily a growth field, renting can actually be a better deal than owning. You cannot lose any equity in a rent because there is none. Often these complexes have swimming pools and sometimes a club room. The apartments with club rooms are more likely to have a swinging, drinking crowd than those lacking them, but the pool attracts nice, healthy people.

RENTING HOUSES

Rents on good, brick ranch houses with fireplaces, two baths, and air run very high nearly everywhere, typically $750 to $1,500 a month or more. The small older bungalow, mill house, Cape Cod, or minimum ranch house in a lower-middle- or working-class neighborhood is what you will get for $350 a month. It will have two or three bedrooms, one bath and facilities and trim like the $350-a-month apartment. It may not be centrally heated, but if the space heaters are under your own control and none of them are kerosene pot burners you can manage OK. The little house probably has connections for washer and dryer. It may have a carport or a one-car garage with the door raised by hand. It will cost more to heat and cool than most apartments; there will be a lawn to mow and, in the north, snow to shovel. But you can use the yard for fun, for cookouts, maybe a vegetable garden, to hold yard sales, and to work on things.

Big, older houses rent for about the same as smaller ones, but costs for heating or air can be extraordinary, maybe more than $500 a month. Avoid them as rentals. For economy, stick to the well-insulated single-story or story-and-a-half home, preferably under 1,000 square feet. The neighborhoods these homes are in vary greatly. Some of these homes are found out in the country on one- to five-acre lots. There you can raise a fine garden. Crime may be a serious problem both in suburbs and in the country now. Ask around, note whether you still see women and young people out walking at night when you drive by. Look for burglar-alarm signs, fierce dogs, and chain-link fences.

Trailers or mobile homes may also be rented, and they usually need no furniture. But many trailer parks have bad reputations; the residents are into all kinds of bad things. Those accepting only senior citizens and not permitting children are better. Usually the lot as well as the trailer is rented by the week and it costs more than an apartment. The management gets trailers to rent for little or nothing from people who abandon them and from repossessions. These trailer parks are seldom bargains. The better trailer to rent, if you like trailers, would be one by itself on its own lot. This might be hard to find. Some people like trailers—I prefer a nice little house.

Right: I was offered this livable Pennsylvania house for $8,000 in 1989. New owner is restoring it.

Far right: Attractive low-cost log house in the pine trees.

Right: This small house overlooking the beautiful Allegheny River has a glassed-in sun porch and a sun deck. It is not for sale but you can find houses like it on the river or build one.

Far right: Smaller houses can be very beautiful. This one is in Vermont.

More good-quality small houses. Right: The gambrel roof house has lots of space and is easy to heat. It is not for sale but plenty more like it can be found these days.

Far right: This type of high-grade architect-designed 1940s house is still affordable in the lower-cost parts of the country; they cost $60,000 or less.

BUYING LOW-COST SMALL HOUSES

Remember how the Volkswagen Beetle always had top resale value among cars? Well, in houses, the good deal is the two- or three-bedroom, one-bathroom, one- or one-and-a-half-story ranch, bungalow, or modified Cape-Cod-style house.

It will have central heat, a real cellar in the North and central air in the South. It will be frame construction and perhaps brick veneer, though this usually puts it above our price range. In the low-cost areas of the country we have listed, great quantities of these good houses are found for $45,000 or less. This is what you want. These houses with full cellars may have the cellar finished off into a family room or even some extra bedrooms, giving you quite a large house at a very low cost. Often there are bedrooms under the eaves, sometimes with dormer windows. Bedrooms can be added and the attic finished off. You could do either of these jobs yourself if you really needed more room. These houses often

Small ranch houses like this are usually the best investment and the best value.

have porches. Often the porch has been fitted with storm windows, insulated, and made into an additional room in the house. Good owners love these houses and are steadily working on them as a hobby. That is the kind of house you should buy.

It is an art to assess the condition of used houses. Ask people and get books on it; we cannot cover it here. The FHA checks a house very carefully for one of their mortgages. It's best, of course, to avoid a mortgage entirely. If you can manage to buy a small house using the money from a house you've sold, you can live worry free and out of debt.

Small houses with two or three bedrooms are usually found in older suburbs with sidewalks, but also out in the country on lots of one to five acres or more. These little rural homesteads can be a very good deal because you can farm or have a business. Here, there is no zoning. The big problem is that someone else can set up a business you might not

Traditional Southern mill house. They are good to live in, and will probably appreciate in time.

like, such as a noisy sawmill that runs all night, an adult book store, a pig pen, or a junk yard right next to you or across the street. Better be sure the neighborhood is full and there are no vacant lots and you like your neighbors before you buy. Some neighbors may be the "fighting and feuding" people you sometimes find way out in the country.

Water access may be a great problem in rural areas. Even good wells have been going dry in recent droughts and heat waves. They cost $7 or more a foot to dig. The bill can run to $20,000 if you need a new well.

Septic tanks are another problem. I'd better not say too much about septic tanks because once I bought a house with no septic tank at all without knowing it. The sewer pipe just went out into the field out back and ended. A working couple lived there before. Strange people—they must have used the toilet at work for all of their serious business. I noticed it was a little swampy out back, but I didn't pay it much attention. But when we arrived with a baby and a washing machine—oh boy! A lawyer made them put a septic tank in for us, but the story is no credit to me, or to the FHA inspector who approved the house.

Mill Houses

Mill houses—built in rows by textile factories about a hundred years ago in what are called "Mill Hills" in the South—can be good buys and are well worth fixing up. Prices run from $18,000 to $45,000. Most sales are private and you have to get to know local people to buy one, because these are good neighborhoods and they want to keep them crime- and drug-free.

HOUSING THAT DOESN'T COST YOU ANY MONEY

Build or buy yourself a small wooden duplex. Finance it. Live in one side and rent the other. The rent from your one tenant should pay for the house. Tenants can be weird people. I had some real turkeys and losers. Having them next door you can, at least, watch them better.

BIG HOUSES

Bigger old houses can be low cost if located in places that are isolated—where there is no industry and no place to go to work. This 3,000-square-foot, double-brick Eastlake Victorian home in good repair sold for $62,000 in 1996 in a rural location. It had two fireplaces, oak paneling, stained glass and beveled windows, a formal dining room, sun porch, and old time electric chandeliers—all authentic. Nothing had been ruined by remodeling. Heat was steam, and the oak kitchen had modern appliances. It was well-insulated between the double-brick walls and in the attic and cellar. It had a complete complement of custom-made wooden storm windows, some curved, that had to be attached and removed every year. Those on the second floor were attached on the inside to save using a ladder. There even was a neat cement block garage that could hold a car and a boat. Look for houses like this. They are still for sale in the more remote places.

This brick Victorian house in rural Pennsylvania sold for $62,000 in 1996. Note the beautiful entrance hall with oak paneling and authentic old-time wallpaper.

HOUSES TO BUILD

These are a lot of fun. Some we show here are quite austere, suitable for living on borrowed land as described in the chapter on living on no money at all. Some are very nice, but they take considerable skill to build. Others are simpler; they can be built by an unskilled person in a short time.

You might make a more temporary shack at first to live in while you are building a good house. Long ago, from 1930 to the 1950s, the more ambitious working man would build his house from scratch while he had a full-time job in a factory. It took all the man's weekends and spare time for a number of years to finish a good-looking Cape Cod or ranch house. Sometimes after they dug the cellar and set the cellar walls, they would put a roof over it and move in and live in the cellar to save paying rent. The people who did this were called "Cellar Dwellers." They would pay for the house with cash saved from their weekly paycheck as they went along, building it piece by piece.

Most of these men are now retired and some are dead. The houses still stand and now are worth 10 times or more what they cost. Building a house this way was characteristic of WW II veterans and people who survived the Depression of the 1930s. I wish more young people still did things like this. Friends and relatives often helped and trades were bartered. For example, if the owner was a mechanic, he would swap auto repair work for having an electrician wire the house, or a plumber put in pipes. I remember Seth Warner with a whole gang of friends and relatives digging a great big hole for the cellar of his new house with picks and shovels.

You can still build your own house in places where the politicians have not yet passed impossible building codes. It might be a very good idea, but these days most people need a little help from an experienced carpenter to make a house that looks neat and is well fitted. A shack covered with tar paper or plywood can be made by anyone in a matter of days. We'll cover both kinds of houses, as well as interesting, pretty log and stone houses and modified trailers.

Basic House for a Small Family—Must Be Carpenter Built

This plan is well proven and has been used for years. It has 768 square feet and costs little to heat or air condition. It is remarkably low cost if the labor to build it does not cost the $75 to $100 an hour that contractors charge.

Do not put in a fireplace, which costs a fortune, and do not make an elaborate tiled kitchen and bathroom, which are expensive. If you want to see a fire burning, use a gas heater that glows, or get a Franklin wood stove, or give up and simply do all your fireside cooking outdoors in a low-cost outdoor fireplace you make of old bricks and stones.

Little house plans must not have many tiny rooms or you will not like to live in them. Do not have large furniture or too much furniture—the rooms always look smaller after you get the furniture in than when they were empty. For several kids of the same sex, use double bunks in the second bedroom; usually the kids prefer the upper bunk.

In the north you get a better insulated house by making walls with thicker studs than 2x4s. Try 2x8-inch studs further apart. Maybe you can find a carpenter that can build this way. Building materials are expensive new. You can save by looking for used building materials in Dumpsters and at construction sites where they are thrown away, and at used building material stores. We paneled our cellar with studding and fine wood paneling a local bank put in a Dumpster last year when they redecorated their offices. It was free and we have materials left over.

Since labor and materials are so variable in cost we can give no fixed price for what a small house like this will cost, but it will be very low. It should cost less than $10,000 for materials, which means you will probably not have to borrow money. A little house like this does have limited storage space, however. Get rid of your excess junk at a yard sale and if you

Here are two ways our basic small house could look. The basic floor plan can be styled different ways. House above has a low roof, a crawl space in the attic, and real redwood siding. There is no cellar. The house below has a substantial attic, which could later be fixed up with two bedrooms. Note the steep roof so snow will run off it and small double-glassed windows characteristic of Maine, Wisconsin, and Minnesota. Construction is frame but log siding makes it look like a log cabin. A cellar has been dug, but the floor is still earth.

still have things to store, keep them in cheap unheated, unwired temporary buildings, or even old truck bodies, for a fraction of the cost of closet space inside a nice house. Then your little house will be quite big enough.

Houses within 100 feet of a dirt road with any traffic will be dusty inside. You will be mopping constantly. Many dirt roads are nearly useless for travel in mud season. You wallow in it. Pay much less for a house on a dirt road.

What Size House Do You Really Need?

The bargain houses are all less than 1,000 square feet, which is ample size for a family. A 400- or 500-square-foot house is fine for a couple even with one or two small children, and as little as 200 square feet is enough for a single person. Remember, a large motor home only has 300 square feet. You may have to get rid of a lot of things. With a smaller house you

The basic small house plan here has 768 square feet and measures 24 by 32 feet. This plan has been very popular since the 1920s. A variation shown below has stairs up and down so you can fix up the attic with two bedrooms and put a family room and a workshop in the basement later. In the single-story plan a washer and dryer may be put where the chimney and hall closet are now and the chimney relocated to the right bedroom closet. In the two-story plan the washer and dryer are in the cellar. These are extremely successful houses. Show this page to an experienced carpenter and he will know what you want. If you find a house like this for sale, buy it.

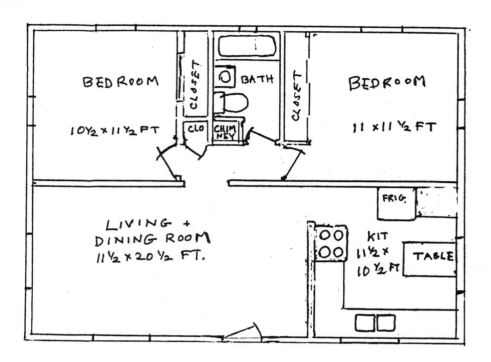

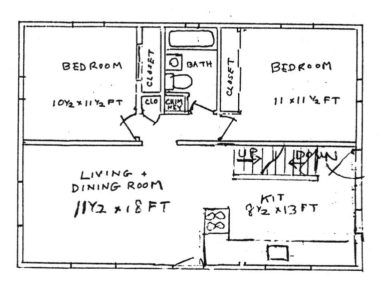

do more out of doors all year—work, cook, eat, read, and study. Sleep in a hammock under a tree in good weather! Let the outdoors be another giant room for you and you'll be much happier and healthier.

An Attractive One-Room Cabin

This is ideally suited to a single person or a couple. The original was a beautifully made 1930s prefab. The plan is good and it resembles a motel room inside. For it to look neat and attractive, you need the assistance of a retired carpenter or builder (easily found in rural areas) who will know how to frame it, plumb, fit doors and windows, and finish off the interior neatly. I urge you not to use cheap plywood, vinyl siding, flush doors, shag carpets, thin panels of imitation wood veneer on the interior walls, fake plastic beams, or foam ceilings, or it will be no more attractive than a cheap trailer. Give it real wood clapboards outside, novelty siding of solid knotty pine inside or at least real wood veneer, Celotex, or Sheetrock. The body of any wood house must be raised a foot or more off the earth on cement or stone pillars or on a perimeter foundation wall or it will rot. Pillars look best with lattice between them.

Log Cabins

Log cabins are beautiful and substantial buildings. Unfortunately, one built from a kit will cost as much as a brick house of the same size. They require a lot of labor and a lot of heavy lifting. If you cut your own logs you must do it the year before you build so they can dry and be peeled. They are easier to pull around when there is snow on the ground. Log cabins are generally made with a chain saw today.

It is easier to make the gable ends of clapboards or shingles than logs as

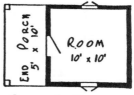

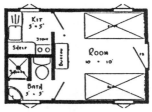

Camp A, Plan 1 —

This 1930s-era cabin is extremely small. Three suitable plans are shown. B-1 has a bath and kitchen if you have running water and septic tank. Choose A3 if your bath is outside. I have stayed in little tourist cabins like this and enjoyed them.

Camp B, Plan 1

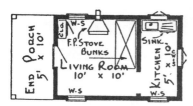

Camp A, Plan 3

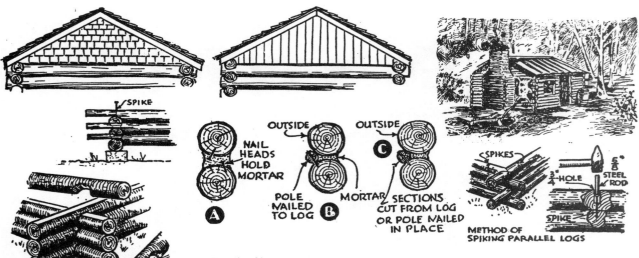

Details of log construction.

An attractive log cabin for year-round living.

shown in the pictures. Many books from the library and the bookstore show how to build them and you can buy videos too. Do not try to build one from just the information in this book.

A new way to make an economical log house is to use a chain saw to make four logs each with two flat sides at 90 degree angle. Erect them vertically at the corners of the house on your sills. Instead of the traditional horizontal logs with notched ends sticking out, you cut flats in the ends of each horizontal log to fit the flat sides of the end logs. Peel the outside of the horizontal logs but leave the inside with bark on them, which will peel off later. Cut windows with a chain saw and frame with 2x8- or 2x10-inch timbers. All this saves a lot of labor.

Stone Houses

I assisted a master stonemason when I was a kid. He could break rocks into square blocks by hitting the grain of them like splitting wood. In ashlar construction the rocks are randomly placed and held together with mortar. The secret appears to be to use a lot more cement in proportion to sand than usual and to wet the rocks thoroughly. We used New England granite.

Stone is a free material if there is plenty on your property. Your only expense is cement and labor. A small house will sit on stone pillars made this way. It also saves cement to use stone for cellars. A stone house is very beautiful, but cold unless you insulate it well and have a separate inside wall supported on 2x4-inch studding. This makes it as expensive as a frame house even with the free stone you have.

The Flagg house is a system of building in stone by unskilled labor using a form and filling it with stone and then moving the form. The

Flagg house shown finished and under construction

Top: A mountain man log cabin, built deep in the woods. It is heavily built to resist bears and vandals.

Middle and Bottom: The secret of making smaller houses attractive is to build in attractive surroundings and keep them neat. Keep junk and trash behind lattice or bushes. These 1930s houses were built long and narrow for a good view from every room. You can do this when land is plentiful. They cost more to heat but it may be worth it.

Flagg house shown here is written up completely in Harold Cary's *Build a Home—Save a Third* and also mentioned in the Reader's Digest book, *Back to Basics: How to Learn and Enjoy Traditional American Skills.*

Florida Houses

Most Florida houses in the lower price range are cement-block construction, the blocks being the inside of the wall as well. The floor is a concrete slab like most garage floors. There is no interior paneling. Pipes, wires, and ducts are buried under the slab. They are well liked in Florida, but in colder climates they are damp and hard to heat, and the pipes sometimes freeze and burst under the solid concrete floor slab. In

Here's a lightweight, well-insulated owner-built house in a mountain meadow in the far West. Note the unusual modern design—quite comfortable. The large, high windows and high ceilings give good views of the towering mountains around it.

A mountain home under construction. Note the plywood sheets. The owners lived in the prefab shed at right while they built it.

I spent several nights in this guide's comfortable cabin.

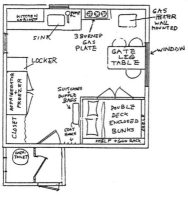

Missouri and North Carolina only cheap rental houses are built this way and tenants avoid them. In Arizona and New Mexico, cement blocks, stucco, and adobe houses are very successful with insulation only in the roof. In a climate with little rainfall, flat roofs are popular.

A Clever Guide's Cabin

This hunting guide, a man of 70 years of age, knew exactly what he wanted. He was still strong and nimble and could climb over rocks in search of the upland deer with the best of them. His house measured about 16 feet square. It was made of plywood covered with tar paper, very neatly done with new materials and good construction, straight and level.

The bathroom with only a chemical toilet was off the entrance vestibule, which was closed in with a second door to act as an air lock in cold weather. The dwelling was heated by a gas space heater run from a propane tank. This man, like me, had spent enough years of chopping wood for a fire, so he wanted no more of it. The cabin was heavily insulated and weather-tight with no drafty cracks. Windows were double-glazed.

For privacy for two men staying there, he built two enclosed double bunks, one over the other like old time Pullman berths, but with a wide knotty-pine door instead of a curtain. The two beds were each the width of a small double bed with good innerspring mattresses. Shelves above them held personal belongings and books. Each bunk had a rack for hunting rifles. The bed compartments had no windows so you could sleep in the daytime. The cabin had a well with an electric pump and a sink with a faucet, so he didn't have to pump by hand. Hot water was heated in a kettle on the cookstove, which was a two- or three-burner gas plate.

The good old man would take a bath when he visited his married daughter in town while he did his laundry in her washer and dryer. His wash was mostly suits of long johns, which he wore constantly. There was a nice old gateleg table to eat on, write letters, and clean guns. A mirror on the wall in a picture frame was used for shaving. There was no TV, just a portable radio. He had electric power. He had a very good life and I found his unique cabin to be more comfortable than most motel rooms.

You might want to build one just like it since this is a proven floor plan. He had a lot of insulation in it since the bottled gas heat was expensive. These days you might want to make the walls with thicker studs than 2x4-inches. Make them six or eight inches thick, put a foot of insulation in the roof and insulate under the floor and your camp will feel wonderfully solid and comfortable in summer or winter.

Low-Cost Cabins and Shacks to Build Yourself

The shack or shanty is the cheapest to build. They used to be called tar paper shacks because tar roofing paper on the outside covered the cracks and knotholes in old boards. Now they are often covered with wallboard, shingles, or siding. The little houses are built out of second-hand building materials from abandoned or demolished buildings. You can use any old gray wood as long as it is not soft and rotten. Usually $1,000 at most covers the expense for the building, not including lot, well, and septic tank or privy. Make your shack with 2x4s 24 inches apart—not the standard 16 inches since the walls carry little weight. Make a 2x4 out

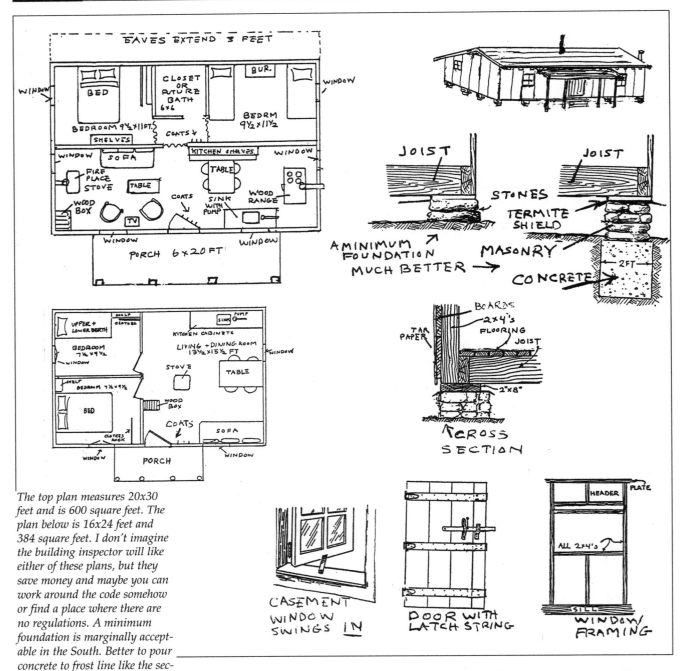

The top plan measures 20x30 feet and is 600 square feet. The plan below is 16x24 feet and 384 square feet. I don't imagine the building inspector will like either of these plans, but they save money and maybe you can work around the code somehow or find a place where there are no regulations. A minimum foundation is marginally acceptable in the South. Better to pour concrete to frost line like the second foundation pier. Termite shield is a square of sheet metal flashing. Note the window-framing details to prevent the roof from sagging and jamming window. Study garages and sheds near you for construction details and size and strength of roof needed locally. Plywood or outdoor particleboard may be substituted for boards. Use secondhand materials to save money.

of two smaller boards nailed together if you lack one, or use a small, squared-off log in odd places for a stud to save buying lumber.

There will be no sub-flooring, just one layer of floorboards. Use old boards or plywood (they don't have to be tongue and groove) for the floor, put tar paper over to cover the cracks, and secondhand linoleum on top of that. Outside walls are random-sized secondhand boards or plywood scraps with tar paper again to cover the cracks and knot holes. Hold it down with thin wooden strips if it is to be the outside covering. For a luxury, you can cover it with shingles or sheets of wallboard. Consider heavy-duty outdoor chipboard, too. In this type of construction long, sharp-pointed Phillips screws are put in with a battery-powered drill with a screwdriver bit. They cost about $60. You may be able to rent one—they save a lot of time. Also, angle pieces and brackets are used to fit joists and rafters. But to really save money, stick to old-fashioned nails. Instead of buying new nails, use bent nails you've pulled out of old wood and straighten them with a heavy hammer. Lots of people who could afford shingles or clapboards used to leave the tar paper on the outside because they feared if they made the house look nice, the tax collector would raise the assessment.

The roof may be a slanting, shack-type roof without ridgepole, or the regular ranch-house-style with a peak. It may have a very low pitch with the ridge three or four feet higher than the walls depending on its size. The roof will span only 12 to 20 feet to reduce weight on the walls. Try to have a partition in the center of the house to support the roof. The best materials and construction will go into roof rafters and floor joists. The rafters will be thicker and closer together in areas of snow and high winds. Examine older garages and small buildings in your location to see what is used there. If the single layer of boards for your roof has knotholes or cracks, the tar paper roofing, which is all you use, will keep the house tight.

Sometimes these houses are paneled with old cardboard cartons inside and they may be insulated with foam chips and foam scraps found at the dump. Insulation is now much more important than 30 years ago because energy costs have risen greatly and will probably go up more. Newspapers were sometimes used long ago to insulate, but there may be a fire risk.

The foundation will be pillars of stone or solid cement blocks. You can make the roof much lower than the normal height on the side of the cabin where there are no doors, perhaps four or five feet high inside if you wish. This makes for a cozy, easy-to-heat cabin. Many of these houses have seven-foot ceilings. The old-timers would put a porch out front with an old wooden bench or some junk car seats where they could sit and rest and drink ginger switchel from glass jars on a hot day. In back you want eaves about three feet longer than the house to store firewood, junk car motors, and other things.

Some little houses have a lean-to carport against the back to work on cars and motorcycles in the rain or snow. A very small house should have the toilet outdoors or off the porch to avoid odors. It may be a chemical toilet. Water probably comes from a dug well and you can put the hand pump in the kitchen to save carrying water.

Give your cabin adequate windows. Use simple single-window sashes, bought used, most of them set into the wall permanently so they do not open. If your windows are high like cellar windows it is harder to break in, you have more privacy, and it is easier to place furniture inside. Some windows may be arranged to swing in (as shown in the drawing) or up against the ceiling. Always nail screen wire over the outside of the window frame and reinforce it with heavy fence mesh if you need to prevent vandalism from humans or wild animals. You can make up heavy frames of wood to bolt over windows like shutters if you wish. In winter you tack on transparent plastic for insulation.

The front door is made of heavy boards as shown in the illustration. If you fear break-ins, drive lots of nails into the door to make it hard to chop through. Padlock it when you are away and give it a bolt inside or make a lift latch with a string, as shown in the illustration. When you pull in the latch string, callers know you are in bed or busy other ways. A screen door is a nice luxury touch. There is no back door and there may be no doors to the rooms and closets inside, just curtains. If you had doors you would have to get a heater for each room to stay warm in winter.

FURNISHING YOUR SMALL WOODLAND HOME OR SHACK

This is how they did it long ago; few people would be this austere today.

A sheet-metal wood stove bought new at a local hardware store will heat your little house. Keep the stove three feet from the wall and any flammable objects. Put sheet tin on the floor under it and put sand in the bottom so the fire will not eat through the sheet-metal sides. Used stoves of this type are usually rusted out or have holes. Be careful.

Your bed will be a thrift-shop reconditioned mattress and inner-spring set right on the floor on 2x4s. There is little headroom. Clothes are generally kept in cardboard cartons, not a bureau. If there is a bureau it will be a small pine one of the type sold as unfinished furniture, or it may be made of heavy wallpapered cardboard, which is less successful. Clothes are hung on wire hooks. Shelves for storage are simply flat boards nailed to the studs or sometimes boards separated by bricks. There will be a sofa, which is either a used one maybe badly worn with torn places patched with duct tape with a blanket thrown over it, or perhaps the seat and back from the rear of an old car. Chairs are second-hand folding or kitchen chairs repaired as needed.

Long ago we would put new plywood or fiber seats in old, spoiled dining room cane-bottom chairs. There will be a kitchen cabinet covered with oilcloth to put the dish pan, if there is no running water. The dining table may be a trestle table, or boards, or plywood hinged at one end to fold up into the wall like an ironing board. It may also be an old, folding auditorium table. The icebox is placed on the porch in winter. Lighting is oil lamps, maybe an Aladdin mantle lamp, or candles.

You can cook on the heating stove in winter. In summer you can use a wick-type kerosene stove—but never use a Primus or Coleman indoors. Cook out of doors on an outdoor fireplace as much as possible. Kept clean and neat, a little house like this is fine. Dirty and dark, it has the traditional look of rural poverty.

Your shack might have one room for a couple or two bedrooms for a family. See the two typical plans here. These houses were very common in the 1930s. Now they are rarely found except in extreme wilderness, like West Virginia, or way off in the woods on dirt roads. You can tell to read this that I know them pretty well. As a teenager, I loved to spend weekends on the river in a summer camp like this that belonged to friends. About 1965, I stayed in the unique guide's cabin of tar paper in Whitefield, New Hampshire, above the White Mountains, which we described. And I have visited many tiny houses when I was a salesman. Actually these little houses are much nicer than they look, which may be an advantage in this modern world.

Low-cost interiors and some appliances typical of simple camps.

OTHER WAYS TO GET A LOW-COST HOUSE

You can buy a good smaller house that is in the way of new highway construction for $1,000 or less and then move it. Since you have to pay for land, septic tank, water, foundation, moving cost, and possible repairs if it is damaged in moving, the house must be very cheap. Find these houses by visiting new construction sites and watching the classified ads. It takes cash to buy them.

Convert a Trailer

Trailers 8, 10, or 12 feet wide and 40 to 50 feet long are quite low cost if they are in poor repair—around $500 to $1,000. Many cheap trailer parks with them have been condemned and closed, so they are in great surplus. Buy two of them, have them fumigated, and put them together. Knock a door between them. Erect poles at the corners and put on a roof that will not leak. Now sheath the sides with thick Styrofoam and siding. You will have a pretty good house. Of course there will be two kitchens, but you can make the second one into an office. The two baths you will like. The total cost is very low if you do most of the work yourself.

Mobile home with house-type roof and insulated sides.

The minimum family housing that I have seen on my travels in the United States and Canada is this pole house in Canada. A family was actually living in it. It is made like a log fence with the logs stuck into the ground with an earth floor. It is too wasteful of wood.

A-FRAME HOUSES AND A-HUTS

These are unique and quite popular. If you do not borrow money, you will be less restricted in what you can build. Note in the pictures, the A-frame house with second-story living quarters and a garage below—with a classic tail-fin Chevy Impala in it! You will get a better view of distant mountains with the living quarters on an upper floor. The next A-frame house is a luxury home in the West of considerable charm, but still affordable for many people.

A-frame house with garage below.

Luxury A-frame house.

Building an A-Hut

A good minimalist A-hut is this tiny 60-degree triangular hut measuring about 12 by 14 feet. It is easy to build in a few days and provides living space for one or two people and storage. A-huts are smaller than A-frames. I have not seen them in use, recently, but if our standard of living drops, they may be used again. You make the simplest version by spiking a timber or log between two tree trunks. Then you nail studs of logs or 2x3s or 2x4s to it and place them to make a 60-degree triangle. In the quick version these timbers go right in the ground. Nail boards, plywood, or whatever you have to them horizontally for siding. Dig a ditch for the water to run off. Roof it with tar paper, shingles, or anything good you can find. You can insulate the A-hut inside with corrugated cardboard. Insulation bats tacked in and wallboard inside would be a luxury. Such a dwelling will probably be built for no cost but your labor. You will want to spend most of your time out of doors and only use it for sleeping and storage.

Conrad Meinecke, a great woodsman and outdoor writer of the 1930s, drew this more sophisticated A-hut, "The Squatter." Long ago, when lumber was cheap, they set it right on the ground. Today you would want to set it on a raised wood floor with joists and floorboards

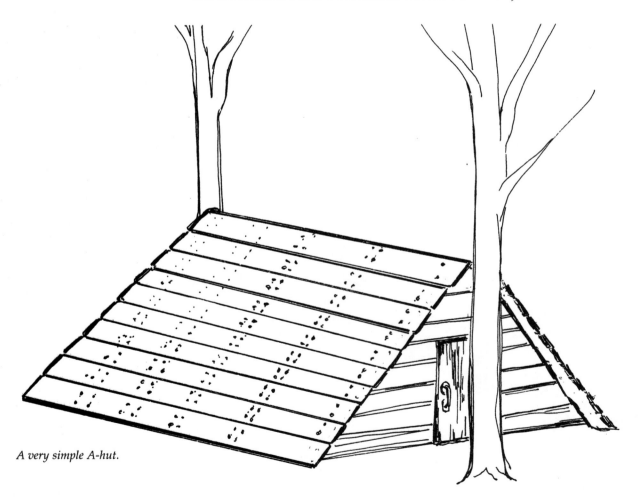

A very simple A-hut.

Conrad Meinecke's A-hut.

like the other log cabins. It should be supported on posts of flat rocks or cement. This more refined A-hut is self-supporting. No trees are needed. You will give the little house a real window and door and make built-in beds and wood shelves and cupboards for storage under the eaves. You sleep on the side bunks on mattress pads in sleeping bags since there is full headroom only in the center. It can be a very good little shelter. If the roof, which is most of the house, is shingled or tar papered and extended several feet at the ends to conceal the glint of windows and shelter the door, the little A-hut will be impossible to see from any distance or from the air—a good idea in these troubled violence-filled times.

An underground home.

Underground Homes

Underground houses evolved from the experiences of people who lived in the cellar of an unfinished house. Usually they are open on one end with windows and a door. The temperature stays about 50 degrees all year without heat so they use less energy to raise or lower the temperature than an aboveground house.

Water leakage is a problem. Cellar walls may have stones in them but must be all cement on the inside for the seams not to leak. If the floor happens to be built over a spring you will have endless leaks. Be sure a person who knows how to waterproof concrete builds it.

If it is well done, it is quite inexpensive and you will like the underground house very much. They are particularly good in the desert.

Abandoned Homes

In the 1930s, during the Depression, people, good people, lived in junked streetcars and old buses. A family even lived in a junked four-motor Fokker airplane body in Wheeling, West Virginia, until the 1935 flood took it out. Some also lived in abandoned houses and we will tell how that is done, too.

Simply select the best part of the home to live in and seal up the broken windows and open places with black or transparent plastic sheeting, duct tape, and shingle nails. If the floor is about to collapse, jack it up with a car jack and put in extra timbers cut from logs extending from the floor joists to the cellar floor. Do the same with the roof—lay tar paper or plastic if it leaks and put plywood or old boards over big holes in the floor or roof. You will be surprised to discover that snow will filter through leaks and cracks too small for rain to penetrate. In winter you will find little snow piles indoors after a snowstorm. I have played in abandoned houses like this as a kid and slept in them as a hunter.

You can save money by building your new house over an old cellar hole. About 1939, Felix Bachmann bought a big, ugly, old house in the center of a fine town on a good lot. He took it apart carefully, sold some of the materials, and used the rest of the timbers to build a very attractive Cape Cod house that arose like a Phoenix from the ruins of the old house. You can often get around red tape from building inspectors by rebuilding from the shell of an old house using retired workers instead of initiating new construction.

Tree Houses

These are fascinating wilderness dwellings that need no foundation. They are good if you have a fine view or want to watch animals. Remember, animals and people seldom look UP. Being high off the ground, these homes are hard to burglarize. It is best to use two healthy, substantial trees as shown in the pictures.

Tree house construction.

Chapter 11

Mobile Shelters

PICKUP TRUCKS

It is possible to live and sleep inside a pickup truck with a bed at least 6 feet long covered with a cap. It is good if the cap has screened windows. If the truck is a big, wide one, you store your gear along the side. If it is a small truck, like a Ranger or small Toyota, you may have to throw most of your things in the cab when you go to bed. Advantages over a tent are that pickups are warmer, drier, there is no danger from bears, and there's no chance of being run over by a 4WD or motor home while sleeping. Used caps for pickups are in the $100-$200 range. Another good way of camping is to have a carryall or minivan with seats removed and a plywood platform on legs about a foot high installed. The packs and stuff go under. You sleep on top. We did this with our wooden Ford Beach Wagon long ago.

At one time pickup campers that mounted on top of a pickup truck were popular. This is not a cap, but a structure with sides and a floor you can stand up in, with a dinette and a kitchen with gas stove, refrigerator, sink with water tank above, a bunk over the cab, and sometimes a toilet and even a shower. These campers overloaded older trucks and made them top-heavy so people disliked them. They can be found for less than $1,000, and are often set up on blocks off the ground so you can live in them like a house. We saw a fine one for sale recently for $600 in New Mexico.

Top: A pickup camper.
Above: An old Dodge van camper with raised roof. It was bought by a friend recently for $900.
Left: Dodge Carryall with bed platform inside.

123

Converted Gerstenslager Bookmobile makes a rugged off-road motor home.

VANS

You can convert a big van like a UPS or a bread truck into a motor home and live in it. My friend Charles Swimmer paid $1,500 for this surplus Gerstenslager Bookmobile and converted it into an excellent motor home particularly suited to hunting and camping. These bookmobile vans are made by the Gerstenslager Corp. in Ohio. There are thousands of bookmobiles around and they show up in surplus auctions fairly often. This one has 20-inch wheels and large tires for good traction. It came with a 4kw generator, which makes it self-contained. It has real household appliances. He added an evaporative cooler and a woodstove so it can be used all year. The bookmobile was built eight feet tall inside to hold many books, which gives it a spacious interior and permits a double-decker bed arrangement.

Step vans such as bread trucks are often converted, too. People find them not as smooth and pleasant to drive as a modern pickup truck on a long trip, but they are very roomy—comfortable to live in and cheap. I know one flea market dealer who disguised his converted step van so it didn't look like anyone lived in it. It had only skylights and the standard back windows and the privacy shield for the back looked commercial too. He could park it anywhere and no one noticed it. It looked like any ordinary commercial truck. This saved a lot of RV park fees.

SCHOOL BUSES

A surplus school bus may be purchased cheaply and converted to a home. It is a lot of work removing all those seats, so it may be better to buy it converted than do the work yourself. Most school buses have small motors, look funny, ride poorly, and are slow. They are better left in one place, the owners soon discover. Often they are for sale very cheaply, under $3,000 converted, $1,000 unmodified with bus seats still in place.

They are best bought from local school districts that sell them sur-

This converted school bus in the ghost town of Oatman, Arizona, is well done, but not fancy. Note the two-inch timbers to reinforce the sides. White paint makes it cooler in the desert sun.

plus at auctions. Some buses will not run, so your only competitor in buying them is the junk dealer; a few hundred dollars will get them. Bid low. Tires are very important. If they show age cracks, it can cost $600 or more to replace all six tires. Brakes can cost as much as $1,000 to overhaul. Some people simply have their school buses towed to permanent sites and never fix them up to drive. Do a Yahoo! search for school-bus conversion Web sites on the Internet. They provide many resources, have groups of people who discuss them, show pictures of buses for sale, and identify the few makes with motors that are troublesome. Diesel school buses with manual transmission get the best gas mileage, sometimes more than 10 mpg. Gasoline buses with automatic transmissions are the poorest—as low as 5 mpg, less in hilly country. If you want to tour the country driving hundreds of miles a day and stopping at a different place every night, a school-bus conversion is not for you. But if you take it to a lake or a convention-site destination and leave it there for a while, it might be ideal.

Important features to add are a roof rack on top, and for side protection and greater strength, have some long 2x8-inch timbers bolted to each side of the bus.

I saw another school bus where people were living in Alaska a few miles off the road between Anchorage and Fairbanks near Talkeetna. It looked cozy inside on a cold, clear Alaska morning with its wood stove puffing through a long stovepipe let out a side window. Most windows had been blocked in or painted white and it looked really fixed up well inside. I wish I had taken a picture of it for you.

CAMPER TRAILERS

We owned an 18-foot 1971 Airstream in the 1980s that we bought used. These are classics now and quite collectible. It did not tow well at all behind our 1984 Crown Victoria with 302 cu. in. motor and four-speed automatic. But it pulled fine behind our Ford 1971 LTD with 351

Classic 18-foot Airstream trailer.

cu. in. motor and three-speed automatic, and it would be ideal to tow with a full-size pickup truck or a surplus police cruiser.

The Airstream was surprisingly heavy for its size—more than 3,000 pounds. We had many problems with it at first, annoying at the time but funny afterwards. We took it to a park in Virginia during a terrific heat wave with temperatures above 100 degrees. The park was packed with trailers and motor homes, all running their air conditioners. That would soon overload the park electrical wiring and the power would go dead. Then most of the people would turn their air off and the power would start up again. Then the air conditioners would all start up until the fuses blew again. This kept up all night, on and off, on and off. It was not a cheap, two-star park, either.

The Airstream also had an annoying habit of freezing its retro-fitted roof-mount air conditioner after steady running. Then the cool would quit, we would turn it off and it would drip ice water on us from above. When you used the shower, it wet the whole bathroom. We dreaded using the tiny flush toilet and usually went elsewhere. But Airstream is really a classic, with a fine club and many exclusive Airstream parks at reasonable prices. You will like Airstream people very much, as we do.

MOTOR HOMES

Greedy salesmen often persuade retired couples to sell their homes and pay $100,000 or more for motor homes. This is often a mistake. Motor homes are vehicles and depreciate rapidly, unlike a home, and they have a limited life. And a serious illness can put an end to travel. They cost a lot more than simply staying in motels and resorts. Note that the interest on the $100,000 used to buy them is at least $7,000 a year and that sum could pay for 100 motel rooms at $70 a night. The park will cost $20 or more a night anyway, and you have to hitch up a messy sewer line, water, and electricity every night and jack it to level it. This may be more work than unloading your car and carrying your stuff into a motel room. And gas mileage is usually below 10 mpg.

Increasing gas costs could make many of these motor homes too expensive to drive, and there may soon be a lot of them flooding the market. Their depreciation is extraordinary. Many older motor homes are as low as $3,000. A lot of them look dirty and drab and need fumigation, complete refinishing, and reupholstering, new carpets, and linoleum to be livable. Some smell of cats or babies—or worse. They have many mechanical problems, leaks, plumbing, and electrical problems. Repairs, particularly if you are traveling, can be very expensive—often $300 or more for simple jobs of an

Cottonwood RV Park in Truth or Consequences, New Mexico, is comfortable, spacious, and low cost.

hour or so. You are at the mercy of the dealers. If a motor home breaks down on the highway, it can cost $200 just to have it towed in a short way for repair. This just happened to our preacher.

Some people do like these big RVs a lot. They love the cleanliness of sleeping in their own sheets, the fellowship of nice motor home parks, and the opportunity to make many friends. They also enjoy the challenge of driving such a large vehicle and coping with its mechanical problems. Some also enjoy the status of parking them in front of their houses. Such expensive motor homes as the Bluebird and the Prevost are really luxurious.

MOBILE HOMES

Mobile homes, on the other hand, are large trailers that are seldom moved and are used as permanent housing. They are cheaper than small houses and they seem to be taking their place. In the 1950s they were limited to 8 feet wide, then they became 10, 12, or 14 feet wide, and now even larger ones are found in some states. Narrower ones are very cheap these days. A double-wide is two of these units hitched together permanently at the site. They will be 20 or more feet wide. Often they are well built and it is hard to tell them from a real house.

They were asking $3,500 for this old motor home, then dropped the price. It could probably be bought for much less.

Buying a Mobile Home

They can be $3,000 or less used without a lot. I've seen really good ones for $1,000. The shorter 8-, 10-, and 12-foot-wide models are cheapest. Often they are cheap because they look filthy, or have been trashed. Trailer owners do not take care of them. They are fairly easy to clean and fix up, so a bad-looking one can be a good deal. Try $500 for a private sale.

Roofs have to be tarred or recovered every few years, but you can put a house-type gabled, shingled roof on a trailer. Trailers 50 years old can be good today. The old shiny aluminum Ranger trailer made by North American Aviation about 1948 is an excellent unit, beautifully built and becoming collectible. Look for one. They are still around.

Do not keep a pot-type oil furnace in a mobile home. It is dangerous. Fire is a serious trailer risk, often fatal. Windstorms ruin trailers. They need to be bolted to the ground with cables run over the top. See a trailer accessory dealer. Often the lot costs more than a used trailer. Be sure you have a place for it first. A trailer already set up on an individual small lot by itself with water, septic tank, and power costs much more than a bare trailer—$6,000 to $30,000. It may be less in low-cost areas like West Virginia or more in vacation areas like Florida. Used double-wides cost more, as much as $60,000, since they are popular.

LIVE ON A BOAT—WHY NOT ?

Along the Maurice River in New Jersey, people moor old boats and live in them. They try to find old wooden yachts too shaky for a long voyage for $3,000 or less. The interior appointments of these craft are luxurious. The mooring dock costs them $450 a year. The boat can be left in the water all winter because the slightly salty water never freezes solid. You pay no real estate taxes on a boat. These are interesting and unusual people that it would be fun to know. The one serious disadvantage is that you are not allowed to throw any wastes overboard. You have to tank them and carry them off. There are similar houseboat settlements along the Inland Waterway to Florida and in the Pacific Northwest. Some of the boats seen here are old fiberglass houseboats.

Darius Robinson, an experienced yachtsman who took the boat pictures, reminds us that fiberglass boats are very cheap now because they made too many of them and they never wore out. Many boat owners get sick of them and sell out after a few years, usually because the wife does not like sailing. About $3,500 will buy you a nice sailboat about 25 feet long with a cabin with sleeping berths and a galley. If the fiberglass looks old, you can sand, polish, and repaint it with automobile paint, he says. In fact, with a trailerable boat, an auto paint shop can do the job.

I just met a man in Florida who likes to buy old fiberglass trawler yachts for about $50,000 apiece. He lives on them as he's fixing them up and then sells them for much more than he paid.

Build a Houseboat

The plans here are from a 70-year-old *Harper's Book for Boys*, which the library discarded to make room for liberal kid books. The boat

People live in these boats.

This luxury 1930s Consolidated yacht is still going strong in 2001, Robinson reports. Here the 65-year-old wooden boat is under way, moving very slowly and leaving a cloud of smoke behind it. It is worth about $12,000 today.

should work OK today if you can get the lumber cheaply enough, or maybe you can take a ruined building apart for timber. Waterproof plywood could be substituted for planking so you wouldn't have to caulk the joints as shown in fig 4.

Use fiberglass tape between the plywood panels. Note fig 5 showing needed supports for the deck on each side of the centerpiece. The houseboat is 8 feet wide by 24 feet long. A very small outboard could move it slowly. In calm waters, even an electric motor would work. Cousin George Bryne moved a loaded 100-foot barge across Boston Harbor with a 22-hp Johnson outboard motor when all the tug boats were out on strike. It took all day. Cousin George was a fine old yachtsman and a true friend who taught me a lot about boats when I was very young.

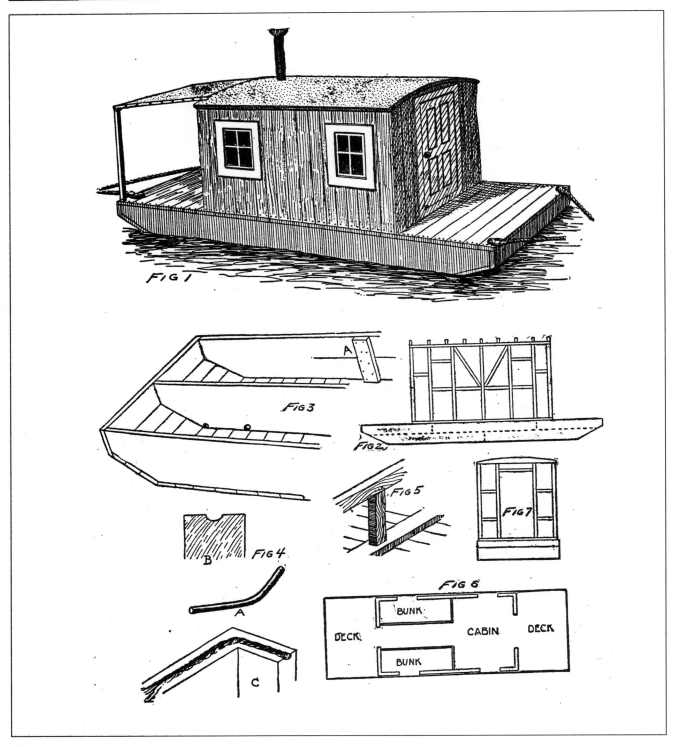

Old-time houseboat construction.

Chapter 12

Save on Utilities or Do Without

DOING WITHOUT

You save the most by going without electric power entirely. It can save $600 a year or more. Most people find it easier to do so in the cold North than the South. Electricity is really needed for air conditioning and to keep food cool.

In the description of the shack, we told you to heat with wood, illuminate with kerosene, and cook with a wick stove. You may cook on an outdoor fireplace in summer and on the heating stove in winter. If you have no heat in the house you can not have running water pipes running indoors; they will freeze. But you can have a shallow well pump in the kitchen that you pump by hand. You heat water in winter on the stove and take a shower in a plastic tub. You stand and pour water over yourself with a pitcher. You can build the simple solar water heater shower shown below. Solar showers work well all year in Florida, and the Southwest, but only in summer elsewhere.

Building a Solar-Heated Hot Water System and Shower

This is one of the few practical solar-heating projects I know. Select a place on your property where it is sunny all the time—no shadows from trees or buildings. This is easy in Nevada!

Rent a post-hole digger and place four strong poles into the ground in a four-foot square. On top, about 7 feet up, build a 4x8-foot frame of 2x6-inch timbers or flattened logs like the picture. This size will hold about 20 gallons with water 1-inch deep. It may be made larger or smaller, of course. The water frame is cantilevered to save material. Level it with a carpenter's level and shims as needed.

Get free hot water from this simple solar-heated shower.

There is a cross-joist timber in the center of the top, indicated by the dotted line in the drawing. The structure must be strong, because the water you are going to put up top will weigh as much as a person, and you will want to climb up there for cleaning and repairs yourself. Now floor it with boards or a 4x8-foot piece of exterior plywood, and make sides to it like a box out of 2x3-inch timbers. Waterproof this box, which holds your water, as you would waterproof a boat, or put plastic sheeting inside it. Now make a cover, which will have two sheets of Mylar or Lexan plastic with a 2- to 3-inch hollow air space between. Tie the cover down somehow. I used wire wound around nails and a canvas hinge.

The big secret is the air gap between the two sheets of plastic, which works as a storm window does. The water is heated by radiant heat of the sun's rays, which pass easily though the two layers of transparent plastic. When the water is heated up, the heat cannot escape from it because water does not radiate heat. Put a pipe in the center to a faucet and showerhead. If the water is too hot, open the top or dilute by adding cold water up top. You need an overflow and a means of filling it with a hose, which will be a hole in the side. You can also remove the top when it rains and let rainwater fill it or you can fill it with pails of water if you lack running water.

The system heats fastest with about an inch of water in it. The water will stay warm longer if you insulate the water box outside with foam insulation and make an insulated foam cover for it for night. If you need privacy, you can put boards or plastic around the sides of your shower and give it a curtain. You could lead an insulated pipe indoors to an indoor shower and hot water faucet and use the system as a water heater, if you prefer. The effectiveness of these showers is greatest in climates like New Mexico or Florida but they will work all through the Southern part of the United States and in the summer months up North. A feasibility test before building the whole works is to wrap foam around a pan holding an inch of water. Place the pan in the sun covered by two layers of transparent plastic with an air space between. See how long it takes to heat up, and how hot the water gets. These water heaters are common in Third-World countries. Another simpler water heater for warm climates is a 50-foot or longer section of dark-colored garden hose put on the roof and kept filled.

Free Refrigeration Without Power

Old-timers used a spring house to keep food cold. This is a stone house partly underground with a spring in it. They are very beautiful. We keep our meat and butter cool without ice by sinking a metal pail containing the food into a running stream. Even as far south as Tennessee, mountain streams are cold. You can make cold boxes cooled by brook water. You will also find a cellar, a well, or a hole in the ground surprisingly cold and good to keep fresh food. Measure its temperature with a thermometer. You do not need much of an icebox in winter if you keep frozen food in a box on the windowsill or on the porch as they do in northern Minnesota, Maine, New Hampshire, and Vermont. Foods like milk that you do not want to freeze solid are kept in the shed.

WATER

If you want to live in a remote place and want water and power, always price what they will cost before buying property and settling down. It can be expensive to put in a power line on poles running just to your property. Water can also be very expensive. Sometimes a well must be dug more than 1,000 feet deep to get any! Digging a deep well can cost $15,000 or more. Existing wells often go dry as the climate changes and the water table falls. Maybe this is why the previous owners wanted to sell so badly.

In some soils, septic tanks and pit toilets do not work well, or are prohibited. Electric incinerating toilets that use no water are available, but expensive. You need to study in books from the government, or in your local library, to find out how to get pure water, how to treat water, and about septic tanks and privies and where to put them. If the sewerage gets too close to the water supply, people will get sick. This matter is very important, but we lack space to cover it here in the detail it needs.

AIR CONDITIONING

In the South, low electric power costs are essential because you use a lot of power for air conditioning.

There is an evaporative air cooler you can make that costs less to buy and run than an air conditioner. It consists of a big fan with wicks of cloth in front of it fed from a water tank above. It works well in low humidity areas, particularly the Southwest. We saw a small one in a thrift shop there for $10. Big ones are about $500 new, less used. In 1985, in the middle of summer, I traveled through Nevada, Wyoming, Utah, and Colorado in an old car cooled with an evaporative cooler set in the window; it worked OK. I put an evaporative cooler in an apartment in North Carolina with semi-success. Humidity was too high. An evaporative cooler can be powered with a gasoline engine if well-muffled with a long exhaust pipe, so the fumes do not get in the air intake to the house.

There are room air conditioners that also heat. Some have electric heating coils; others work like a heat pump. They are liked in the South. Secondhand room air conditioners are very cheap in the South since nearly all suburban middle-class houses have converted to central air conditioning. They are in great surplus. I paid $75 in a pawnshop for a fine 8,000 BTU unit which would have been at least $150 in the North. Go down South to buy one. It is better to have central air and natural gas than a heat pump, in both cost and service life. A heat pump has pistons like a car motor and wears out the same way in time. No room air conditioner, no matter how many BTU, seems to cool more than one room at a time. Central air can actually be cheaper to run than several window units.

COMMUNICATIONS

Replacing the Telephone
A phone will cost you $300 a year or more. You do not need one if

POWER AND HEAT FROM THE PUBLIC UTILITIES. Pipeline natural gas is the cheapest way of heating a house, cooking, and heating hot water. The gas mains do not run way out in the country, so check on its availability. Having natural gas in one place and not in another can make a difference of between $1,000 and $2,000 a year on your heating bill. Parts of New Hampshire without natural gas have very high fuel costs—at least twice the rates of Pennsylvania, where natural gas is abundant. Gas prices have been rising recently. It is wisest to have a small, well-insulated house.

you have a neighbor who can take calls for you in an emergency. (Do some favor for your neighbor in return.)

If you miss chatting with people, or live way out in the middle of nowhere and need emergency communication, I suggest citizens band (CB) radio. CB is one great big party line. Older units are available in quantity now that cellular phones are in vogue, yet they work as well as new CBs and seldom are used enough to wear out. Pay $25 or less for a working 12-volt 23-channel CB with antenna. The automobile whip antenna only works on a metal roof, or with a counterpoise, you must remember.

You can make a house CB antenna with a few cents worth of wire in doublet form. See ham radio books or ask a ham. Your antenna should be as high as possible. One make of CB is as good as another as long as it is full 5-watt input. CBs may not work at all if you live deep in a valley. Their dependable range is about 10 miles in the country, but sometimes you can talk all over the world. Power your CB radio with a lantern battery, car battery, or any 12-volt power source described here. CBs that plug into house current are also sold, or you can run your 12-volt CB on house current with an adapter—also a flea market item.

Get a battery-operated shortwave receiver, too, if you do not like the programs on local radio stations. They are $1 to $5 at flea markets. Sometimes you have to clean or replace the battery contacts if they are corroded. See Radio Shack for parts. Like most used appliances, the whole radio is often dirty and gummy; clean with detergent and put Armor All on its leatherette case. Antique-tube shortwave radios like the Zenith and Hallicrafters are still usable if you have 117-volt AC power and are quite collectible as well. There could be a fire risk if the wiring is frayed—check them carefully.

A Free or Nearly Free Cellular Phone

I have bought several older briefcase-size Motorola cellular phones in working condition for $5 or $10 in local yard sales. The batteries on these may have to be replaced for true portable use, but you can plug them into the cigarette lighter of a car, a storage battery, or run them on a 12-volt power supply without a battery. The unusual thing about these units is that they are all set up to be able to call the emergency number 911, even if you do not pay to have them connected; the maker does not want anyone to be denied emergency service for not paying a bill, you see. I keep my cell phone in the car for use only if I see a serious accident or a fire or something. They may not work way out in the wilderness. You have to find out. In some areas you must have a digital cell phone. If the cell phone does work at your homestead, that is the way to have a real phone just for emergencies for free. And because you are not in any phone book, you cannot be bothered by incoming calls. You may also want to look into the various rates from phone companies for regular use of your cell phone. Some cellular services cost less than a home phone if you use your phone very little.

Ham Radio

Ham radio will let you talk to interesting people worldwide. The license is free. Used equipment is quite reasonable—usually less than $300 for a station of older equipment. Most of it can be made to work on 12-volt power too. I suggest a Heath HW-12, a TenTec or a Drake TR-3 or TR-4 single sideband transceiver. Local ham radio clubs will teach you free and the license is free, too. You no longer need to know high-speed Morse code, which is difficult. They now accept 5 words per minute, which is easy, for the General Class license. Ham radio conventions and flea markets are called "Hamfests" and are listed in QST, the ham radio magazine. Hamfests are where you get good cheap equipment. I am a ham, N4DFX, active since 1964. Contact the ARRL (American Radio Relay League), the national association for amateur radio, at www.arrl.org for more information and addresses of radio clubs near you.

POWERING WITH GASOLINE, PROPANE, AND STORAGE BATTERIES

Appliances

If you lack electricity and gas, you can buy a new kerosene refrigerator and freezer for about $1,559, a propane refrigerator for $1,149, wood stoves to cook and warm the house and heat water for $600 and up, a new Speed Queen gasoline motor-powered washing machine for $995, Aladdin kerosene mantle lamps from $60 to $400, a propane iron, and chemical toilets and pumps. These gas and kerosene appliances do cost more and are very hard to find used.

All these items and more are available from Lehman's, Box 41 Kidron OH 44636. The mail-order catalog is $2, or visit their Web site at www.lehmans.com. The merchandise is *new*, made for the traditional Amish and for missionaries in the Third World. The Aladdin mantle lamp is the only kerosene lamp bright enough for serious reading and fine work at night; it is equal to a 60-watt bulb. Or you can use a storage battery and fluorescent as described below.

Ice box, kerosene stove, mantle lamp, battery-powered TV, and CB radio enable you to live without power and telephone.

12-Volt Power Systems with Storage Batteries

A 12-volt storage battery from a car will run a few lights in a small house and power small appliances. It must be recharged regularly. You can put it in your car to charge off the car alternator, have it charged in town, or charge it with solar cells, a windmill, or water wheel. Solar cells are very expensive new. But you may find them, and many other electronic goodies, cheap in surplus sales. Look for ads in magazines such as *Popular Science*. They work well in the Southwest where it is usually sunny.

Lacking solar or wind power, you can charge a storage battery with a used Briggs and Stratton gasoline engine driving an old automobile alternator with a belt. Some people use an engine run on propane so they do not have to handle gasoline. This system develops considerable amperage (60A 720w) but is quite noisy. Here are some of the appliances you can power with a 12-volt storage battery: Any stereo boom box or car stereo works on 12 volts or less; some sound very good. A 12-volt black and white battery-powered TV is very cheap used, a small 12-volt color set is about $150 new, much less used. Video recorders for 12 volts are available and you can use any VHS camcorder to play videotapes, of course. There are small 12-volt refrigerators, toasters, coffeepots, fluorescent lights, and many other appliances sold for trailers by RV dealers and by JC Whitney and other mail-order vendors. A tiny 12-volt refrigerator of 1 cu. foot or less can make you quite comfortable. All you really need cold is butter, orange juice, and ice cubes for drinks. You can get 12-volt lamp bulbs, dome light fixtures, and sockets out of junk cars, and the wire and switches as well. Use them to wire your own 12-volt electric lighting system for your camp. A sealed-beam headlight bulb from an old car makes a nice outdoor floodlight for emergency work at night. The heater fan from an old car could provide ventilation. There are inverters to change 12-volt DC to 117-volt AC that run fluorescent lights, electric shavers, small tools, and other smaller appliances. They have problems including severe electrical interference used with stereo or video and erratic voltage. A 12-volt battery system is much cheaper than new kerosene refrigerators, Aladdin lamps, and water heaters.

Propane Gas

For a bigger refrigerator and a hot-water heater, you can use bottled gas. There are two types, one with a large bulk tank filled by a truck, the other with round cylinders of gas wheeled in by the gas man. Either is good and you should price both systems. This pressurized gas can also supply gas mantle lamps that are as bright as electric lights. Bottled gas heat for a one-room cabin is much more convenient and clean than wood and not particularly expensive if the hut is well-insulated with walls six or eight inches thick. This is done a lot now with new construction in Maine. You can heat your cabin with a vented gas heater and never have to chop wood again! The guide's hut I stayed in was gas heated. A gas hot plate is a better stove for the kitchen than kerosene. You can buy gas appliances used in flea market or new in RV stores or from JC Whitney or Sears. Be sure your appliances are for bottled gas, not natural gas, although you can have them converted. Better get help from your local bottled gas company.

If you have a running spring from a higher elevation, as we had in one house, you can have running water without a pump. Also, windmills and gasoline pumps have been used to pump water to elevated holding tanks or cisterns. Plumbing work is much easier today with plastic pipe than it used to be with iron or copper pipe. But still you need to pay some skilled local moonlighter to help you with these systems, if you have not worked on them before.

117-Volt AC Gasoline Engine Generators

All small 117-volt AC generators are noisy, expensive, and require frequent maintenance. If you want power all the time instantly on demand, you have to leave the generator running constantly. You need it running, wasting gas, for just one lamp and the TV set. Generating your own power costs 10 times as much as buying it from the power company. It is seldom advisable to do it, except in tiny quantities, less than a kilowatt hour a day. Maybe you only run the generator a few hours each evening as they do in Third World countries. Incidentally, 117-volt AC generators and other emergency items are quite cheap now that the Y2K scare is past. Never run a generator indoors and keep the exhaust far from any air intake.

USED HOUSEHOLD APPLIANCES

Older used refrigerators are cheap—like $25—if they are not frost-free, and have a small frozen-food storage area. They seem to last forever. My parents kept their GE refrigerator 35 years and it was still running when I sold the house. It never had to be repaired. In cold climates in winter a regular refrigerator left on a porch set to coldest, will get as cold as a real freezer. Maine people do this. Used stoves, washers, and dryers are a good deal too. All these items should be tested before you buy. They last longer than most people care to keep them.

Chapter 13

Save on Transportation

Far too much money and attention is devoted to cars. It doesn't take much of a car to last you well and give you good service if you live out in the country and do not drive all over the place. We know an RFD mail carrier who drove a 1960s Nash Rambler 600,000 miles—wearing out three motors over many years. Newer cars can be very durable too. There is no reason a good car cannot last 60 years or 600,000 miles.

After housing, the automobile is the biggest expense for most families. Each family member who works or drives to school has to have a reliable car. Usually cars are driven 15,000 to 20,000 miles a year, much of it commuting in heavy traffic. Cars cost 25 to 35 cents a mile including gas, tires, depreciation, taxes, insurance, repairs, and everything. Thus the budget for cars will run from about $3,500 a year to $10,000 or more for the aver-

This 1927 Dodge is still used in regular service as a taxi in Skagway, Alaska. It takes people from the cruise ships into town. The car still has its original engine.

I photographed this 1930 Oldsmobile touring car recently in Lisbon, Portugal. It is used in good weather to take tourists to the old fort on top of the mountain. The original tires and headlights have been replaced with larger equipment. Mileage is unknown.

age family. A family with a Mercedes, Cadillac, fancy 4WD SUV, truck, or sporty car will spend much more.

Here are some ways you can cut your cost for transportation. The best way is to walk, ride a bus, or get a bicycle or a small motorcycle or moped. You cut your transportation cost by cutting your car mileage; if you are out of work or work at home, there is no more commuting cost. If you can walk to grocery stores, the post office, and church you save even more money on transportation. It is well worth finding a place to live where you can do this. If you plan your trips carefully and combine them and ride with other people whenever possible, you cut your car mileage so your car will last a long time. If you have two cars and get rid of one and let one family member use a bicycle or moped, you will save lots of money.

If you own two cars, it is much cheaper for only one to be a recent model that depreciates instead of having both cars new. The first person out, or the person going the longest distance, takes the newest car. It will get a lot of miles, which may justify its high cost. The second car will be used only if the first car is busy. It can be a low-cost 10-year-old car or one that eats a lot of gas. Since it will be driven very little, perhaps 2,000 miles a year, it will last a long time. At 2,000 miles a year, even a car that gets only 14 miles per gallon will only use $200 worth of gas in a year. You have to be very rich to own two new cars at once.

There has been little improvement, except in gas mileage, in cars over the last 35 years. A 1966 car is quite as comfortable as a 2001 car. The difference between them is only in styling and status. You are less likely to have an old car stolen, or to be dragged out of it and assaulted when you go to the city. Gas mileage is not as good on older cars, but remember, gas is a much smaller part of the cost of owning a car than depreciation or car payments. The age of the car is not important; the condition of the car is everything. Unfortunately, poor people usually buy the lowest-priced most recent car they can afford, which is usually a defective car. Good Japanese cars and big old American V8 cars have drive trains that last 150,000 miles or more. Such a car at 100,000 miles will have years of life left.

Assessing the condition of a used car is difficult. I have made mistakes. Generally a good car will be neat and clean with no haywire temporary repairs and no rust showing on the body. Small things such as door handles, windshield washers, and backup lights will all be working. We may think wishfully that these small details can easily be fixed—that is not the point. An owner whose car has broken back-up lights and windshield washers probably also ran it for a year or more without changing the oil or greasing the front end. This kind of negligence will ruin a new car in two or three years. It is bad if the owner let the car be scratched and did not touch up the scratches with paint. A car with rust showing has many more serious problems that you cannot see, you may be sure. *Consumer Reports* magazines found in libraries have good evaluations of the merits and problems of particular makes and years of used cars. They also tell a lot about how to size up a used car and how to buy one. They are well worth reading. Also check the Internet for Usenet bulletin boards discussing various makes of cars and their problems.

There are plenty of good used cars for less than $1,500. If you pay more, you are probably foolish, unless it is a fantastic car. Plenty of good cars are a few hundred dollars. Warren Taylor's son answered an ad in a shopping publication in New Hampshire offering a car listed as suitable for parts—for just $25. When he saw it, it was a 1972 Ford LTD wagon, loaded, with air and power that ran and looked very fine. The older lady had taken it to the dealer to trade in and the salesman had told her he didn't want it, that it was "only good for parts." So that is how the dear lady worded her ad. Taylor's son started it up easily and drove the car home from where he bought it under its own power and found it quite a good car—for $25. It seldom happens this way. It is worth checking out all used car ads from individuals. Some are rare buys. Some of your relatives may give you an older car like this, too.

Cars can be too expensive in used car lots with a well-dressed sales force and expensive premises. The overhead and the salespersons' commissions mean they have to get at least $2,500 for a worthless car to break even. They tend not to display cars selling for less than $4,000. Find lower-priced cars in ads by individuals in the classified pages of the newspaper, on the Internet, or in local shoppers. You find many good lower-priced cars in a junkyard. Often they set aside older cars that are too good to crush and sell them for a few hundred dollars. These junkyards are sometimes able to take a car with a burnt-out motor and put another motor in it from a car that was wrecked, creating one very good car. If you know cars, you may want to buy one with a bad drive train and do an engine swap. I have lifted out motors with a come-along hoist from the Taylor Rental people and a length of chain hitched to a tree limb. This is what the real country people do! It is a pile of fun.

OLDER CARS

The main reason to buy older cars is because the depreciation, interest payments, and insurance on new cars are too high. These fixed costs run $2,000-$3,000 the first year for any new car. They drop the second and third year. But if you buy a $1,500 10-year-old car, even if it costs you $500 a year for repairs, (which hopefully it will not), you will be way ahead financially. Financing a new car for four or five years is particularly expensive. Thousands of dollars are thrown away for bank interest. When you own a low-cost older car, you keep no fire, theft, or collision insurance at all and the minimum liability. It saves a lot of money. One caution: If you get in an accident, insurance will not pay enough on an older car to be worth having. Dad had a 20-year-old V8 Ford totaled when he was rear-ended by an oil truck. He had bought it from a retired mechanic. Nearly everything on it, including the engine, was new or rebuilt. But all he could get for it was $150—and the claims adjuster even balked at that. To avoid accidents and to make cars last longer, we should not drive over the speed limit or when exhausted or distressed. Tell your insurance company you no longer commute to work. They will cut your rate. I like low-cost AARP insurance.

Keeping the car you own now is good if it is not a luxury car. Any car you own, even if only driven a few thousand miles a year, will cost at least $1,000 a year. Often the cost is much more. You should keep records of car expenses—you will be surprised. You also need to keep a car diary or logbook of maintenance and repair with each car so you will not neglect it. If you sell, you will then know how much you have invested in the car so you can set a price.

THREE COMPETING SYSTEMS FOR OWNING CHEAP CARS

Men in coffee shops argue about the merits of each system.

1. Buy very cheap cars near the end of their lives and run them to destruction, one after the other, and then let the crusher have them. Never do any repairs at all, since repairs are one of the biggest expenses of owning a car and seldom return what they cost. If the car dies, discard it.
2. To avoid the depreciation, buy a car that is fully depreciated and will be valuable later. Take good care of it and keep the mileage low.
3. Buy an unusual or foreign car that is very cheap because no one wants it or because parts for it cannot be easily found. A man we know bought a 1980s VW Jetta for only $600 privately in better than average condition. If it were a Taurus it would have been $2,000. Fiats, Renaults, Saabs, Opals, AMCs, and cars like that can be very cheap too. Get parts mail order and do your own work.

LIVING WITHOUT OWNING A CAR

If owning a car costs too much money, alternatives include walking, taking the bus, or riding a bicycle, moped, or motorcycle. Secondhand bicycles are $50 or less. Some prefer mountain bikes, which cost more. Mopeds are $300 to $500 used. No license or insurance is required in most states. Gas mileage is extraordinary—over 100 mpg. Mopeds are quite dangerous because they do not go fast enough to keep up with traffic. They are too slow climbing hills for use in hilly country and useless in snow. Scooters are possible but tend to cost more. A small motorcycle is much better than a scooter if you can afford it.

HOW TO BUY MOPEDS AND MOTORCYCLES CHEAP

Cars need expensive garages or parking spaces. When they are no longer needed, they are sold, not kept around. But a moped or a motorcycle takes little space leaning up against the wall in a garage or cellar. It will be kept for years after the owner stops riding. People usually give up riding motorcycles for one of these reasons: They have had a bad scare;

they get too old to ride; they buy a car; or they get married or have a change of interests. Sometimes they buy a bigger motorcycle and keep the small one because the dealer will not give them enough on it at trade-in time. You find these idle machines by asking around and by placing want ads in local shoppers or weekly newspapers. Motorcycles sold by car or motorcycle dealers are much more expensive. Dealers do not like to keep a $500 used cycle around that could cost them the sale of a $7,500 new machine. There are independent motorcycle repair shops that also sell used motorcycles; they may give you a better deal. Flea market dealers sometimes have mopeds or motorcycles and they will let you ride them. I got mine in a yard sale. Always buy used helmets for about $5 in flea markets, never a new one. Buy trim, parts, and accessories used, also.

I've owned a number of motorcycles, first the 250cc Harley Sprint shown here, then a 125cc Honda and now a 1978 185cc Honda Twinstar. It cost $650 with 3,500 miles on it, in mint condition. The motorcycle takes the place of a second car. Its luggage rack will accept a pack or a large item. Avoid motorcycles over 500cc or over 400 pounds—these are costly to buy, run, and insure. They are too heavy to lift over a stone wall in the woods or to load into the trunk of a car. Honda and other well-known Japanese makes are the best buys in a motorcycle. The cycles can be used year round in the dry Southwest.

Checking Out a Cycle

Here is how to check out a motorcycle. If you can crank a cycle over, the motor is not frozen. They need fresh gas to start if left a year or more. Often the battery is gone. Get new batteries from Sears or a motorcycle shop. Always check the oil and replace if it is dark and dirty. Use the recommended oil.

Motor knocks and transmissions that refuse to shift are expensive. Chains are easily replaced. Out-of-round wheels and broken spokes are serious. A dented or scarred tank reduces sale price but is no consequence except appearance. Motorcycle chrome rusts quickly compared to cars, particularly on the muffler. But this is a cosmetic problem, too.

Precautions

A Honda or similar machine with its overhead cam, roller bearings, and 10,000 rpm motor really needs to be fixed by a motorcycle repair person. It is too complicated for the general handyman mechanic. But once running, the cycles last like outboard motors. Theft is a problem. Store it indoors and carry a chain of hardened steel and a good padlock to chain it to a pole when you park it. Like most everything else you buy, the good buys in cycles all must be bought with cash. Your small nest egg of $2,000 or so is vital to your economic survival. Stay out of debt.

RENT A CAR OR TRUCK

Some people walk or use a bicycle or motorcycle locally. When they take a long trip or need to move something heavy, they rent a car or a truck. It requires a credit card or a large deposit. For as much as two week's use a year it is cheaper to rent than own a vehicle.

A small motorcycle saves money, can even take the place of a car.

A TRUCK OR A TRAILER?

Pickup trucks are extremely popular and have a macho image. That makes them too costly used, unless you buy an older model with two-wheel drive and a six or small V8 motor. I suspect they will soon be worth much less if gas prices rise greatly. A car towing a small trailer, which may be rented, will carry just as much as a pickup and is lower and easier to load. But trailers are hard to back up and tow poorly off the road, and they are unsafe in snow or ice; these are their only limitations. I prefer a rental trailer to a truck when I move antiques or goods. I try to buy trailer hitches in flea markets where they cost $10 to $20. New installed they cost $150 or more. They may also be ordered from JC Whitney. Big old V8 cars can handle the biggest trailers. Front-wheel drive four-cylinder cars only tow small trailers. If you use a cargo trailer often, homemade ones are sold by individuals locally for a few hundred dollars.

Make a Pickup Truck

Since pickups cost more than cars used, this makes sense. Take a big old sedan with a frame. Have a welder cut off the rear body. Make the pickup bed out of wood. Add air shocks or helper springs (mail ordered from JC Whitney) if you plan to carry heavy loads, such as a cord of wood. Country people have been doing this for 80 years or more. The truck on the TV show *The Beverly Hillbillies*, made from a 1923 Oldsmobile touring car, was quite authentic. The truck shown here is for show, too. Yours could be plainer. Won't you enjoy parking it next to some spendthrift's new $30,000 diesel pickup?

Homemade pickup truck from Murphy, North Carolina.

VANS

Vans tend to be cheaper than pickup trucks of the same size. The engines are harder to work on, and they are less fun to drive. Like pickups, they use a lot of gas. You may want one.

WHAT KIND OF CAR TO BUY

There is a lot of guesswork and chance here and though I have had my share of lemons myself, I know enough of auto mechanics to let me rebuild motors. A lot of car lore is mostly opinion, too. The most durable cars are the Mercedes Benz, Lexus, and Volvo, which are usually too expensive and worn out if they're offered as used cars. Big, older American V8 cars such as the Ford LTD, Crown Victoria, Chevy Caprice, and similar Mercury, Buick, and Pontiac cars are next in durability. Chrysler Fifth Avenue V8 and Dodge and Plymouth V8 equivalents are almost as good. Four-door sedans and wagons are the cheapest, and also the most useful body styles in these big cars.

Avoid buying most small American front-wheel drive cars, except for Plymouth Sundances or minivans with Japanese motors and transmissions, or equivalent Dodge or Chrysler models, which are about the best of them. If you like to tinker and can get parts by mail or through the Internet, you can try very unusual, small, foreign cars at low prices. The AMC Renault Alliance, a front-wheel drive circa 1990, is very cheap used—$300 or less for a good one, but repair parts are difficult to find. Tiny Renault R5s or LeCars are a few hundred dollars used for a nice one, if you like to tinker with cars. We toured England with a rented one. A Ford Fiesta, Festiva, or Geo Metro is a good buy. Dodge Colt is OK. Ten-year-old VW diesel Rabbits are about $1,500, get 50 mpg and have ultimate reliability. Long ago I had Beetles, Nash Metropolitans, a Simca 1204, MGA and MG-TD, Fiat Spyder, Saab 95, and a Datsun B210 hatchback. Dad had a Crosley. But these cars are now too collectible to consider today, unless bought very cheaply. Used Cadillacs and Lincolns have too many headaches for most people, but 1980s Lincolns are used as taxis. At least they have dependable Ford drive trains.

The mid-South is the best place to buy clean, rust-free used cars. Florida has too much ocean salt and some Florida cars are actually rusty Yankee cars brought down by sunbirds. Atlanta cars are good, but may have a lot of mileage since the city is spread out like Los Angeles now. Kentucky and Virginia cars may have salt damage. So Georgia and the Carolinas are the best car marts of all. I have helped friends buy good lower-priced cars in the Carolinas, and all of them so far have been successful. The dealer will do all the paperwork and give you a temporary plate to drive home.

This 1982 AMC Concord had 34,000 miles on it. It cost the author $1,750 in 1992. No rust since it came from South Carolina. It was sold at a profit.

The Austin Mini is a very fine small car. Highly collectible, too. Maybe you will find one at a bargain price. This car, which I rented, is a Mini 1000.

AGE VS. CARE

The age of a car makes little difference—it is the quality of the previous ownership that is most important. Was the oil changed regularly? Cars drop in value until they are 10 years old then rise again as they are perceived as antiques beginning at about 20 years of age. Buying a fully depreciated 10-year-old car is usually the best way to go. In 1981, I bought a big 1971 Ford LTD hardtop with air from Saluda, South Carolina, for $1,200. Previously, it was upper-middle-class owned and was nearly perfect, though it had 88,000 miles. It had no salt damage. Eleven years later it had 134,000 miles and has had only small repairs, the biggest being universal joints, motor mounts, a rebuilt starter and a carb. I sold it in 1993. This old car was completely dependable. We drove it on several 2,000-mile trips and towed an Airstream trailer with it with no problems. Early Ford LTDs rust very badly. The car could never be driven in snow, which is the main reason I sold it.

To replace it I bought a 1982 AMC Concord with 34,000 original miles in near-mint condition for $1,750. I kept it two years and sold it at a small profit. It gave no trouble. AMC and Rambler cars were often quite good and sold cheaply used since they were an off brand. My present car is a Saturn, bought new in 1997, too costly for this book, but bought because I was too busy to work on cars. It has been good. Saturns may be good used buys later.

Engines and transmissions should last 150,000 miles or more in an American V8 car. Honda Accord, Plymouth Sundance, Datsun B210, Toyota Corolla, and many similar small, Japanese four-cylinder cars last as long. This fact was not recognized until recently. Japanese four-cylinder cars with 100,000 miles on them used to be sold for a few hundred dollars. Now that people know they last so long, the price has risen considerably. Automatic transmissions are quite reliable now. Avoid like the plague all Chrysler family four-speed automatic transmissions of any size. Manual shift cars have often been abused by hot-rod driving. They are a second choice to the automatic shift.

CONVERTIBLES

Convertibles are very nice. I bought this big 1968 Ford Galaxie 500 convertible for $1,200 in 1977. Then it had 150,000 miles on it. It is a rust-free South Carolina car, too. The engine was poor so I gave it a Ford rebuilt motor just after buying it. I have had it repainted and reupholstered, and have given it a new top and some new chrome. It looks show grade now in 2001 and has a book value of $7,000, which is about what I have in it. It now has 222,000 miles on it and runs perfectly. I keep it under a carport and out of snow and salt, of course. A convertible really is a very practical, economical car—and sporty, too. What you pay extra when you buy one used, you always get back when you sell—so the luxury costs you nothing.

This 1968 Ford Galaxie 500 convertible has logged 222,000 miles.

Good Convertible Buys

Right now, four-cylinder Dodge and Chrysler convertibles of the early '80s are only about $2,000 used and are sure to go up in value while you drive and enjoy them. Buy convertibles in winter when they are cheaper! The tiny Dodge Shadow convertible based on the Sundance platform is nice. Wives and girlfriends love a convertible. You have more status than someone in a $35,000 macho car! American V8 convertibles of the early 1970s such as Ford LTD, Buick, Olds, and Pontiac are still fairly cheap and are fine cars. A convertible is one way to own an old car and retain prestige. A ragtop makes a most practical old car. I've carried beds, storm windows, giant bookcases, ladders, and other bulky items in my

WHAT ABOUT GAS MILEAGE? As this is written, gas is selling for $1.55 a gallon and going up. Recently it was a dollar a gallon or less. This can make running a big dual-wheel, twin-cab pickup very expensive. Sports utilities are also big gas eaters. It is interesting that the spendthrift public has a mania to buy these trucks just before a gas shortage. In 1980, after the last oil crisis, they only wanted four-cylinder economy cars, and even put V6s in big Cadillacs. Bigger cars were in great surplus then. If you only drive 2,000 miles a year, gas mileage doesn't make much difference to your budget. If you drive more, it might be serious. It might make you prefer a small Toyota, a Metro, or a Saturn to a V8 car. Gas shortages could again cause a surplus in big pickups, SUVs, and V8 cars. I am not certain what is going to happen, which is why we own both a Saturn and a big V8.

This type of Chevy Caprice is already a good used buy.

convertible by pulling out the back seat and standing them up, with the top folded down. It often tows a big U-Haul trailer. Open cars do not leak nowadays. The thick nylon tops last five years outdoors, and indefinitely if the car is garaged. Convertibles are tight and warm in winter.

V8s

Big V8s are nice; the egg-shaped, 1992-and-later Chevy Caprices seem to be good cars. Few were sold and they were carefully made on a slow-moving production line. The motor and chassis have been time-tested over many years. They are desirable used buys if you like a big car. Full-size four-door sedans like this are cheaper than coupes and smaller sporty cars such as the T-Bird, Mustang, or Camaro. Big, conservative four-door sedans are most likely to have been owned and driven by careful people, and are the best buys. It is worth studying what kind of cars are used as taxis in your area. In the South, taxi owners buy big used V8 cars, just as I do. A friend towed a trailer cross-country with a two-year-old Ford police cruiser he bought for $1,800 at a state auction. Your state legislator will give you information about state surplus sales. Your congressional representative has this data for federal sales; there is no need to pay for this information.

Body rust is a serious problem in the North. Hopefully you'll get rid of the car before it rusts out. It is good to sell before any expensive series of repairs, but this is easier said than done. I have kept cars too long until the motors failed or the floors rusted out. And I have traded cars that the next owner then ran trouble free for years. I do not always guess it right. You can leave cars outdoors all year and they last a long time anyway. Be sure they are kept clean and waxed. This makes all the difference. A garage is not vitally important, but nice to have.

Body rust holes may be fixed by screwing or riveting on sheet-metal patches. They may not look pretty, but they will hold. JC Whitney sells new fenders and rocker panels of metal and fiberglass that may save a car. They are not cheap. Oil undercoating of the chassis may help. You have the oil sprayed on or use your old drain oil and do it yourself. The franchises that do this oiling charge too much. Have an independent do it. Ask locally. In Vermont, where road salt was severe, the Cadillac dealer had a big cellar where he stored all the wealthier people's Cadillacs for the winter. They drove pickup trucks, Jeeps, or older vehicles in snow.

DRIVING IN SNOW AND OFF THE ROAD

Four-wheel drive trucks and Jeeps are very expensive. The AMC Eagle is a low-cost four-wheel drive, but its body is not rugged like a Jeep. The 4WD Dodge Colt and the Suburu are interesting 4WD vehicles. Old tire chains, found in flea markets, will get a rear-wheel drive car through most any snow. A VW Beetle, Dune Buggy, or any front-wheel drive car will go almost anywhere a Jeep will. Once long ago I broke the rear universal joint on a Dodge Powerwagon. Parts were slow to arrive so I had to drive it for some time with only front-wheel drive. It seemed just as good; traction was superb. The front wheels do most of the pulling in 4WD. A big American V8 sedan will do very well if you keep moving and straddle the ruts and put some cement blocks in the trunk. Remember the police have wonderful success with the big Ford Crown Victoria and Chevrolet Caprice. They jump curbs and medians, drive ferociously, and go anywhere with them.

Actually, the motorcycle is the most practical off-the-road vehicle. A pair of one-foot diameter trees three feet apart will stop any four-wheel drive truck. But a cycle passes between them easily. This is a fact often forgotten. Avoid ATVs for the same reason.

SAVING ON MAINTENANCE

You should change the oil and filter, and check and add brake fluid, transmission fluid, and antifreeze yourself to save money. Change oil as the owner's manual suggests or more often, even if you are poor. Use a high grade of oil as recommended for the car. It does not pay to scrimp here. Your loving care will reward you with a smooth-starting, dependable car. Spark plugs and ignition points (found on older cars) are easy to replace. Get new parts and fluids from stores like Western Auto, Kmart, Auto Zone, Wal-Mart, or Sears, or buy mail order from JC Whitney (Box 1000, LaSalle, IL 61301-0100 or www.jcwhitney.com). You will pay more for parts at a new car dealer or a parts house selling to garages, like NAPA, unless they give you a discount. I have had a general machine shop rebuild old car parts successfully. It will usually cost much less than a replacement. Junkyard parts can save you money, too. Cosmetic parts should always be from a junkyard, but use caution with mechanical parts. Put used motor oil in gallon milk cartons. Use it for lubrication of most anything that squeaks and for rust-proofing your car underneath. Hemming's Motor News, an antique car trading publication (Box 256 Bennington Vermont 05201 or www.hemmings.com) has parts and services for most older cars. Surprisingly they cost no more than parts for new cars.

ANTIQUE CARS

This beautiful 1948 Pontiac Streamliner was photographed in 1999 on a street in South Carolina. It is worth about $5,000, should have zero depreciation. Compare this with a five-year-old used car for the same $5,000 which will soon drop to $1,000 or less. This more recent antique is highly reliable. Its powerful straight-eight motor is even good for turnpike speeds. Fairly modern antiques are good transportation, if you don't use them more than about 2,000 miles a year.

Were antique cars more durable than cars today? Not really. The bodies were superior, but the mechanical parts gave more trouble. Dad kept a 1928 Ford for 150,000 miles and I ran a well-used 1929 Ford Model A coupe about 20,000 very hard miles as a teen in the early 1950s. I drove several 1936 and '37 V8 Fords, including two woody wagons, for over 100,000 good miles between 1954 and 1964. Dad had a 1940 V8 Ford that ran up 180,000 miles with the original engine with few repairs. It burned a lot of oil by then. I worked on all these cars a lot. For low-mileage country use, Model A Fords and six-cylinder 1954 and earlier Chevy or Dodge pickups are still excellent transportation if you can get along without air conditioning and automatic transmissions. They have zero depreciation, you remember. Tom Watson drives a 1948 Nash Ambassador in regular everyday use around Hayesville, North Carolina. The savings in old cars are in low-cost antique insurance and plates and, of course, antique cars will appreciate. There will be *no* savings unless you keep a good stock of parts on hand and like to tinker, as I do. Keep all old cars strictly original. Allow no modifications, no late-model engines, trim, or wheels, which look foolish and make them hard to sell. Sealed-beam headlight conversions should be added to update older headlights. Hydraulic brakes are

essential on all but very light cars, like Model A Fords. It is out of the question to own and use antique cars for transportation if you live in the North where it snows and the roads are salted.

REPAIRING A CAR FOR FREE

To do more elaborate work on cars buy a Chilton's book on repair or take a course at your community college. You need a few tools. For American cars, 3/8-, 7/16-, 1/2-, 9/16-, and 5/8-inch open-end and box wrenches, a bigger Crescent wrench, files, pliers, vise grips, plain and Phillips screwdrivers, and thickness gauges are essential. A 3/8-inch socket-wrench set is nice. Foreign cars have different metric sizes. Buy well-known Craftsman, Snap-on, Crescent, Stanley, and other good American tools, used if you can, and never cast-iron imports from Asia. Note that some Sears Craftsman tools now come from Asia and are not as good as they used to be. Sometimes the widow of a mechanic will sell you a good tool kit. You need a very strong garage jack and jack stands, or blocks of wood. Never use cement blocks or a bumper jack to support a car. They can break. People have been crushed by cars that fell on them while they were working under them. More expensive, seldom-used tools such as wheel pullers should be rented as needed. Many community colleges have the students repair cars for the public and they only charge the cost of the parts. Check with them and maybe they will fix your car for free. It may take some time.

Chapter 14

Save on Education, Entertainment, and Vacations

We will discuss entertainment first. Remember that most of the best entertainment is educational, too.

ENTERTAINMENT

Radio

If you get a boom-box portable stereo for less than $100 new, $10 used, you can record all your favorite music off the radio on tape cassettes costing less than a dollar each and never have to buy another CD. People's tastes in music changes fast—the top tune they love one day they want to throw out the next. It saves a lot of money to simply get all your music off the radio and record it. My kids started doing it at about 11 years of age. One way to get a good stereo for very little money is to buy an old Magnavox or RCA console stereo in a big wooden cabinet in a thrift shop for about $30 and modernize it. Get a new or used CD Walkman and mount it inside the record storage bin of the stereo and run cables to the accessory inputs in the back. Power your Walkman with a small 12-volt power supply. Now you can play CDs. If it sounds weak in the treble, as some older stereos do, add a pair of Radio Shack super tweeters. To play tape cassettes mount an accessory tape player removed from a junk car inside the cabinet.

We own a high-grade 1960s Marantz stereo bought for $35 at the Kiwanis flea market. We also listen to shortwave on a 10-year-old Sony all-wave set.

A cheaper home music system is a car stereo with cassette player removed from a junk car or bought in the flea market for $25 or less. It can be powered with a 12-volt power pack if you have a power line. Its antenna will be a short piece of wire about as long as a car antenna. Mount it in a cabinet. Use the old car speakers mounted in separate cabinets.

There must be something to classical music and good literature. Those who love it are successful, upscale people. Most of us would love to be like them. Yachts, trips to Europe, and debutante balls cost a fortune, but a tape of a Mozart or Beethoven symphony is within the reach of all of us. Try it. Learn to love the classics. It will do you good.

Television

Much TV is a waste of time, but cable stations have some good programs; it might be worth its cost even on limited budgets. In extreme rural areas without cable you must have a satellite dish to receive a signal. I would own a $25 used black-and-white TV if we only received the networks.

Small-screen sets last longer than big-screen sets since the plate voltage for the picture tube is lower. Plenty of secondhand color TV sets are available as low as $25. A VCR also is desirable to record good movies off the TV and to play educational video tapes on such subjects as plumbing and auto tune-up, which you need, as well as great classics such as the plays of Shakespeare and wonderful operas.

Musical Instruments

If you have inherited a piano, save it and get someone in your family to learn how to play it. Guitars and banjos of the cheaper non-electric variety are easy to play and bring out hidden talent. It is just what you need to play when people are gathered around the fireplace or a campfire! The cheapest musical instrument and the easiest to play is the harmonica. Even I can play one! Hohner's Marine Band model, for about $25 new and $12 or less used, is the standard. It fits in a pocket! You have to have a little fun, a little beauty, a little music, no matter how poor you are. When I was a kid, men walking to work, postmen, and delivery men knew how to whistle, some quite musically. It seems to be a lost art, one that should be revived.

Used electronic organs are as cheap as $100. They are easily fixed. Usually all that is wrong is that the key and pedal contacts need cleaning with a spray can of TV-tuner cleaner. Wurlitzer, Baldwin, and Hammond are good makes. I have bought them and fixed them up to give to small churches. I maintain the Wurlitzer organ in our church now for free. Pianos are cheap in places like West Virginia and New Mexico. We saw one advertised for $300. Darius Robinson bought a fine Steinway Grand for $350! It is amazing how low people price what they sell in classified ads.

Social Events

Much of the entertainment and social life of people in the country comes from the church and from social organizations like the Grange.

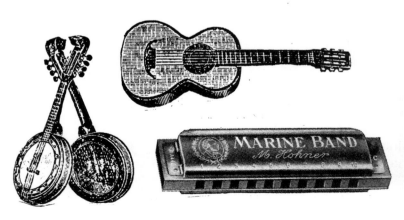

They have covered-dish suppers where each family brings a casserole or a pie. There will be a speaker and a program. The cost is very low. If you accept the lifestyle of country people you will have a wonderful life. If not, it might go like the TV couple who moved to Green Acres.

Sports and Games

A much better game than expensive bowling or golf is croquet played with wooden balls, mallets, and wickets on a beautiful lawn. Another fine lawn game is badminton—like tennis, but a lawn game with feathered shuttlecocks instead of balls. I loved both games as a teenager. The English aristocracy used to enjoy badminton and croquet at their great country houses. You will, too. The English working people play darts in their pubs. A set of darts and a board costs a fraction the price of a stupid video game. It is much more fun. Try to buy these old games cheap at flea markets and yard sales.

Board Games

My wife's family loves Trivial Pursuit and they are much better at it than I am. It's a fine game. Chess and checkers appeal to many good people. Monopoly teaches business values. If you no longer use your high intelligence on the job, board games will keep you mentally active. Buy these games in thrift shops and yard sales, too.

Art

All it takes to be an artist is talent and a paper and pencil, or an ink pen and paper. You will never know if you have talent if you do not try. Watch instruction in drawing and painting on ETV and on videos. That is how the drawings for this book were made, with pen and ink, by a talented young housewife who lives nearby.

Toys for the Kids

You often feel humiliated when you are poor and wealthier in-laws give your kids toys you cannot afford. But often the kids prefer your older, cheaper toys so there is no problem. If the kids start nagging you to buy them things you cannot afford, you must put a stop to it emphati-

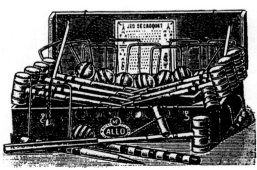

Darts and croquet are fine games.

cally or your kids will become big spender, consumer-mentality people who cannot resist a sales pitch. Kids who are slaves to peer pressure and status will never make or keep any money, and are likely to have trouble all their lives.

Kids love cloth dolls and stuffed animals. A favorite of mine was a cloth elephant with button eyes my mother sewed up for me out of an old dress. It was unique. Raggedy Ann dolls are beloved possessions. If the kid has only one or two cloth animals, the imagination soon makes real personalities out of them. Now kids have dozens of teddy bears, sometimes a whole room full, and their imaginations cannot make them seem real anymore. They are more like cushions. Restrict your kid's toys.

Toy guns are a problem. We favor giving kids only water pistols that squirt, never a gun that only makes a noise, and teaching them gun safety early with toy guns. Do not allow them to point a gun at any one. I dislike science fiction, which usually is bad science as well as bad fiction. There is a plastic space toy called a "Transformer" that changes from a fighter plane to a robot figure as one moves its different parts around. It never existed in reality and probably never will. Yet kids think that is what a transformer is! A real transformer changes voltage and current by the turn ratio of its coils, which is fun for kids to calculate. They are around the house in battery chargers, power supplies for battery radios, and many other places. It is a pity to confuse American kids who are already weak on science with so much junk science from the media.

Dad let me take apart old radios, clocks, and telescopes as a kid. I learned enough to fix radios and build a telescope by age 14. Today, transistor radios are giveaway items. If battery powered, they are safe for a kid, unlike older AC radios. Buy your kid a soldering iron and a cheap test meter (under $20) from Radio Shack, $5 to $10 used, and the kid will be able to take electronics apart, learn the parts, and do all sorts of experiments. They learn to make new circuits out of the old parts, even including a shortwave receiver and transmitter. Old Mac, Commodore, and Tandy computers are giveaway items and fun for experimenters, too.

Kids like to make wooden models far more than playing with plastic kits. With wood, a knife, and some paint, glue, and fasteners you'll be surprised what they can create. Gasoline-powered model airplanes are fun to build. Girls should also make things. Women do wonderful work building satellites and computers—there is no reason why girls should not make models. Some ship models are worth $20,000 !

Modern kids refuse to play with a toy after it has a few scratches on it

Kids like toys that are a challenge, like these. Buy them in flea markets..

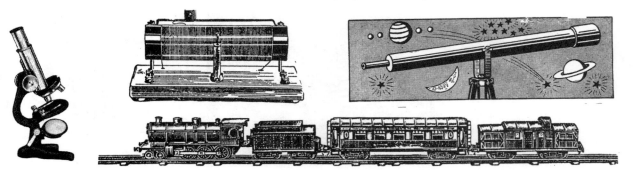

so there are great quantities of toys available at low cost in flea markets and thrift shops. Most only need cleaning and adjustment. Buy them up. I found an HO electric train outfit for $15 recently. One car had a bad wheel. The factory sent us another free, which restored it. We ran it under the tree one Christmas and then gave it away. I learned basic electricity from a set of electric trains as a kid. Give younger kids a bank that does tricks like the old cast iron ones to teach them the value of saving money.

For outdoor life, kids need their own sleeping bags, canteens, packs, and things like that.

Schoolbooks are terrible these days. We give the kids of friends and relatives sets of McGuffey readers, which are fun to read. Old mechanical typewriters are interesting to take apart and also to learn to type on. Some kids learn to type before they can write well, as I did. Dad made me some pull-toys out of old boards. I remember a battleship he made with broomstick smokestacks and castor wheels. We made wonderful playhouses out of stacks of old cartons. There is no reason for kids to suffer if you are poor. The only real poverty is poverty of mind.

Animals to Love

Kids cannot learn to be kind to real animals from watching cartoon figures like Bugs Bunny and Donald Duck. The Beatrix Potter books are about real-looking animals. Kids should have pets but they should be responsible for their care. Always get your pet from a shelter or adopt a stray—save money and save a life! Punish kids for hurting a cat or a dog as you would punish them for attacking a smaller child.

EDUCATION

The best way to get ahead and to stay active mentally is to learn new things.

Literature

The public library is a fine resource for pleasure and education. Nothing entertains better, if you can read well, than a book. You will never be alone, never be bored if you love books. If you read for pleasure you will soon be reading fast. Keep your library card and use the library often.

Libraries have book sales of discards. The librarians often throw out the best old books, it seems. Dealers buy them up to resell; you can too. I've found rare $100 books for 25 cents in library discard sales. See your librarian for dates and location of these sales. You can also buy very low-cost books at secondhand book stores and paperback book exchanges and in flea markets.

Encyclopedias

One can become a scholar in many branches of knowledge, English, history, geography, religion, philosophy, mathematics, logic, anthropology, psychology, architecture, art, music, and many other fields by reading an earlier Encyclopedia Britannica. You do not want a recent 15th edition with two sets of books, one easy and one harder. The older books are more scholarly. The traditional Britannica from the 1890s to about 1970 is what you want. Get a 14th edition or earlier. The 11th and 14th editions are the best of all, but any older Britannica is good. It will not be up to date for science or political geography, but for everything else, it has more scholarship than the current edition. It is fun to take a volume at random and read the sections that appeal to you. Britannicas usually cost $35 to $100 at flea markets, thrift shops, and secondhand book dealers, but can be much less. I give them to young people. My last one, a 14th edition Brittanica in beautiful shape, cost only $5 at our local humane society thrift shop.

The Encyclopedia Americana is acceptable but other encyclopedias, such as World Book, and Collier's, are not nearly as good. Avoid Brittanica Jr. and other children's encyclopedias, which are quickly outgrown. The Harvard Classics five-foot shelf of books may be cheap used, particularly if a few titles are missing. It is quite good on the whole, although not every book is essential. We have a partial set. You can also buy the classics in other matched sets. We bought a 20-volume set published by Random House in 1950 for $5. Fine leatherbound volumes of Shakespeare plays and the great English poets are common used. We love our set of Waverley Novels with steel engravings, which the public library discarded. Most importantly, you need a Bible. For science you need to visit a college library and read periodicals, because science changes so fast. No encyclopedia or bound textbook is sufficient by itself. A good way to get a home library is to buy all the books from the estate of a good old doctor, preacher, or professor. If the heirs are liberal or not too bright, as often happens, they discard all the old books, or sell them for a few dollars. See Chapter 5 for how to buy estates.

You Can Learn Languages Free

Japanese, Chinese, Spanish, German, and many other valuable languages are taught through shortwave radio. A battery radio costing as little as $5 used in a flea market and $40 to $120 new gets international broadcasts from most countries in the world. You need at least 4 to 12MHz coverage or bands from 49 to 25 meters. Sony ICF-7600 is good. We have a policy never to buy a radio or boom box without shortwave. The foreign-language stations will send you text and workbooks free if you write to an address they give over the air. Then you listen to the spoken language by radio and do the written work in the workbooks. The news and cultural programs, from BBC London, Radio Netherlands, Voice of America, Canadian Broadcast Corp., HCJB (call sign of Voice of the Andes) in Ecuador, and many other countries are fascinating. You can make tapes of the broadcasts with a patch cord to your shortwave radio. You can also borrow language tapes, records, and video courses from your public library.

The Internet has good language instruction, too. There are many courses you can take by computer, including some for college credit. Use a search engine to look for them.

Technical Education

Local two-year community colleges and technical institutes are highly recommended. Unlike college professors, the instructors are required to teach so the students can understand them and their courses must meet an expressed need of business and industry for trained workers so the student can be guaranteed a job upon graduation.

Most correspondence courses are good, too. Home study does cost more than going to school, surprisingly, due to the individual attention they give you. I once worked for the old International Correspondence Schools (ICS) and found it an excellent company. Used correspondence courses are very cheap, if you can find one, and a good bet. We had ICS students who learned subjects such as accounting/CPA, carpenter work, plumbing, surveying, electrical contracting, radio/TV, and many other subjects. The great Walter P. Chrysler, who founded the Chrysler Corporation, learned mechanical engineering from ICS, as did many other famous and successful people. We placed a graduate of the ICS high school course in MIT when I worked there.

The 1930s were really the years of home study and self-improvement. The struggling young people of those bleak years became the successful business owners of the postwar period. This type of education works. Incidentally, anyone reading this book without a high school education is smart enough to take the ABE (Adult Basic Education) program at a community college and get the GED (General Education Development) high-school diploma easily. Go for it!

What About College?

Only degrees in law, medicine, accounting, engineering, computer science, and the physical and biological sciences are worthwhile these days. Liberal college counselors lure students into liberal arts, education, and the social sciences. The kids prefer liberal courses to more substantial courses because they are easier and they get higher marks. They have to study much less in these programs, but what they learn is mostly left-wing political indoctrination and secular humanism. It is a pity that parents pay for this kind of education and banks loan money against it. They will be sorry.

People in the 1930s loved to study and learn. See these old ads.

College students still are forced to learn Marxism in America—long after Russia has discarded it. The professors, however, call it "Economic Democracy." The college students study Sinclair Lewis' *Main Street* to learn to hate the American community, *Elmer Gantry* so they will hate religion, John Steinbeck's *Grapes of Wrath* so they will hate capitalism, Arthur Miller's *Death of a Salesman* so they will hate business, Ibsen and Strindberg so they will hate the family, and Ken Kesey's *One Flew Over the Cuckoo's Nest,* now called a classic, to make them accept craziness as a positive value. Then using the existentialists and logical positivists, the students are conditioned to doubt their ability to think. After they are mentally paralyzed, they are taught atheism, socialism, and sexology—with reverence! B.F. Skinner's *Walden Two* commune is taught as the Good Life. They are taught crazy modern art and sheet-metal sculpture. The kids soon learn to hate America, hate business executives, and hate work and become people who are totally useless, unemployable, and impossible to have around. If you are looking for a college for your kids, do not just look at the beautiful campus. You must read the bulletin boards, talk with the professors and go in the bookstore and actually read in the texts your son or daughter will be studying. You will be shocked. Why pay to have your kids ruined?

I have an MA degree myself so I know the problems well. Much of my education was a waste of time, but I had a few good courses where I learned math and I learned how to write and to do research. They had an excellent library and I learned the most there, reading literature, history, and philosophy in dusty books that no one else read, reading on my own to counteract the secular humanism we were fed in class. *I would have acquired nearly as much real knowledge if I had not taken any college classes at all but had simply been given a library card to read in the college library.* Often you can actually get a courtesy library card from a college near you. This may be the best way of all to get an education. Don't expect you will get a lot of individual attention in college. In my five years of study I was only inside one professor's house—and he got drunk!

A college education can cost as much as $150,000 for four years. Unless the prospective student is highly qualified, takes the harder courses, and works very hard, it is not advised. If the $150,000 were invested in good stocks and bonds, or a small business instead, it would probably earn more money over a lifetime. It is like real estate. They used to say that owning a house was a sure investment that could only go up in value. We know now that is not true. Now we are finding out that a college degree is not an automatic ticket to promotion and success, but often simply confuses the student and leaves him or her four years behind the kids who decided to go to work. One possible exception for Southern people is a business course (not science) in a Christian college such as Bob Jones University where the students have a reputation as loyal hard workers of high moral caliber. Many employers, particularly in the South, still have good jobs ready for these students. Babson College, Stetson University, and Grove City College are excellent smaller colleges, too.

If you cut off your kid's education at high school graduation, you should not feel guilty. Here is one alternative to consider. If four years of college costs $100,000 to $150,000, consider what that money could do in a family business in which you and your kid work. The kid could read in the library or study accounting at night. $100,000 gives you a pretty good start in a restaurant franchise, specialty store, used car dealership, video rental, poultry farm, or printing shop. People become millionaires in these businesses. It is something to think about.

What Kind of Kid Is a Good College Prospect?

Most of college learning consists of reading many books or taking notes rapidly and skillfully in lectures. If a kid is a real bookworm, always has his or her nose in a book and you worry that he or she is not getting enough exercise or outdoor sunlight, then that is the kid you want to send to college. If the kid is always working mathematical puzzles and experimenting with electricity, chemistry, robots, computers, or things like that, that is a good sign. If the high school kid has part-time jobs or a home business, that is a very good sign.

I've done guidance counseling in a college and I would estimate that only about a quarter of the population can master traditional college work. By traditional college work, I mean that a serious college graduate knows foreign languages, can write a report or essay good enough to be published, knows how to find abstruse information in libraries or on the Internet, knows higher math (at least through trig and statistics), understands college-level physics, chemistry, astronomy, and biology, and knows enough history to talk intelligently about the Thirty-Years' War or the Dred Scott decision. Unfortunately many colleges now permit a student to take very easy courses and to graduate with no languages, no math, and no serious science. Then the unfortunate graduate ends up working for McDonald's. Why people who really don't like to read and study go to college is a mystery to me. Low marks in high school are not necessarily serious if the SAT scores are high. This happens fairly often, particularly if the teachers are extremely liberal and the kid is not.

Graduate Programs

People who graduate after four years and are unable to get a job often enroll in graduate school. They think the master's degree will help them get a job. Actually a skilled recruiter looking at a resume can spot a person who only went to graduate school because he or she could not find a job. That person will not be hired. Instead of a *stepping stone*, a graduate degree is apt to be a *millstone*. It is ill advised to borrow money for any advanced education except medical school.

VACATIONS

Free and Low-Cost Vacations

Really free vacations are usually limited to kids. There are good camps for low-income kids and scholarships so that families of limited means may send kids to Boy Scout camp, church camps, and similar paid camps. These are offered by churches and service clubs. You have to ask around and read the local newspaper to find them.

If you, an adult, are willing to work during your vacation, there are lots of openings as camp counselors, clerical help, kitchen help, maintenance workers, and other volunteer positions with church and charity camps and at camp meetings where you do some work and vacation also. People who are reduced in income often want to rediscover their religious roots with a more fundamentalist church. The Christian camp meeting, or retreat, is an old time institution, popular in both the North and the South, and low cost for the whole family, which church members find a real blessing. Get to know about all these opportunities.

People interested in the environment also volunteer in various service programs. The National Parks Service has a volunteer host program that gives a family free camping in return for being a sort of chaperone for a smaller unstaffed park. Those volunteers I have talked to liked the work. Write your congressional representative about these opportunities, which change rapidly. Many state and city parks will give a reliable person a free RV hookup and utilities to watch the place. Some people even consider working in a resort location to be a vacation.

Camping

Camping in state and federal parks is the big vacation bargain. Fees are $10 to $20 a night. You need a tent costing $100 to $250 new (maybe $25 secondhand) Often the wife does not like camping so the tent is sold. You must get sleeping bags for each family member. Buy the type of bag that can also be used as a quilt in your home; they are about $30 each. Put foam pads or cheap air mattresses underneath, $5 each. You need a single-burner propane or unleaded gas stove—about $35 new. (Most of this stuff, except the sleeping bags, can be bought used very cheaply.) Use plastic plates, and older pots and pans and cutlery. You need a big flashlight and a lantern or candle, a hot dog grill for the fire, plastic pail and dish pan, and camp ice box. People who bring more stuff to camp

Volkswagen Camper Vans like this one have been popular for years, in spite of being a bit slow.

are silly, like people who take five suitcases to Europe. If you backpack, you need knapsacks, a canteen, a compass, and a waterproof matchbox. So you see, $350 will buy a fine outfit that lasts 10 to 20 years.

It is dangerous and unpleasant to set up a tent in parks near motor home and trailer parking. Their generators, air conditioners, and TVs keep you awake and a motor home can easily run over people in a tent on the ground. It happens fairly often. So be sure your tent can be placed in a grove of trees with some separation between the next sites. The best tent is made of 8-ounce canvas if it is to last any time at all. These are too heavy to backpack, however. I like simple, easy-to-raise tents and prefer enough headroom to dress standing up inside.

The Best Parks

These parks will have toilets and usually hot showers. We have found state and federal parks in Arcadia, Virginia; Starved Rock, Illinois; Lake Shetek, Minnesota; Table Rock, South Carolina; Lake Hartwell, Georgia; The Outer Bank of North Carolina; Bethany Beach, Delaware; Cook Forest, Pennsylvania; Greenfield, New Hampshire; Gifford Woods, Vermont; and Baxter State Park, Maine, to be particularly excellent in the East and Midwest. In the Southwest and West, famous parks such as Yosemite, and the Grand Canyon tend to be crowded. Choose parks near lesser-known attractions. For example in New Mexico, Elephant Butte, Caballo Lake or the many small parks along the Rio Grande, or in North Dakota, the Badlands (instead of Mount Rushmore) would be fine choices. In the Far West, even roadside parks have plenty of vacancies and are nice places.

Private camps including KOA and Yogi Bear's Jellystone are good, too, but cost more. KOA rents little huts where you supply bedding so you can try their facilities without buying a tent and see how you like them. The huts are expensive. There are plenty of vacancies in parks during the week but they fill up on weekends. For many parks you need to get in by Friday noon. But if you are out of work, you can just as well go on weekdays when you find a better crowd, fewer macho types with loud rock music and quarreling kids. Directories for these parks with much valuable information are sold in newsstands and bookstores. You need one of these directories if you plan to camp. Some parks have furnished log cabins and cottages to rent reasonably. Others have very beautiful big log inns built by CCC labor in the last Depression. Reservations are usually required well in advance to stay in an indoor park building of any sort.

Any kind of car can be used for camping. It doesn't have to be a wagon or pickup. If you have four people in a small car you need a roof rack from Sears or Wal-Mart or rented from U-Haul to hold the camping outfit. The parks have various facilities. People fish, swim, hike, bicycle, rest, and read. I wrote a book while staying in parks. It is quiet and peaceful. There are fascinating tourist sites and good antique shops and flea markets to visit near the parks as well. With a family you save more than $100 a night on motels and restaurant food. The campfire is an important part of camping. Firewood must be bought and can cost as

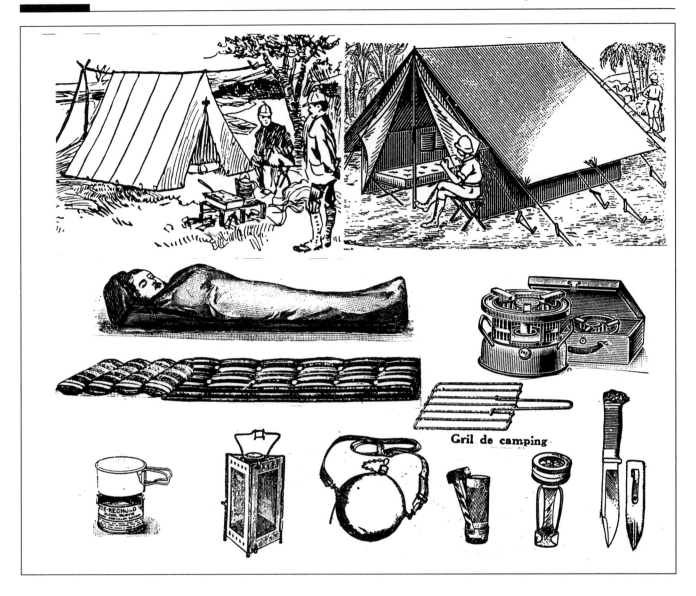

Gril de camping

These are old drawings but the same items are sold today. We have used the tent at top left for years. Note sleeping bag, air mattress, gasoline stove and grill in center. At bottom, see Sterno stove (slow but safe), candle lantern, canteen, matchbox, compass, and knife.

much as $5 a bundle. If you pay it, the country people will be laughing at you as they take your money. Bring your own firewood from home or gather it from the roadside as you drive. Dry, weathered wood burns best. Pick up fallen branches intact and put them in your trunk. Break them up later. You seldom need an axe for wood for a cooking fire. Break the sticks with your knee or by putting them on a rock or log and jumping on them.

SAVING ON FOOD WHILE TRAVELING

Buy submarine sandwiches or hoagies in supermarkets where they are cheaper, not in restaurants or convenience stores. Keep a canteen of water and small cans of fruit juice in the car. You can cook on a car motor as we explained in the food chapter.

ATTRACTIVE VACATION RESORTS

If you like the beach, the Florida Panhandle is fairly low cost. You will like Destin, Panama City, and that vicinity. Unsold Florida condominiums are often rented daily or weekly at low rates. See the beautiful "House on the Rock" in the Wisconsin Dells to see what imagination and persistence can do. Eureka Springs, Arkansas, is a real fun resort with something for everyone. It offers the famous Passion Play, several country music halls that present Grand Old Opry-style shows, antique shops, gift shops, and fine places to eat. There are many good hotels and motels. It is not cheap, but a lot cheaper than Disneyland, Opry Land in Nashville, Tennessee, Branson, Missouri, or Gatlinburg, Tennessee, which have a similar appeal. The Armagosa Opera House in Death Valley Junction, California, has great appeal to those who like old-time theater.

TRAVEL CROSS-COUNTRY FREE

There are services advertised in large cities that deliver a person's car cross-country. They are used by people moving to a new location who lack the time to drive. A person with good references will be paid by these firms to drive a customer's car. It's a good vacation. Look in the classified pages of large newspapers for their ads.

BOATING

Top: I got this 1929 17-foot mahogany Airship speedboat in trade for a camera worth about $250. It went very fast with a small outboard motor.

Bottom: A rubber boat with a small motor is quite successful. You can even backpack it in to a mountain lake on a pack frame in two trips.

Boating is great fun and need not be costly. Some friends bought a big aluminum canoe with a hole in it for $50 and patched it easily with pop rivets. They love it. Older lighter boats of 12 or 14 feet are low cost. They can travel on a car top so you need no trailer. We carried our 17-foot Airship mahogany speedboat on a carefully padded U-Haul trailer, which we sunk in water to float it off. I doubt U-Haul would approve!

Rubber boats with motors are fun. Be sure they are made of woven rubber cloth, not plastic film. We had a Lidair Flores with a 6-hp motor that traveled to Florida in a car trunk. Good makes today are Avon and Zodiac.

Houseboats have been made from oil drums attached to a wooden platform.

Small fiberglass sailboats are low cost used; we just sold our 17-foot O'Day with trailer for $1,200.

Pull-start outboard motors of 25 hp or less are very cheap to buy and run. Outboards need not be recent—I bought my 1974 Evinrude 10-hp outboard for $100 in 1990 in a flea market. Now in 2001, I have a 1990 Mercury pull-start 25-hp outboard motor, which has never given any

trouble. It is on a 14-foot aluminum boat with high sides. It is ideal for most any freshwater lake or river, no matter how large. This boat has no carpet, upholstered seats, or fancy trim to deteriorate, so it can be left outdoors all winter. No storage battery to go dead either. We put clamp-on upholstered stadium seats on it and use flashlight battery-powered running lights when we go out. This type of boat is typical of those used by Maine fishing guides.

In Maine camps, they store aluminum outboard boats and canoes all winter by sinking them in the lake under the ice. When a foot or more of ice covers them, no one can steal them! They are very durable. These smaller boats are fine for rivers or lakes.

Boats like this are the best buys and most practical, but modern men prefer $25,000 macho boats with swivel chairs, sonar, and 200-hp outboards! Try to get a round-bottom boat with a bow that looks like a real boat.

Older people we know tell us that the Great Depression was not all misery, that some of their happiest years were when they had very little money and had only simple pleasures to enjoy. I hope this becomes true for you, too.

Chapter 15

Protect Your Investments and Make Them Grow

Maybe I shouldn't write a chapter like this, I thought, because I never made any big money. But then I realized I have never had any big losses either. So the first part of this chapter is my advice on how not to lose money. The second part, which is brand new in 2001, is compiled from notes made after a nice two-hour lunch in New York with a very fine older man who has really made a lot of money. He told me how he did it (after I shared some of my antiques-business secrets with him). He said I could publish his story as long as I kept his name out of it.

HOW YOU CAN TELL IF YOUR BANK IS GOING BROKE

The bank certainly won't tell you. The government won't tell you—their politicians cover up all bad news. And the media works closely with the government, so they won't tell you either. You cannot tell much from a bank's audits and financial statements because the quality of their bank loans is an opinion, not a fact, and it can easily be slanted to make the bank look better. But there is one sure way to spot trouble: *Bank officers and directors sell their stock before the bank goes broke.* So watch the stock of your bank in the financial pages and if it drops a lot, you'd better get all your money out of the bank and run.

HOW PEOPLE LOST THEIR LIFE SAVINGS

Dad remembered the Great Depression and warned me before he died that another big depression was coming soon. There were a lot of widowed aunts and old-timers in our family, some who were rendered penniless by the Depression and some who did all right. Those who lost everything made one of the following mistakes. This applies to you today, so study their mistakes carefully.

They Sought Too High an Interest Rate

If a bond pays 12 percent when other bonds pay 7 percent or 8 percent, there is something wrong with it. If a stock pays a dividend of 8 percent or 9 percent when other stocks in similar companies pay 2.5 percent to 4 percent, it is probably in trouble and going to reduce or suspend the dividend soon. In the long run there are *no* free rides. The tragedy is that poor or old people who need more money to live on are most likely to risk their future on high-yield junk securities. Rule of thumb: *Any* stock or bond paying much more than average should be suspect.

They Trusted Fiduciaries

People lost (and will lose) their money in a recession or depression because they let a fiduciary hold their investment. People in our family had their money with Lee Higginson, a broker in the 1930s. This firm kept the stock certificates and paid them the dividends as most brokers do today. When the firm failed, the money and the stock were nowhere to be found. A mutual fund is another form of fiduciary, as is a money-market fund. In hard times, there will be a run on the open-end mutual fund, just as on a bank. To raise money the fund is forced to sell securities they bought when the market was high at the bottom of the market, with huge losses.

They Bought Open-Ended Mutual Funds

All open-ended mutual funds perished in the last Depression. What happened was the shareholders redeemed all their shares when the market was at rock bottom so the funds were forced to sacrifice fundamentally sound positions at pennies on the dollar. It is risky to buy such a fund today. Most mutual funds advertised are open-ended. A few are closed-end funds, which cannot be redeemed from the firm at net-asset value but simply trade like other stocks on the various stock exchanges. These closed-end firms cannot be forced to liquidate assets by stockholders who want their money back in a crisis.

The Gold Scam Got Them

One of the silliest things otherwise intelligent people do is to buy gold or silver coins from a firm that promises to store them in a protected warehouse. Generally that firm simply spends the money and never buys your coin or bullion at all. It is a scam. Gold might be good someday if you took possession of it, or used a large international bank, but never trust someone you do not know to hold your gold for you.

They Trusted Brokers

People continue to trust brokers too much. Brokers are always telling you to buy more stock; they will never tell you that the market will soon crash. Grandfather lost a lot of money when Morton Prince failed in the 1890s. Yet Granny continued to trust brokers. To avoid a fiduciary relationship, *never* let your broker keep your stock certificates. How do you know he or she ever bought them? Make the broker give them to you to take home and put in the safe or lock box. *Never* take the advice of a broker—it is almost always self-serving.

They Traded Too Much

Don't trade often. In the stock market, avoid frequent trades and buying at market peaks. A good friend of ours, a widow, lost half of a $200,000 inheritance in a year or two in a time when the market was rising. She gave her broker power of attorney to trade as he saw fit. He made great numbers of trades for no good reason simply to increase his commissions. He bought junk bonds and marginal stocks at high prices and sold them when they went down. Then he bought more junk and let it go down. If you have computer online trading, it is tempting to trade too much yourself.

They Failed To Diversify

Don't put all your eggs in one basket. Loyal Western Pennsylvania people put all their money in Columbia Gas, which suspended its dividend at one time, and in Quaker State, Westinghouse, and in U.S. Steel (now USX), which have all done poorly. Another sad case is the employee of Sears who holds thousands of shares of their stock bought through payroll deduction over many years. Sears is now badly mismanaged and his stock has not gone up in value like most other stocks. It is too risky to hold that much stock in any one firm.

Inflation Got Them

Don't get whipped by inflation because you trust only life insurance and bank deposits. A famous life insurance company used to advertise how you could retire on $250 a month. It showed the retired couple on a steamship cruise! Today, fixed income CDs pay so little you are actually losing capital if you spend the interest. A life insurance company is another form of fiduciary relationship, that danger we warned you about in a previous paragraph. Ordinary life policies often return less than if you simply saved your money in a bank. We had an uncle who bought an annuity paying $400 a month in 1960. He and his wife lived until their 90s into the 1990s and were quite poor trying to live on $400 per month then. We had to help them.

They Took Tax Losses

Don't let the IRS make you do stupid investing. People should be willing to take losses because they can take it off their taxes, the IRS says. You can only deduct about a third of the loss, actually, so you are really losing two thirds and that is bad. People also sell investments in the fall, when the market is low, to juggle their taxes to take a gain or loss this year rather than the next. It is better to let market price and the health of your stock, not the IRS, determine when you sell. People also keep large quantities of a weak stock they should sell because, if they sold it, the capital gains tax would be high. Let the market, not your tax status, determine how you buy and sell stock.

They Trusted the Investment Media

Distrust financial advice in magazines and newspapers. The investment advisors were all wrong in 1929, I discovered in old newspapers, all of them except our cousin, Roger Babson.

For example, in the late 1960s when gold was $35 an ounce, newspaper financial columnist Sylvia Porter told people *not* to buy it, that it *never* would go up. She was wrong; gold went to $800 an ounce briefly and now is near $300.

Time, Newsweek, and the newsstand business magazines are nearly always wrong in their forecasts. *Barron's* is about the best for financial news and advice, but a bit pessimistic. *The Wall Street Journal* is pretty good, and you need their statistics.

GOOD ADVICE

We have now told you a lot of things you should not do. What you *should* do is more difficult to explain and, frankly, no one is sure. I am not sure either. If a market rises rapidly it may mean hyperinflation is ahead and *not* an economic boom. It is just recalibrating stock prices to a weaker dollar. That is actually what happened in the 1965-1992 period. I really do not know what is going to happen next. Now that I have told you what not to do, here is some advice below from a man who is a winner in life. Enjoy.

How You Should Invest:
Ed's Notes after a Long Lunch with a Happy Millionaire

This good and generous man, in effect, wrote the rest of this chapter for me while I listened. Here is a paraphrase of what he told me.

****

I inherited a little money in the 1960s when I was younger and I had saved some too, about $60,000. I wondered what to do with it. Everyone had different advice and most of it was obviously self-serving.

Then, at the Rotary, a good friend asked me if I had ever thought of selling mutual funds. He thought I had many good contacts—which I did. He told me I would have to take a course at their headquarters and pass an SEC exam and become certified, and that it could be done part-time while I kept my regular job. I decided to give it a try.

The course was taught by the firm's sales manager and was extremely valuable. He told me some amazing things. The general approach was simply foot in the door. He said that when you called on an M.D. in his office he would keep all his patients waiting while he talked to you because doctors were so interested in money. I am not sure if this is true or not. He told me to buttonhole all my family and friends and not to let them leave until they bought into the funds. Anyway, I competed the course and passed the SEC exam and was given my franchise and the sales kit. That was in 1965 and the Dow Jones had just hit 1,000.

Then I began to think. Who will I sell the funds to? Aunt Clara, maybe? She had some money but what if the fund lost money for her? How could I ever face her if she lost half or more of her investment, instead of it growing like wildfire as I was supposed to promise her? And Uncle Winston? I know he'd be enthusiastic. He'd even borrow money to buy my funds. But if the market crashed, he would lose everything. They'd repossess his house, put him out on the street. No, I'll leave him off the list. And as I went on I eliminated one person after another from my list of prospects until I had none left. The problem with all open-ended mutual funds like this one is they grow like crazy in good times, and that is when the people buy most of the stock—at high market prices. But if hard times come, then the people will make a run on the mutual fund and it will be forced to sell stock at low, recession prices. A mutual fund is as unstable as a bank in the days before banks were regulated by the SEC.

Then I thought to myself, if I didn't feel it was right to sell the fund and I had paid for the course, could I buy it myself? So I looked at its portfolio, looked up some of the stocks in the Moody's and Standard and Poor's and Value Line financial services in big books in the library. The fund I was supposed to plug owned a lot of stuff like Occidental Petroleum, Benguet Consolidated, and Ling Temco Vought that didn't look exactly blue chip to me. They were companies with lots of hype but no dividends. So I decided I'd not buy any for myself. That was in 1965. It is lucky I didn't. Over the next 15 years or so the market went into a terrible decline all through the 1970s and didn't get back to Dow Jones 1,000 until the early 1980s. I could have lost a bundle for myself and my friends and family in that fund.

But I could tell that great inflation was coming. Cash in banks was not enough. What could I do? Then I got on to a principle I have used many times since. General Motors was a large and stable company then. Most of their cars, like the Chevy Impala were very fine, but attacks by Ralph Nader on the safety of their Corvair car had cut the price of GM stock in half. It was about 66. The dividend was huge. I didn't think the stock was that bad, or that the company was ruined. So I put all of my money into it, a good sum. In about a year I sold it at 85. Not a big profit, but with the size of investment I had, it was tens of thousands of dollars. And the dividend was huge then. By 1968 I thought the stock market was too unsafe to invest in any more. I had no confidence in the economic policies of Lyndon Johnson or Nixon. What could I do?

I would have liked to have bought gold coins in Canada, then selling in the Montreal airport store for a little more than $35 an ounce. But it was illegal then. I knew the dollar was losing its value rapidly in the face of great inflation. I had to have some other standard of value. Mexico, surprisingly, was quite stable then. So I bought a lot of Telmex—Mexican Telephone Stock—a blue chip by Mexican standards. It paid 11 percent interest. I also bought South African gold stocks, Welkom, Blyvoor, and President Brand, which paid huge dividends, too, and promised to go up. I kept this stuff through most of the 1970s, received huge dividends, and my principal did not go down as it would have with U.S. stocks. Note, I was willing to take many more chances when I was young than I do now. Now, with more money, I am very conservative. I also bought small amounts of U.S. blue chips including U.S. Steel and DuPont in the 1960s. This was a mistake. When I began to lose money in Steel I quickly sold it. I had learned never to let a loss continue. DuPont I kept until I needed the money for something else. The gold stocks I sold at about break-even around 1980 when I could see South Africa had serious political troubles. At least the dividends had been extremely good and some went up a little.

By 1980 the United States was in horrible condition, banks were paying 12 to 15 percent interest and good stocks were incredibly low. The Ayatollah was holding American hostages, President Carter was paralyzed, and the people were demoralized. The Dow Jones average stayed below 1,000. I could see a Republican president would be elected and I doubted the fundamentals were that bad. So I sold everything foreign and bought GE, IBM, Xerox, Exxon, AT&T, and several power companies at historically low prices, and some high interest T-bills as well. I watched it all grow. At times it went even lower than I paid for it, but then the rise began. I culled out Xerox and IBM because they did not grow as fast as the others, and I thought the black-suited IBM repairman who came to our office was arrogant.

Then in 1983 came the AT&T crisis and break up. The government split it up into seven different phone companies. Most brokers and advisers said stockholders should sell before the break up. They thought the government had ruined AT&T and it could never be the same. Some said to keep AT&T and sell the regional companies. But I talked to a telephone executive I knew well and she said no problem, they'd all do just fine and she was continuing to keep her stock for retirement and would let it be split into Baby Bells, the new regional phone companies. I studied all this and decided only AT&T had problems. Their scientists made wonderful inventions at Bell Labs, but management gave them away without proper patent protection. They should have tied the transistor, which they invented, up in patents, as RCA did the vacuum tube. They were restricting the growth of two-way radio excessively. And they were trying to manufacture office machines and computers, which looked stupid to me. So I sold the AT&T and kept the Baby Bells. I still have most of them and the appreciation over 18 years has been astonishing, well over 10x. I did sell US West, which seemed less successful than the rest. In addition I had all the Baby Bell dividends automatically reinvested. Now I have thousands of shares of each Baby Bell and I love it! ATT has gone up too, but it has not done so well.

GE has been a good stock in good times, but it is rather cyclical. I just keep it and usually it keeps on growing. It is reinvested too. Exxon-Mobil is OK, too, and I keep it also.

The next thing that happened was in Summer 1987; I felt a crash was coming. Poor people were bragging about their stock profits and guys like [market analyst] Bob Prechter were going wild. So I sold enough stock to have money to buy in after the crash when prices would be cheap. I sold mostly GE, and that was a mistake; I paid a huge capital gains tax. It would have been better to have sold some of the other stocks. Sure enough, the crash came in October 1987, and that winter I bought Detroit Edison, Citibank, American Electric Power, Texas Utilities, and Ford Motor at historically low prices. I sold Ford by 1989 at a profit. I didn't think it was very well run then; it is better now. I continued holding these other stocks, reinvesting dividends until about 1991 when I sold some more of them and bought German T-bills paying 7.5 percent interest when U.S. interest rates were much lower. I would have done better if I had kept more stock then, but I am very conservative. I get a capital gain on the D Marks.

In the late '80s I was reading everywhere that Mexico was highly unstable, that there were gangs of leftist guerrillas grouping in the hills, that there would soon be revolution. Mexican stocks were incredibly low. There had been a devaluation of the peso, which luckily I missed. My favorite, Telmex, was now 2 1/2. I knew people in Mexico and I wondered if perhaps some big U.S. political interests were badmouthing Mexico and driving the stocks down, hoping to buy them all cheap. I bought a good amount of Telmex again at 2 1/2 and sold it at about 40 a few years later. Shortly after I sold, another devaluation occurred and I was lucky to miss it. Sure enough when the Telmex was riding high at about 40, all the brokers started hyping it and saying what a growth opportunity it was. They kept their mouths shut when it was cheap. That is what they usually do. If a man has any really good financial information, he will keep it for himself and his family. And if he had any real money, he would not have to print little investor newsletters and mail them out.

The next crisis came when Clinton was elected president. Many of my friends thought it was such terrible news that they should sell all their stocks. I had a gut feeling that although Clinton was a threat to our moral values, he and his wife liked to trade and invest also, and they wouldn't do anything to kill the stock market. So I held tight. I was right. I had some near misses—I sold Public Service of New Hampshire, and Amoskeag Bank at a break even, and they both went bankrupt shortly after. I sold some stocks I should not have sold—Chrysler at about 3 when it was ailing. It went to 60 or so after. But if you are right more often than you are wrong in the market, and resolve never to take a loss, but to sell, in the long run you will do OK

The next investment opportunity came in 1993 and '94. Hillary Clinton was plotting to nationalize health care. The big drug companies were under attack. I guessed correctly that her health care program would be put down by Congress, and I bought all I could afford of Bristol Myers Squib, Schering Plough, Warner Lambert, and Mylan Labs. These were bought at historically low prices and have had a great appreciation—all except Mylan Labs. The CEO of that company died suddenly and it went into a sharp decline. I sold as quickly as I heard the news. I still have most of the others.

From then on the market has been rising astonishingly and I have simply held on and enjoyed it. I did buy and add to a few conservative stocks, Duke Power in particular.

My portfolio started with about $60,000 in 1966. It has grown much more than the Dow Jones average has in the years since. I never took chances with stuff like AOL, eBay, Microsoft, or Amazon.com. I like to sleep nights, and I sleep very well.

My advice to my friends is to always avoid open-end mutual funds. Never borrow money to buy stocks. You'd have to be a genius at investing to make more than the interest they charge. Avoid options, except maybe to sell them on stock you keep. Few are ever exercised. Buy a few good stocks even if you have as little as $10,000 to invest. Don't own more than about a dozen stocks no matter how much money you have—it is too hard to follow them all, and they tend to regress to where you might as well be owning an index fund. Use direct-investment plans and reinvest the dividends. Plan to keep the money invested permanently. This must be money you won't need suddenly. I can't tell you what to buy, what will happen next, but I expect inflation, another recession, maybe a war, high food costs and energy costs, energy shortages, maybe like the 1970s again. But I am not putting all my money on that hunch, not at all!

Stocks are generally cheaper in October, higher in springtime, but not always. Buying and selling stocks online is convenient, and you'll avoid broker hype and high pressure. Morgan Stanley Dean Witter is a popular Internet service that does this for you. You can make paper trades—just note what you would buy, but don't buy it. This will tell you how good a trader you are. But beware, all stocks go up in a big bull market and if you profit then, you may not really be as good a trader as you think you are.

If you:

Buy investment-grade stocks paying good dividends;

Remain flexible, buying in the face of bad news when the advisers and the financial media tell you not to, but when you know the fundamentals are good;

Resolve never to take a loss and sell if you made a mistake;

Resolve that sometimes you may have to stay out of U.S. markets for many, many years; and

Pay all your taxes,

You will probably be successful.

****

Ed continues: Another possibility for investors is in Treasury bills.

If you are very conservative or think this is time to get out of the market, you can buy Treasury bills and bonds directly from the Treasury Department and save the $50 or so the bank charges you as a fee. The minimum investment is $1,000. You order them by mail enclosing a bank check for the full amount. The price is determined at auction and you get a refund, which is your discount or interest. At maturity you get the full amount returned to you. You can also fill out a form to reinvest the whole amount automatically for one or more times. These bills and bonds are exempt from state tax and are considered quite safe.

Contact the Bureau of Public Debt at Box 9150, Minneapolis, MN 55480-9159, or www.treasurydirect.gov. Addresses of government agencies do change quite rapidly. If this one should change, contact the office of your representative in congress. T-bills have been a favorite of old and sophisticated families who keep their money. But, hyperinflation and political instability could change all this.

Chapter 16

Save on Health and Medical Care

This is the most pessimistic chapter of all. If you are poor you simply have to stay healthy—that is about the size of it. Medical insurance is typically about $7,000 a year for a small, healthy family. If your company has Blue Cross and you leave, often you can pick it up on your own, but then it is more expensive. Some go without insurance and gamble they will save money by living healthier than most people. Federal and State charity medical care is an interesting situation and varies from state to state. Massachusetts gives free sex-change operations. New Mexico gives Medicaid to a family of two adults and two children earning as much as $40,000 a year—not poor at all, in my humble opinion.

FREE MEDICAL CARE

Free medical care can be obtained by volunteering for medical experiments. The doctors test a new drug and its placebo and also give you physical exams and a variety of other medical services. Most of these programs are near medical schools or large cities.

A few renowned doctors and clinics will treat a limited number of patients free. Radiotherapy Clinics of Georgia is one. Their prostate cancer therapy is world-class. Several hotels offer free rooms to patients undergoing treatment. See their Web site at www.prostrcision.com.

Veterans Administration

The Veterans Administration hospitals treat veterans even if they were not in combat during war. The illness need not be service-related. The VA will supply prescription medicines and outpatient services, which often are good quality. Care and medicines are absolutely free. Depending on funding and regulations, outpatient and non-service connected disability medical care may or may not be available at a given time or location.

There has been wide publicity given to complaints of poor medical care in VA hospitals. Patients who are senile, brain-damaged, or chronically ill seem to run the greatest risk of mistreatment. Some VA surgeons have poor records. You take your chances. It is necessary to apply for benefits several months in advance of your first VA appointment. My experience with them has been very good.

MEDICAL INSURANCE

If you qualify under poverty or Social Security guidelines you may receive Medicare, Medicaid, and other services that may be quite valuable. People have given their homes to their children and hidden their money to qualify for health care and benefits. Then sometimes the heir sells the house, or refinances it to buy a Corvette, a Rolex, and a motor home for himself or herself and spends all the money. Beware!

People have had a family member take a low-level salaried job just to get the family health-care benefits that go with the job. There is a lot of good health care information you can use in books and in the media. We cannot cover it here, and can do no better than suggest you take a look at it.

STAYING HEALTHY

You keep yourself in good health by watching your weight, eating a proper diet, getting exercise, and not smoking. Excessive drinking is very bad. Avoid sunlight; it ages women's skin more than anything. Wearing sunglasses will prevent wrinkles around the eyes and a broad-brimmed hat or old-time sunbonnet and covering the body will do more than any cosmetic to keep a woman looking young, my wife says.

Avoid auto accidents by driving carefully. Become safety conscious in all you do.

Vitamins seem to improve health. Generic vitamins sold at great discount by mail-order firms are equal quality to name brands like One-A-Day. Most patent medicines are fakes or placebos. Aspirin is good, but name brands like Bayer are no better than generic aspirin or a store brand. Alka-Seltzer is aspirin plus soda. You save a lot of money by putting a generic aspirin in water with a teaspoon of soda if you like this kind of thing.

Prune juice is as good a laxative as any pill you can buy. Epsom salts are a laxative and also a good antiseptic to soak infected feet and hands. Some take vinegar and honey for good health. The best burn treatment is immediate application of cold water. Farmers used to put veterinary penicillin on themselves when a barbed-wire fence or a sickle had cut them. It requires no prescription. Herbal medicines can be good.

Working men spit a lot because they eat very salty food and seldom drink water and it makes their saliva taste terrible to them. If they cut down the salt in their diet, they would not need to spit all the time and they would feel better. This is not generally realized. We all should cut down on salt and sugar and drink many glasses of water a day. A wealthy man who hired a lot of people once told me he would never hire a person who put salt on his food without tasting it first. That person would show hasty judgment in business matters, too.

Granny glasses you buy in drug store racks or by mail are just as good optically as prescription glasses. I learned to fit glasses once when I was a lab assistant. We needed older volunteers with 20-20 vision and the only way to get them was with temporary spectacles. It was quite easy. Get your eyes checked by an MD for glaucoma, detached retinas, cataracts, and other serious problems. But if you have the usual middle-aged farsighted vision with both eyes needing about the same power of lens, and no astigmatism, drug-store reading glasses will be all you need. I wear them myself for very close work.

Hearing is easily damaged by loud stereos and portables radios with headphones, as well as by chain saws, circular saws, and gunfire. Nothing makes a person seem really old more than being hard of hearing. Many modern liberal kids will soon be partially deaf. Be careful of your ears, use ear plugs when shooting or using power tools.

If you live in the Southwest you can go to Mexico for very low-cost medical and dental care. Prescription medicine can be bought at lower prices without a prescription, sometimes 25 percent of U.S. prices, in my experience. Many Americans are doing this. Some say Canada is a bargain for medicine and medical care too.

Free prescription medicine can be found in Dumpsters if you are brave. It is surprising how much is thrown away. Antibiotics and certain volatile drugs such as insulin and nitroglycerin are perishable, but most drugs are highly stable for several years at least. You have to read drug manuals and know what you are doing. The risk is high and you are on your own if you try this.

Avoiding sugar prevents dental problems. So does dental floss. You can use the thin, white string that people use to wrap packages to floss your teeth and save money. Be sure it is clean. I've done this. I've also saved infected teeth from being pulled by having an M.D. give me an injection of antibiotics. They can give stronger antibiotics than dentists. Some frugal people have all their teeth removed to save dental bills. I'd feel like a dreadfully old tiger if they pulled all my fangs!

SANITATION

Sanitation is important for country or wilderness living. A spring or stream high on a hill with no civilization above it usually provides safe drinking water, but it could be polluted if, for example, a porcupine fell into it and died and decomposed. Polluted water can look and taste fine. Government agencies will check wells. Find out locally where to reach them and have it done. Clorox, iodine, or Halazone tablets from GI surplus stores will kill bacteria in water. Charcoal will filter it. There is more to learn about safe springs, wells, septic tanks and privies than we can cover here. Read military training manuals and U.S. government publications or a good encyclopedia for the finer details. Dishes must be washed, not just wiped. Human wastes must be buried. Always wash your hands after going to the toilet.

Chapter 17

Fix Things and Make Them Last

If you want to save money, it is vital that you become really good at doing your own repairs and keeping old things going for years. Here are the real and seldom-told repair secrets.

REPAIR-TRADE SECRETS

These real repair-trade secrets are closely held and not widely known. I learned these secrets myself only after a lot of travel and many years of experience. Writing about these secrets as applied to fixing cameras, radios, and cars gave me a good living for years. But they work with most everything else you repair. I am publishing them here only because I am tired of making repairs myself after 40 years of it—and I now own enough good cars, tools, boats, radios, cameras, antiques, and appliances to last me 75 years or more—longer than I will live. So here are all the repair secrets I know—with my very best wishes. Note: Readers Digest publishes some excellent do-it-yourself repair guides that can help you with many repair jobs.

Difficulties Fixing Things

The usual approach to repairing manufactured things is that each part has a parts number and there is a big parts list or book. To fix the car, gun, motorcycle, outboard motor, camera, clock, or whatever you are repairing, you must know the maker, the name and model, and perhaps the serial number. Then you must locate and identify the part that broke. Then you look up the part in the manufacturer's parts book and you will see it has a number and you order it by the parts number. This system has several problems.

Often the manufacturer is out of business or has discontinued selling parts for your broken item because it is too old.

Your car or appliance will be out of action two weeks or more while the part is ordered and comes by UPS.

The part costs a lot of money because it is costly to store parts a long time and sell them individually. For example, a $25,000 Ford Taurus would cost $150,000 if you bought each part out of the parts book. The replacement repair system is labor intensive, hence costly. A car is built in about 20 hours in a factory by mass production. It takes about 1,000 hours to rebuild an old car by craftsmen working on it individually. Repairs are costly in time and money.

There is another really nasty problem: The manufacturer is tempted to make sure that repair parts are expensive or unavailable so the customer will discard the old product and buy a new model. Sometimes, as in camera repair, the whole repair technology was kept secret—until I let the cat out of the bag in my camera repair book in 1975. Obviously there is a better way to fix things than to depend on ordering new parts from the manufacturer.

Is Full Restoration Needed? Is Restoration Really Successful?

By restoration I mean taking an item like a car or a boat completely apart down to the frame, examining each part, rebuilding each part or replacing it with a new part so each part is equal to new, then reassembling the whole thing. In refinishing the parts, all paint or finish on each part is removed down to bare metal and new plating and finishes are applied. Full restorations of anything are expensive and time-consuming.

In antique cars restored like this, the parts never fit back together quite right, and the restored cars are never as reliable as a new car. I've been on several antique auto tours where we drove a whole caravan of old cars 100 to 250 miles and each time at least one of the most expensively restored and best-looking cars broke down. A $25,000 frame-up restoration job did not help the reliability of that car at all. On the same trips, simple low-cost mechanical restorations of low-mileage original cars did better. These old cars held together. For some reason car show judges insist on 100 percent cosmetic restoration, which is laughed at when done to guns, coins, silver, and other serious antiques. Sanding an antique gun to bare metal and chrome-plating it ruins its value, as does scraping down and refinishing an old colonial table. It does not pay to over-restore any item. Never replace nickel-plate with chrome. I realize most of you may not repair valuable antiques but the principle is important. You face the same problems if you take anything that you own too far apart and do too much work on it. You may hurt it more than you help it. "If it ain't broke—don't fix it," is often a good slogan.

Repair Economics

Do not think in terms of depreciation when evaluating whether to repair or replace things. Any running car should be considered as valuable as a new car for as long as it is doing the job of a new car. The moment it fails to do so, its value drops instantly to zero or to its scrap value. If your older car is doing the job of a new car, treat it as well as a new car—drive it carefully, limit your motor speed, and change the oil regularly as if it were actually a new car. Then you will not be destroying it ahead of time merely because you want an excuse to buy a newer model.

One is tempted to discard a car when the cost of repairs needed is greater than the price of a similar used car. However, one must think that if the new repair gives 20,000 miles more of trouble-free service, what will be its cost in cents per mile then? Will it then be cheaper than another car? Often you will decide to fix the old car anyway. Almost anything on a car can be fixed except a ruined body and frame if you are willing to pay enough or work hard enough. The question is not "Can you fix it?" but "Do you want to?" The same repair principles apply to radios, appliances, tractors, and most other mechanical things. On some things that are progressing rapidly and improving—such as computers—having a recent model is important, but with cars and most appliances that are static in design, old models are as good as new models. The differences are only styling.

Do Preventive Maintenance Inspection
and Replacement Schedules Prevent Breakdowns?

There is evidence they do not. There is no improvement in highway safety in those states where all cars are inspected annually compared to those without an inspection program. When I worked on radar in the Army, at first we believed all radio tubes had a life of 1,000 hours and should be replaced at that time. But it did not help, the tubes still failed and the sets still broke. Some tubes last 100 hours, others 10,000 hours, you see. The 1,000 hours was just an average life; the curve was bimodal. I have put many new parts such as carbs, generators, fuel pumps, and starters onto 20-year-old cars simply because I had the parts and I had bought them for nearly nothing. It didn't seem to make the cars any more reliable. A corollary to this principle is that a car or appliance that breaks down a lot when you first own it is not necessarily a hopeless lemon—*if every defect is corrected properly.*

Schedules of lubrication and inspection are essential and must be obeyed, but you cannot prevent trouble by replacing parts for no good reason. Many people believe old things are no good and this false belief can profit you greatly when you buy a used item from such a person. Make them admit the gas stove or vacuum cleaner they are offering you is 20 years old and they will practically give it to you. But, as you know, it is actually use and care a thing is given, not age, that determines its value.

Control Your Emotions

You cannot get angry at a thing—it will never know it. You cannot intimidate it or frighten it. It will not feel anything if you hit it, or hammer it, or throw it against the wall. Getting angry at a car that won't start or a stereo that will not play is a bad character defect that can cripple a repairperson and make a repair career impossible. Only living creatures can hate. Things cannot hate you. Your broken car or TV set is not your enemy.

You do good work only when you are able to work on things calmly. Quit and do something else for a while if you are tired or angry. Do not hire a person who swears to work for you. He will smash property of yours and your customers "by accident" in his excessive anger.

When I had only one car that I needed to commute to work, I used to

A MODERN PIONEER. When I was crossing the country in 1959, we camped near a giant boulder on a state road in Wyoming. A 10-year-old Dodge pickup truck was stopped there, too, with an older working man and wife and some young kids who sat in the enclosed cap on back of the truck. The man seemed to be working on the motor. After awhile we began to talk and I had a look at it. He had dropped the oil pan from the flathead six on to the ground in the shade of the big boulder in what was actually an American desert. And he was cleaning it out. He had an assortment of old insert rod bearings and he was assembling and fitting pairs of them, trying patiently to find a combination that would stop the knock in the motor from a bad rod bearing and restore oil pressure. The old bearing had failed in the extremely hot weather. None of his family, even the kids, were frightened although this was a serious problem that would certainly destroy the crankshaft and leave them stranded without transportation in the middle of nowhere if he could not fix it. They seemed to have full confidence in him. The family amused themselves, the wife read or sewed, and the kids played nicely while the father worked on the old truck. I asked him if he needed tools, which I carried, or water or oil, or my help, or if he wanted me to get help at the next town. He declined all of my offers politely. I waited to leave until he drove off with the old truck, now running fairly quietly, going in the opposite direction. I always remembered that man and his family. *That was the spirit of the pioneers alive today that I had witnessed.* Look for it yourself, encourage it. Be like that.

make mistakes when fixing it. I would hurry too much. I do poorly when a car is broken down on the road compared to how I think and work in the garage at home. Owning more than one car these days, the pressure is off and I do much better work. Do not do low-quality, sloppy repair work on a thing just because it is old—such carelessness as leaving out some of the bolts to save time, hammering on things, using pliers or visegrips on bolt heads, ruining screw slots with the wrong size driver, or forcing sheet metal parts together instead of fitting them carefully. Many old cars and other old things I see have actually had their life shortened more by poor repairs than by the wear-and-tear of age. You can learn a lot about how good, old-time craftsmen mechanics worked from the old Gus Wilson stories, and from Old Bill, the machinist shop foreman in *Popular Science* magazines between 1933 and 1950. More articles like that need to be written today.

A SENSIBLE SYSTEM OF REPAIR

It is difficult to explain our system of practical, low-cost, effective repair, but I can probably do it best by relating all the unusual experiences I had to go through to learn it. You will have to read this section several times and then apply it to your own repair jobs. It is not as easy as the rest of this book. I learned the system from people in many different trades after many years and after traveling to many countries.

How They Fix Atomic Submarines Under Water

This information came from a man who had been on a nuclear submarine. These undersea boats must spend several months to a year under the seas without surfacing. As with any complex device, things will break down over this length of time. They cannot keep spares for all of the thousands of parts on board and, obviously, they cannot send for a part by mail from under the water. So each submarine has a little machine shop with a Unimat lathe, a drill press, grinder, and some brass and steel rods, tubing, threaded rods, sheet and bar stock and a machinist on board who makes the replacement parts. So in imitation of a wise idea, I bought a Unimat lathe myself and learned to make little tapered pins, shafts, keyways, and bearings. It worked and it usually saved me money and often allowed me to fix otherwise hopeless things.

Repair Secrets From The Azores

I was further encouraged to make my own parts after a trip of several weeks to the Portuguese Azores, those tiny islands in the Atlantic, where I stayed with friends at the Lajes air base and visited Ponta Delgada. The Portuguese people there are very intelligent and lively and they can make almost anything. They have to, because the islands are so isolated.

Here is an example: My friend, an air force major, drove a British Ford Anglia. The tiny four-cylinder engine required a rebuild. No pistons were available. The clever island machine shop workers actually turned down pistons from a larger car to size, cut slots for rings from another car, then bored the Ford Anglia block to fit. This whole job was quite inexpensive. They did similar jobs on diesel boat motors, refrigerators, compressors, and many other pieces of island machinery. It was amazing to see the Portuguese file a hammer or a trigger for a fine old double-barreled shotgun from a block of steel by hand.

So following their example, I started fixing many more old things with parts I made myself. I never told anyone how I fixed these things until years later. That was my trade secret. I made good money buying up all kinds of old things that did not work, making them work, and then selling them. It made me begin to dream of quitting my regular job. I also learned to use a local machine shop to make parts I could not make myself for antique cars and motorcycles, and that worked out very well too.

Texas Epoxy Work

In the Dallas-Fort Worth area on other business, I called on a shop that repaired broken oil-well drilling and pumping machinery. Knowing that I lived far away and would never compete with them, the owners told me, with considerable pride, the secrets of how they did the work. Their specialty was doing major repair work very fast and doing it on location so the oil-well work would not be held up—which would be a great financial loss to the company that was drilling the well. The owners showed me 8x10-inch photos of a 1,000-hp diesel engine on a drilling rig they repaired. The engine was about 10 feet long—a giant thing. Its crankshaft had broken. Believe it or not, they actually repaired the cracked crankshaft with *epoxy*. They put the crank back together and held it together with bolts they drilled and tapped into it while it cured. They used a special metal bonding epoxy from the Devcon company that could be machined. They could also build up a worn crankshaft by welding or spraying metal on it where it was worn and they would regrind the journal with a portable grinder that went winding around it while it was in place. They did not have to take the crank out of the engine.

The Epoxy Mercedes

At times I wondered if these men were pulling my leg, but when I returned home I sent for the Devcon epoxy catalog and tried some of their techniques on my own jobs and they worked. Soon I heard reports of other remarkable epoxy repairs. This was about 1962. One repair was done by an engineer customer of mine. He discovered a Mercedes four-cylinder car that summer people had left in a camp in Vermont all winter. The block had frozen and cracked. It was not cracked in the cylinder, fortunately, but just in the water jacket, a large hole where a big piece of cast iron had broken out of it. My friend put screen wire across this big hole and held it in place with little screws tapped into the block. Then he mixed up a batch of epoxy and iron filings and applied it to the screening with a putty knife just as you spread plaster over metal lath in plastering a wall in a house. He cured the epoxy with a heat lamp and the car ran beautifully and the repair held for many years. That is the only Mercedes I ever heard of that was bought for $150. That was what he paid for the car! This man had also restored a WW II Army liaison airplane, which he flew, so I took him seriously when he told me about all this.

Money-Making Repairs

Soon I had an opportunity for a similar repair myself. Chrysler goofed when they built my new Plymouth—one head stud was loose and would not tighten. They had drilled too far into the block when they made the motor and it ruined the female threads down inside the block. I considered making a fuss with the dealer, but I decided to try to fix it myself first. I took out the stud, filled the hole with epoxy, stuck the stud back in with no nut on top, and ran the motor a few hours slowly to cure the epoxy. Then after a few days I installed the nut and torqued it down to a full 60 foot pounds—a tremendous force for a glue. The car lasted at least 80,000 miles that I know of, with the epoxied stud in place, and the second owner was as delighted with the car as I was.

There was more epoxy in that old car, too. At the company picnic, I tore the aluminum gas tank by backing carelessly into an old stone wall. It had a thin crack about three inches long that leaked slowly. No welder could weld it and Chrysler wanted $200 for a new gas tank. So I drained all the gas in pails, dried and cleaned the tank, and widened the crack with pliers and a cold chisel until I could work epoxy into it. I bent prongs in the aluminum so it would hold. Then I mixed up a batch of epoxy and steel wool and rammed it into the hole and cured it with a heat lamp overnight. This epoxy repair also held perfectly for the full life of the car. I have done many similar repairs on other cars over the years.

I soon found that epoxy applied with a toothpick could fix smaller things like clocks, jewelry, electric trains, and cameras. One could build up a worn part on a lever or cam by epoxying a metal shim in place. I found bits of razor blades worked well used as little shims or shoes. The epoxy also stuck well holding loose pins and keys in shafts. I could buy up all kinds of nonworking but valuable old things for a few dollars each, fix them with epoxy and sell them for a good price now. No one ever complained to me that they broke or worked poorly. How I fixed them was my trade secret until years later when I started writing about repair.

Epoxy is also good to hold the dowels in their holes in the backs and legs of wobbly old antique chairs so they will not squeak, or to hold dried-out dovetailed bureau drawers together, fix plaster ornaments on old mirrors, icons, and picture frames, and to repair great numbers of other damaged antique treasures. Mixed with corn starch, epoxy makes a pretty good putty to fill in dents and screw holes. Mixed with some actual wood from the antique, it is far better than plastic wood to cover holes and defects. By making parts with a lathe or jig saw and mending them or building them up with epoxy, it was seldom necessary to buy a part any more. I also had a lot of fun rebuilding old wooden Beach Wagons and reinforcing them with fiberglass. Epoxy held our old wooden speedboat together pretty well too but I soon traded it for something else. Today such wooden cars and speedboats are extremely valuable.

Flush Cleaning

The next great repair secret involves modern detergents and solvents. I discovered that all GM car dealers sell a carbon-cleaning solvent that actually removes the carbon from inside a car motor when poured down the carburetor. The carbon shoots out the exhaust pipe in back in a giant cloud of black smoke and soot that is heavy and noxious enough to make the neighbors angry if you do the job with the car parked in front of your house. Gumout solvent fed into a carburetor with tubing using a little kit they sell will clean the carburetor as well as taking it apart. It is risky taking a modern carb apart; there are so many tiny parts. Other solvents also free up stuck valves and rings. Liquid Wrench loosens rusty nuts and bolts, and WD-40 just sprayed on lubricates many things without taking them apart. TV-tuner cleaner is remarkable for freeing up all kinds of switches and switch-operated things like electric organs and computer keyboards. Solvents enable you to flush-clean assemblies in place. They clean watches and cameras and computer keyboards this way, too, by flushing them with a spray can. When you pay to have a watch cleaned, it is not all taken apart, you know. It is simply sprayed or dipped and usually it is lubricated at the same time by a little oil mixed in the dip like a two-cycle outboard motor oil system.

Cannibalize, Cannibalize, Cannibalize

Rusty old cars and smashed-up cars have good motors to put into other cars with nice bodies but ruined motors to make them run like new again. The lens from a camera with a bad shutter can be put into another camera to replace a scratched lens if you know how to collimate it. I used to buy a Speed Graphic professional camera with a ruined lens for $25, get the lens off a ruined 3A Kodak for $5, combine the two and sell the Graphic for $200 or more. Now I do the same thing with Nikon and other makes. A good watch movement in a scratched, dented case can be used to replace a rusty movement in a clean shiny case. Use junk parts and know where to find them. Keep old things for parts.

Do not be intimidated by technology. A complex thing has simple parts you can deal with one at a time. An item with digital chips, like a computer, VCR, electronic organ, or complex autofocus camera like the Maxxum probably failed because the keyboard, the controls, or a mechanical relay or solenoid failed. These parts, being mechanical, fail more often than electronics, but they are also easier to fix.

Do not become too dependent on repair manuals written for a specific brand of product. All older U.S. V8 car motors are quite similar. Many makes of cars have Bendix brakes and if you know one, you know them all. American Motors cars, though an unusual make, have parts common to most other cars. So they are quite easy to fix. There is little difference between one ignition system with coil and points and another. We used to laugh at the repairperson who was always running to look at a manual. Learn repair by systems, not brand names. I've seen men who knew theory and systems fix a circuit defect in a complex, poorly made tube TV set with 20 or more tubes very quickly without any wiring diagram. That is really difficult. The concepts in this chapter enable you to fix most anything for yourself and save a lot of money, and they may also give you an extraordinarily good living in industry.

Summary

Our successful five-step repair program:

- Make the parts; do not buy them.
- Repair parts with machine-shop work and epoxy.
- Flush-clean assemblies with good, modern chemical solvents instead of taking them apart and often lubricate with sprays or dips, too.
- Cannibalize and use junk parts.
- Analyze a device with a systems approach; do not be a slave to manuals and parts lists and do not let the so-called experts intimidate you and make you give up.

REPAIR HINTS FOR COMMONLY USED ITEMS

Air-Conditioners	Leave them alone unless you have special training and tools. The thermostat and controls may sometimes be fixed.
Oil stoves and small oil furnaces	Leave them alone. The carburetor floats stick on pot-type burners and they set houses on fire. Avoid them. Gun-type furnaces are OK, but you need training to do safe repairs.
Gas stoves and heaters	Fix leaks in pipes with epoxy. Valves and parts are available. Have your gas man check your work and test for leaks.
Electric stoves, heaters, toasters, roasters, and broilers	Repair broken heating elements and replace wires or buy new elements. Clean or replace switches and thermostats. Keep cords from discarded appliances for replacements. Replace a cord that has a socket plug that goes into the appliance and a plug on the other end by bypassing the appliance socket internally and simply soldering the cord permanently in place. Sometimes switches on small appliances can be bypassed and you can turn them on or off by pulling the plugs. Simple controls on appliances (no complex push buttons or gadgets) are most reliable.[1]
Heavy motor-driven appliances (washers, dryers, dishwashers, etc.)	Get a repair manual and a parts list—you will need them. Study the appliances and you may be able to fix them. Sometimes you can save an electric motor from one ruined appliance to use in another, or use it with your power tools.

1. Before attempting any repairs to electrical appliances, you must know basic electricity: how to check for leakage with a neon test-lamp to ground, how polarity works, and how to determine the correct wire size for the current. No kid in high school should be allowed to pass a general science course without knowing at least this much about electricity. It can save a life. Shock, even from household power lines, can be fatal.

Small motor-driven appliances (fans, mixers, hair clippers, drills, etc.)	Motors fail from dirty slip rings and brushes, which may be cleaned or replaced. Wiring inside and switches may be the problem. You can often fix them. Interchange nicad batteries if your rechargeable appliance fails. Save good nicads from discarded battery-operated devices.
Electronics, stereo, TV, video cameras, etc.	Usually too dense and compact for easy repair today. Switches and tuners may be cleaned and fixed, but these devices are often cheaper to replace than repair. Buy battery-operated appliances like boom boxes and shortwave radios with corroded battery boxes and contacts for a dollar or so. They are easily fixed. These devices will need cleaning and adjustment, which is not too difficult, though the internal workings are dense.
Microwaves	Avoid broken ones unless you've had special training.
Small gasoline-motor appliances	Fun and ideal for home repair. A community-college course might help. This can be a livelihood, too.
Sharpening saws and lawnmowers	A good specialized field.
Gunsmithing	A specialized repair field. Take a course by correspondence or residence first. Profitable.
35mm cameras	Older ones are definitely fixable, but the newer autofocus point-and-shoots are doubtful. They're so cheap today it may be better to discard them and buy another used camera.
Locks and locksmithing	This can provide a nice new career for a well-known local person with a good reputation. Take a course. I change tumblers myself on locks without any training and I have always done so on a rental apartment, since who knows who has a key? I do not tell the landlord. I cannot pick a lock, however.
Computers, typewriters, and office machines	Computers usually have cable connector and mechanical or keyboard switch contact failures—easy to fix. Monitors are quite easy. Some computer work is high-tech and needs expensive test equipment. Study computers, printers, faxes, robots, and all kinds of modern digital electronics through ICS or NRI, or in community colleges or engineering schools. It's possible to fix older typewriters, but they're usually not worth fixing. But very old typewriters like the Oliver or Hammond are highly

collectible. I have bought a lot of very fine 1930s to '50s typewriters for $10 to $15 each. I am keeping them; they may go up later. Xerox-type copiers are too difficult to repair.

Motorcycles, chain saws, and outboard motors	You need schooling to learn engine overhauls but you can tune, adjust, and fix many component parts on these things.
Electric lamps and lighting	These are easy to fix without training and are worth fixing. Sockets, cords, switches, fluorescent boosters, and starters are sold in hardware stores and places like Wal-Mart.
Kerosene and gasoline lamps	Many repair parts are available from Lehman's (see Chapter 12). Coleman also sells parts for old models. See antiques magazines, too. You can convert modernized antique lamps back from electricity to oil or vice versa with parts you can buy easily by mail. This is a good skill to know yourself and interesting and profitable specialty work to make money, too.
Automobiles	Repair is most successful and profitable on older cars and trucks or unusual cars like AMC, Fiat, Alfa, Austin, Morris, Saab, or Renault that you buy very cheaply and mail-order the parts. Find mail-order parts and repair information from sources in Hemmings Motor News described in the auto chapter.
Automobile bodywork, wreck repairing, and painting	These are good trades but I have no aptitude, it seems, and my attempts at painting come out poorly. The insects especially enjoy sitting on anything I paint. I leave bodywork alone but you may succeed. These trades are learned in tech school or on the job.
Upholstery	I can patch vinyl upholstery rips with the special cements sold for this work but I do not reupholster car seats or furniture, unfortunately. Ruined chairs and sofas that are peeled down to just a wood frame and springs are sold at giveaway prices. You can reupholster them and resell them for many times your cost. It is a wonderful trade to know.

Conclusion

Well there you have it, a book that is a toolbox filled with resources and techniques so you can live better on very little money. I hope it helps you. Any comments and suggestions will be welcomed and may help make a better third edition of this book.

With many years of life behind me, it is my observation that most people get out of life just about what they put into it. And that is pretty fair, isn't it? Mental brilliance does not guarantee success without limit. Too many bright people go through life with their brains in idle or park, their perceptions on hold. Many fail because they let others control their fate, to their disadvantage. They sacrifice personal autonomy for security. Since this is a choice, it makes life no less fair.

People are not just reactive or reflective creatures responding to stimuli. They also create and control their environments. There is poverty, but the real poverty, as author Martin Flavin points out in his book *Mr. Littlejohn,* is poverty of soul. There is a message in this book beyond hardware and technique, and that message is for people to reach out and take hold and rise up and build and grow and create for themselves a better life. Doing so encourages others to do likewise and that builds a better world.

The time in which to do this is limited. We must make our mark before old age and debility soften our brains and harden our arteries. But when our time is done and God calls us home, if we have faith, there will be nothing to fear.

About the Author

Edward H. Romney is best known as the author and publisher of a popular series of books on repairing cameras. He has been self-employed since he left his job in 1969. Some of these years have been a difficult and challenging struggle.

Before 1969 he held a variety of middle-level positions in academia, business, and government. In 1960 he wrote *Restoring Traditional Values, the Search For Human Theory* (ISBN 1-886996-50-5), a unique book that explains most of the problems of the dominant liberal ideology and proposes changes. It was ahead of its time. Revised and self-published in 1995, it has attracted some interest among philosophers and thinkers.

Ed has also been a radio technician, FCC-licensed to repair radar and radio broadcast stations, and is the author of a book on radio repair. He has taught electronics, as well as psychology, sociology, and education at the college level. He comes from an old New England family that lost their money in the Great Depression. He remembers the 1930s when he was a small boy. His father had to struggle hard to survive.

He is married to the former Sara Burgess of Gastonia, North Carolina, has lived in South Carolina for some 25 years, and now divides his time between there and New Mexico. He is a past president of the Kiwanis, is active in the Grange, the American Legion, the local no-kill animal shelter, and is a deacon in his church. His hobbies are antique cars, motorcycles, boating, camping, hunting, travel, square dancing, reading, and learning.